A STUDY OF MODERN TELEVISION

Also by Andrew Crisell

Understanding Radio
An Introductory History of British Broadcasting
More than a Music Box: Radio Cultures and Communities in a Multi-Media World

A Study of Modern Television

Thinking Inside the Box

Andrew Crisell

palgrave
macmillan

First published 2006 by
PALGRAVE MACMILLAN
Houndmills, Basingstoke, Hampshire RG21 6XS and
175 Fifth Avenue, New York, N.Y. 10010
Companies and representatives throughout the world

PALGRAVE MACMILLAN is the global academic imprint of the Palgrave Macmillan division of St. Martin's Press, LLC and of Palgrave Macmillan Ltd.
Macmillan® is a registered trademark in the United States, United Kingdom and other countries. Palgrave is a registered trademark in the European Union and other countries.

ISBN-13: 978-0333-96408-8   hardback
ISBN-10: 0333-96408-X   hardback
ISBN-13: 978-0333-96409-5   paperback
ISBN-10: 033396409-8   paperback

This book is printed on paper suitable for recycling and made from fully managed and sustained forest sources.

A catalogue record for this book is available from the British Library.

Library of Congress Cataloging-in-Publication Data

    p. cm.
    Includes bibliographical references and index.

9   8   7   6   5   4   3   2   1
14   13   12   11   10   09   08   07   06

Printed in China

To my brother Peter

Contents

Preface   ix
Acknowledgements   xi
Abbreviations   xiii

Introduction   1

Part I   **The foundations of modern television**   15
1.   Birth and infancy, 1884–1954   17
2.   The age of duopoly, 1955–1982   24
3.   Proliferation and deregulation: the 1970s onwards   30
4.   Modern television: policies and practices   40

Part II   **Television genres**   47
5.   News and current affairs   49
6.   Documentary and features   65
7.   Forms of infotainment   82
8.   Sport   98
9.   Drama and film   110
10.   Comedy and light entertainment   119

Part III   **Television culture**   133
11.   Television: audience uses and effects   133
12.   Globalisation and localism   144
13.   Television, theatricality and public life   153

Conclusion   159

Bibliography   173
Index   179

Preface

Since an important theme of this book is the frequent individuality of broadcasting reception, it is not always helpful to refer collectively to 'the audience', 'the viewers', and so on. Since I do not wish to weary the reader with dualisms such as 'him/her' and 'he/she', and since there are as yet no singular epicene pronouns that will satisfy the gender politicians, I have quite arbitrarily referred to the viewer, listener, broadcaster or whatever, as 'he' at some points and 'she' at others. I therefore assure the reader that when she/he encounters these feminine/masculine pronouns she/he may take it that where one gender is used, the other is also implied.

Acknowledgements

All writers hope that what they have written is readable, and writers of academic books hope it, or should hope it, with a special fervour. But, to invert Sheridan's famous remark, easy reading is vile hard writing, and not just for the writer but his loved ones. If the hope of this vile hard writer has been realised, I owe heartfelt thanks to all who have tolerated my ursine sore-headedness: my wife, Margaret, especially, and my two daughters, Ellen and Harriet; but also those many patient friends who, hearing my groans of despair, sent an encouraging e-mail or poured me another comforting drink while the book's gestation ran its course. Among these, I must single out Professor Richard Madeley, who at frequent intervals provided companionship that was at once light-hearted and thought-provoking.

I owe particular academic debts to Dr Christine Fanthome for providing me with information about programmes on Channel 5 and other networks, along with valuable insights into the phenomenon of reality TV; Dr Peter Goodwin of the University of Westminster for a luminous briefing on digital broadcasting; Judith Moir for answering my query about childcare proceedings; and my colleague, Dr Susan Smith, for her helpful remarks on aspects of cinema history. With cheerful pertinacity, another kind colleague, John Paul Green, tracked some elusive data all the way back to their lair. None of these benefactors should, however, be blamed for any errors of fact or intellectual lapses that the reader may detect. My gratitude is also due to the University of Sunderland for allowing me a semester's study leave to write some of the book. Finally I must give warm thanks to Catherine Gray and Emily Salz, my commissioning editors at Palgrave, whose skills in authorial ego-management are probably unrivalled.

Abbreviations

ABC	American Broadcasting Company
AOL	America On-Line
BBC	British Broadcasting Company, 1922 to 1926; British Broadcasting Corporation, 1927 to the present
BSB	British Satellite Broadcasting
BSkyB	British Sky Broadcasting
CBBC	BBC children's television
CBeebies	BBC television for pre-school children
CCTV	closed-circuit television
CNN	Cable News Network
DBS	direct broadcasting by satellite
DVD	digital versatile disc
EMB	Empire Marketing Board
EMI	Electrical and Musical Industries Ltd
ENG	electronic newsgathering
EU	European Union
GPO	General Post Office
IBA	Independent Broadcasting Authority (successor to the ITA)
ITA	Independent Television Authority (replaced by the IBA)
ITC	Independent Television Commission (successor to the IBA)
ITN	Independent Television News
ITV	independent television
MGM	Metro-Goldwyn-Mayer
MTV	music television
NTL	National Transcommunications Limited
Ofcom	Office of Communications (successor to the ITC)
RCA	Radio Corporation of America
TiVo	blend of TV (= 'television') and i/o (= 'television input/output')
UHF	ultra high frequency
vCJD	variant Creutzfeldt-Jakob Disease
VCR	video cassette recorder
VHF	very high frequency
VLV	Voice of the Listener and Viewer

Introduction

Why do we need to study television? And why does it seem so *hard* to study – so elusive a thing to analyse? The case for studying the medium is based on its importance as the primary, if not the only, source of information, entertainment and cultural enrichment for the great majority of people. As such, it has also had a powerful influence on those whom it observes, whether governments, corporate bodies or private individuals – another good reason for studying it. Moreover its popularity implies that it is generally felt to be adequate in its informative and cultural roles, an assumption this book will test.

Yet television is difficult to capture and explore as a single composite phenomenon (Dahlgren 1995: 24). At one level it is concrete, physical and easy to define: a medium consisting of sounds and moving images which are transmitted to a scattered and largely domesticated mass audience. These sounds and images – which we may collectively call 'content' – can be live or pre-recorded, though they are always 'live' in the sense that television sets receive them at the time of transmission, even if this is not the time at which the audience chooses to watch them. But then the problems multiply. The codes and conventions into which these images and sounds are separately organised are complex in themselves and even more so in combination with each other. TV content is neither a static text like a printed book, nor even, despite the closure of its individual programmes, a concluded text like a cinema film or a stage play. It is continuous and mutates endlessly. To analyse it, one often has to 'freeze' it in both the physical and intellectual senses; but to freeze is to falsify the object of analysis. Moreover, while the TV text quite closely imitates our first-hand sensory experience we are aware that it is not always straightforwardly truthful and realistic.

If we tease out the implications of our definition by comparing television with the older audio-visual medium of cinema, we can get a clearer view of its character yet also begin to understand why the medium is so hard to analyse (Ellis 1982; Abercrombie 1996: 10–19; Casey *et al* 2002: 85–7). When people go to the cinema they take part in a public and collective activity. They pay an admission fee to experience the high quality of its sounds and images and they sit and watch in darkness. To do these things they must be more highly motivated, and with a more specialised interest in what is being shown, than television viewers, who are presented with a hotchpotch of content in their own homes. Television is private and domestic. Since its screen is smaller than a cinema screen its viewers have a more equal relationship with it. They tend to watch with the lights on, and since it competes with the distractions and routine of domestic life it is often disregarded or consigned to the background. Television's sound and pictures are of inferior technical quality to those of the cinema, yet while the latter exploits the power of imagery in the creation of its meanings television seeks to reclaim us from our domestic distractions mainly through its use of *sound*: trailers, theme tunes, station idents, conversational babble. Compared to a cinema soundtrack, the noises that emanate from a TV set often seem 'busy' and clamorous. Moreover its speech, whether scripted or extemporised, seems more explicit, less allusive and elliptical, than the scripted speech of a cinema film.

The live and domestic nature of television also has a significant influence on the form its texts take. When we make an effort to visit the cinema and pay to see a movie, we expect 'escape', whether in the form of entertainment or artistic edification. Hence the typical cinema text is a single, rounded, fictional artefact – a self-contained feature film which deals in make-believe and ends conclusively. Unlike television, which is daily and continuous and requires so many programmes that they have to be created in a highly collective way, cinema movies can be treated as the work of a single, authorial figure: the director. But many of television's fictions, its soaps, serials and sitcoms, mirror the banal, largely domestic circumstances of its viewers, even to the extent that their action takes place in real time. For an uncertainly motivated audience of varying backgrounds they must be easily intelligible and instantly appealing. Their narratives seldom consist of simple stories with neat closure: the instinct of television drama is towards the serial and episodic, its interest less in events and more in character.

But the most crucial difference between cinema and television is that because the latter is both live and continuous it carries *factual* as well as fictional content. The liveness of television, its ability to reach its viewers instantaneously, makes it an obvious and vital medium for current events: but its continuous, or at least daily, character also pushes it towards factual content because it requires so much material that it must draw on the resources of the real world as well as the make-believe one. Hence television provides news, outside broadcasts, educational and documentary material – all of which means that unlike cinema it is often characterised by *direct address*: its announcers, weather-forecasters, newsreaders, reporters and chat-show hosts talk straight to the camera. Thanks to this and the domesticity of the medium, television speech is also distinguished by a certain kind of intimate, often spontaneous register that is not heard in the cinema. Scholars have often remarked that because television is so much a part of our daily domestic life we perceive its performers as 'personalities' rather than 'stars' in the traditional cinematic sense. But this may also be an effect of the medium's partly factual nature. As a performer within a fiction the film star is herself something of a fiction, a remote icon in comparison not just with a player in a TV soap, whom we encounter in daily and less glamorous circumstances, but with the TV presenter or interviewer who looks directly at us, deals in 'real world' matters, and may also talk to us in a spontaneous, unscripted way.

Thus, unlike the other visual media of theatre and cinema, whose content is tailor-made for them, television is a *heterogeneous* medium. Not only does it create its own, largely fictional content, such as dramas, soap operas, gardening, cookery and talk shows, comedy programmes and quiz games; it also acts as a kind of mirror on, or relay mechanism of, events in the outside world. In this role, perhaps as witness of the state opening of Parliament or the last night of the Proms, it seems to be so transparent, so self-effacing, as barely to be worthy or capable of analysis in its own right. Yet it is a curious fact that TV broadcasters seem to pride themselves much more on their factual reportage than their creative content: 'It tends to be central to the identity of television networks, with news bulletins sometimes referred to as "flagship" programmes' (Casey *et al* 2002: 142). And if we were to analyse television only in terms of the content that is provided by the TV networks themselves, in contrast with that which reflects the outside world, we would give a quite inadequate account of its character and functions.

But it is important to remember that even this 'internally' provided content is not wholly its own, for to a considerable extent television borrows material from other media. Indeed, to compound the difficulties of critical analysis, TV ingests even those cinema films we have just been contrasting it with! We might therefore make a tripartite division of its content into:

- content which is made especially for television
- content which is made for other media but which television adopts or adapts, notably cinema movies and stage plays
- content which is not 'made' in the foregoing sense but is there for television to cover in the form of *actuality* or external events – news, politics, current affairs, sporting fixtures, public music concerts and so on.

However we must qualify this division in two ways. First, while it is true that the content of the first two categories is largely fictional and the content of the third mostly factual, we shall see later that the correlation is not absolute. Second and more important, though these categories can give us a way of understanding the heterogeneous character of television, they are by no means watertight. When it is merely used as a live relay of events in the outside world, we sometimes get a sense of the neutrality or passivity of television. Yet few of these events remain totally unaltered by its presence. Indeed such forms of actuality as politics and sport are highly mediated by television: it often sets out to influence and even in some sense to appropriate them. In 1977 an Australian media magnate transformed cricket from an autonomous sport which television occasionally covered into 'Kerry Packer's Cricket Circus' – something which, like a soap opera or a game show, was created expressly for the medium.

Moreover television is highly proactive in its treatment of the news – in its choice and prioritisation of stories, mode of coverage and style of presentation. The programme genre known as *documentary* could be seen as spanning all three of our categories. It deals with external events, yet is highly mediated and could thus be seen as a product of television itself. And even though an individual documentary might be made by and for television, it is clear that the genre as a whole has been borrowed from the older media of cinema and radio. Indeed virtually all those genres which we are inclined to think of as being native to television have their roots in older media. The chat show has developed out of radio interviews and discussion programmes; many competition shows are adaptations of domestic parlour games; soap opera was first enjoyed on the radio, which in turn adapted it from serial magazine fiction; comedy sketch shows would have been recognised by the music hall audiences of the late nineteenth century; and made-for-TV movies are clearly traceable to theatrical plays and cinema feature films. Indeed there is probably no such thing as a wholly original genre in any medium, and when we examine television's genres we shall seek to understand them better by looking at some of their antecedents.

The heterogeneous character of television inevitably raises difficult questions about the artistic and cultural value of its content. For instance, a TV network can be held critically accountable for its broadcast of a bad play but not for its broadcast of a bad soccer match, except in the rather limited sense of the quality of its coverage. And if a station shows a bad cinema film, how do we apportion blame between it and the original producers? Yet even with respect to its home-produced content, is it reasonable to weigh a daytime chat show in the same artistic scale as a major costume drama or documentary series?

One reason that may prompt us to do so is that the domestic and continuous nature of television encourages its audiences to experience it as an undifferentiated stream or *flow* (Williams 1974: 95): they seem not so much to watch television programmes as simply 'watch television'. It is perhaps for this reason that whereas newspapers have specialist theatre critics, film critics, literary critics and so on, they merely employ '*television* critics'. Moreover when television borrows those cinema films we began by contrasting it with, we could say that it 'naturalises' them – turns them from something cinematic into something which is its own. They are no longer publicly and collectively watched; we no longer pay admission to watch them (unless on pay-per-view TV); they no longer offer superior sound and vision; and they are no longer watched in darkness. This means that they may only be experienced in a desultory, distracted way, especially as they are often punctuated by commercial breaks. Yet this naturalisation is never entire: cinema films on the television are still rounded artefacts which appear to be the creation of a single authorial figure and whose images convey a significant part of their meaning.

On the other hand, a considerable number of programmes which are made for television emulate the artefacts of the cinema. They are often, though not necessarily, dramas: the real point of resemblance lies in the fact that they are as carefully crafted as cinema films, using similar production techniques and similarly expressive imagery. They therefore assume motivated viewers and are a recognition that television is *not* always experienced by its audiences as an undifferentiated flow but sometimes viewed in a selective and attentive way (Gripsrud 1998: 27–9). It is hardly surprising, then, that the critics – though 'television' critics – tend to concentrate on these programmes and to ignore the more informal and improvised made-for-TV content that contributes to 'flow', such as breakfast-time and studio chat shows. Nor is it surprising that they also ignore much of the content that originates in other media or is relayed from the outside world, since this is constrained by factors that lie partly outside television's control. Cinema films on television are often previewed but seldom if ever reviewed; and while critics may question the style or even the overall justification of the TV coverage of an outside event, they have to acknowledge that the event itself is not of the medium's making.

Yet even those 'artefactual' forms of television which command their attention pose problems for criticism, especially if we are used to the more traditional critical practices associated with literature, painting or sculpture. While we must not exaggerate these problems, they are all attributable to the medium's existence in time and can be defined in terms of *ephemerality, quantity, authorship* and *accessibility*. We noted earlier that unlike the static, spatial text of a poem or novel the television text is constantly changing and that to seek to fix it for analytical purposes is to run the risk of distorting it. This is, of course, true of any time-based art form, and the abundance of theatre, film and dance critics suggests that the problem is hardly overwhelming. But while broad, impressionistic judgments of plays and films are relatively easy to make (and appreciated by audiences), close and local analysis is more difficult. This explains why theatre and film criticism has a longer pedigree in journalism than in academia. In art forms where the spatial text plays a dominant role in the overall aesthetic effect, as in poetry or fiction or painting, close analysis is perceived to be rather more straightforward. Yet if we reconsider theatre by its synonym 'drama' it becomes an interesting borderline case. In drama the written, 'spatial' text has traditionally been regarded as a rather greater determinant of aesthetic effect than is its equivalent ('the script') in film. In other words, whereas the dramatist is seen as the primary creative force in a stage play and the director, actors, technicians, set designers, costumiers and so on as ancillaries, the scriptwriter is seldom if ever distinguished from these as the primary creative force of a movie. Shakespeare, Ibsen, and even contemporary dramatists like Alan Ayckbourn have a much higher cultural status than most writers of screenplays, whom few of us could even name.

This is, of course, why drama was swiftly annexed by literary criticism and Shakespeare acclaimed as a *literary* rather than a theatrical genius. It is also why, with the birth of '*theatre* studies', a debate soon developed about just how sufficient the play-text is as a determinant of the total aesthetic effect. This was known as the 'page versus stage' debate: plays on the page could be endlessly analysed and evaluated (albeit by neglecting the element of performance); plays on the stage offered a complete aesthetic experience yet all but defied close critical analysis. The debate was rendered somewhat archaic by the development of recording technology (including, of course, cinematography), which in fixing the process of performance could render it susceptible to almost the same level of analysis as the text. Yet the difference between text and performance is ultimately irreducible. Though the latter can be viewed repeatedly, the camera may not have captured all its aspects, and the very act of freezing it destroys that dynamism which is its essence. Time-based texts, whether theatrical or cinematic, are still tainted with the suggestion of ephemerality – and this in turn implies expendability and lack of importance.

The temporal character of television artefacts presents other problems for criticism, at least when compared to spatial artefacts such as those of literature, sculpture and the visual arts. The first of these relates to *quantity*. Because television broadcasts daily, if not round the clock, it gets through an enormous amount of material; and this seems to debase the artistic status or significance of its individual programmes – even the 'artefactual' ones. Since criticism is concerned not only to analyse and interpret but to evaluate, it gravitates towards the occasional, the distinctive, the exceptional. Yet programmes of this kind can sometimes be hard to discern within a virtual torrent of output that broadly aims to provide routine and continuity.

The time-based nature of television can also present critics with a problem of *authorship* and *origination*. A poem is the work of a poet; a painting is the work of a painter: but whose 'work' is a television programme? Since conceiving a programme, realising it and ensuring that it is successfully transmitted are beyond the powers of a single individual, television must resort to collective methods of creation. The person who has the idea for a programme may not be its scriptwriter; and in addition to the scriptwriter, and depending on the particular genre, creative input will be required from an editor, a presenter, actors, researchers, journalists, camera operators, lighting and sound engineers, set and costume designers, make-up artists – in various ways and at varying removes, the entire broadcasting organisation. Moreover, not only is creation a team effort, but the need to fill the air time as efficiently as possible means that teams must often make not just one but a whole series of programmes in a single process. They must, in other words, resort to *mass production*, and this can create a tendency within TV programming towards the formulaic, the tried and tested, rather than the idiosyncratic or extraordinary.

As we saw just now, theatre seems to be a halfway house between the authorial and the collaborative. The literary skills of the dramatist need the practical skills of the actors and stage crew, and those directors who effect a successful marriage between the two can also claim a degree of 'authorship'. This explains why Trevor Nunn, Peter Hall and Terry Hands are almost as famous as dramatists like Tom Stoppard, Alan Ayckbourn and Alan Bennett. But only 'almost': it remains true that the play-text – and its author – are generally given most of the credit for the overall artistic effect. It is also true that as a reflection of its historical association with the theatre, and the lingering belief that drama is a 'writerly' genre, television has its own roster of famous dramatists – among them Alan Bennett (again), Alan Bleasdale, Lynda La Plante, Alan Plater and Dennis Potter. But since individual writers are capable of producing only single plays or relatively short series and serials, such famous names account for a mere fraction of the total drama output, and given the relentless tendency of modern, competitive television towards economies of scale, they may face a bleak future. In much television, as in all cinema, it is not only the case that even more people are needed than in the theatre to realise the scriptwriter's vision: there is often *more than one scriptwriter*. In cinema, whole teams of writers may not only originate different parts of a single script but re-work one another's material: in television, they are needed to churn out scripts for soaps and other extended series. Put crudely, then, the spatial media of painting, sculpture, poetry and novels produce *authorial* artefacts, and the temporal media of radio, television and cinema produce *industrial* artefacts. To risk stating what is obvious: the fewer who are involved in the creation of a work of art, or who are significantly able to modify it in the course of its execution, the greater our sense of its authorship.

So why is an apparent lack of authorship a problem for criticism? Because criticism has traditionally thought of works of art as the product of personal inspiration, thus making it hard for critics to assign authorial responsibility for those that are the product of collective effort. Again, it is important not to exaggerate the problem. It has little relevance to the descriptive and classifying roles of criticism, and even when they form value judgments, the critics are not – and never have been – inhibited by the fact that what they are criticising is the work of many. Nevertheless they do like to see everything in it as part of a single creative vision rather than as incidental or adventitious, and such an assumption is less reliable in respect of artefacts that are the product of teamwork. This helps to explain the application of 'auteur theory' to the highly industrialised products of the cinema. Since the film script is not only felt to make less contribution to the final aesthetic effect than does the play-text, but is itself very often the work of more than one writer, there has been an impulse among critics to assign authorial responsibility to the director. It is the director who oversees more aspects of the production than any other individual and who allows us to treat the film as the work of a single authorial figure. Earlier in this introduction I described cinema films in just these terms. Even so, it is difficult to regard the authorship of the cinema director as equivalent to that of, say, the sculptor or the novelist. But what auteur theory illustrates above all is that while criticism does not *need* to ascribe authorial responsibility, it certainly prefers to.

Finally, the time-based nature of television programmes combines with the quantity in which they are produced to ensure that they 'date' fairly quickly and are relatively soon forgotten by their viewers, even if they are not missed altogether – all of which creates the further critical problem of *accessibility*. A 'quality' programme lasts for at best an hour or two and is then rapidly superseded by countless other programmes. I can recall seeing in 1984 a theatrical performance of *Richard III* by the Royal Shakespeare Company, with Anthony Sher in the title role; but while I undoubtedly saw many television programmes in 1984, or have subsequently seen them in the form of broadcast repeats or commercial videos, I have no *specific* memory of watching any programme during that year. 'Dating' – obsolescence – is, of course, much less of a problem for art forms that exist in space: the print medium, for instance, makes literary artefacts perpetually 'present', so that if a student is about to read a critical study of Wordsworth but has not yet encountered his poems, accessing them is a relatively simple matter.

Yet quite aside from the endless recyclings of the nostalgia channels, television programmes can also exist spatially in the form of video recordings which can be home-made, bought or hired: 'temporal' does not have to mean 'temporary'. Nevertheless, the storage of television content is a much less efficient and rather more costly matter than the storage of literature. All the works of what is rightly or wrongly regarded as 'the literary canon' are in printed form and, if not directly purchasable, are accessible in libraries: the complete writings of Shakespeare exist in a single and modestly priced volume. But the availability of television programmes is much less certain. The ratio of recorded, or at least widely accessible, material to the totality of output is tiny, and each video cassette or videodisc contains at best a few hours of programming. Teachers and critics cannot assume that even those programmes which they regard as artistically important are well known to their students and readers or are widely available, whether commercially or through informal off-air recording. This means that to a much greater extent than books about literature, books about television are obliged to limit their analysis to material which is either contemporary or within the recent memory of their readers, most of whom, it is hoped, managed to view it when it was broadcast.

Even when the material is familiar, there is, despite recording technology, that almost irresistible feeling that because it exists *in* time it merely exists *for* a time – that once transmission has ended, it is out of date. As one critic laments, 'academic writing about specific television programmes is limited by the time it takes to publish an article or book, by when (or so publishers think) the programmes themselves will be of little interest' (Nelson 2001: 8). The only other remedy for the implied obsolescence of broadcast output is illustrated by several major studies of television drama (Tulloch 1990; Brandt 1993; Nelson 1997; Cooke 2003): the critic must devote much space simply to describing what the play or programme was about before attempting an appraisal of it – and the reader cannot always check the accuracy of the description in order to assess the validity of the appraisal.

Yet while it is important to acknowledge (albeit without magnifying them) some of the obstacles to the analysis and appraisal of its content, a study of television which confined itself to content would be inadequate. What is also needed is a recognition of the wider contexts in which TV broadcasting is conducted. We indicated earlier the categories into which television programmes can be roughly divided: self-generated; borrowed from other media; relayed from the outside world. But in what proportions does it draw on these categories? And what influences its choice of content *within* the categories? What, for instance, determines the ratio of 'serious' drama to soap opera, 'hard' news to human interest reportage, classical music recitals to rock concerts? And what determines the amount – and even more important, the style and content – of its coverage of politics?

Television broadcasting is an activity which is both costly and influential. Hence in every country on the globe the attitude to it of those who hold political power is crucial. What does the government want broadcasting to do, and not to do? And – a related question – how does it wish the activity to be paid for and organised: by taxes and as a public utility or by advertising and as a private enterprise? And if the latter, in what ways and to what extent will advertisers be allowed to influence programme content? A further, if narrower, discretion falls to the broadcasting organisations themselves: the management, programme planners, creative and production staff. Within the regulatory framework which has been imposed by the government, and whether as a protected monopoly or in competition with other organisations, how much money and energy are the broadcasters able and willing to invest in programming, whether original or acquired? Finally, and every bit as important, what is the public willing to watch and able to make sense of? Television content could thus be regarded as the outcome of a negotiation between the government which regulates it, those advertisers (if any) who pay for it, the organisation that transmits it, and the people who watch it.

This book is an introductory account of the phenomenon of television and its presence in modern life. Its purpose is to help students understand how television has come to assume its importance in our society; to appreciate the values and attitudes that have shaped it; to develop a critical awareness of its content and its ways of representing the world; to explore its influences and effects both on audiences and on aspects of public and institutional life; and to appraise its cultural and intellectual strengths and limitations. To lend specificity to the study, it will focus on *British* television, but I would suggest that there are two reasons why this will not be needlessly limiting. The first is that the coexistence in Britain of both a strong public service institution, the BBC, and a thriving commercial sector provides a microcosm of broadcasting systems which operate separately if not together in most other countries of the world. Second, many of the conditions under which British television is operating, particularly the more recent ones of globalisation, cultural homogenisation and media convergence, are increasingly universal. As well as the ubiquitous issues of 'television culture', the *types* of programme discussed in this book will be familiar to non-British viewers, even if the programmes themselves are not.

In order to understand the multi-faceted phenomenon of television – not only the variety of its content but the range of technological, cultural, political and economic factors which help to shape that content – the book will adopt a range of approaches. These might be alliteratively summarised as approaches through *context*, *content*, and *consumption and culture* – with a concluding *critique* of the strengths and limitations of the medium.

The first section deals with the past and present contexts of television.

A brief historical account takes the medium's technological development as its core but explores the issues of broadcasting philosophy and political control with which it is indissolubly connected, the institutional forms television has taken, and the social implications it has raised. After an initial, simplified account of its origins and of the social factors that prompted them, this section considers the evolution of television in terms of the questions implicitly asked by those who were first responsible for it: what purposes should this new technology serve? and how should it be paid for?

These questions had already been addressed in the case of television's older sibling, radio, but their continuing relevance is attested by the post-war debate about the respective merits of public service and commercial broadcasting which culminated in the Television Act of 1954 and the birth of ITV. The public service issue will inevitably inform the entire historical account, but the technological evolution of television has increasingly raised other key issues which must also be discussed – socio-political issues of control, (de)regulation and public accountability; of institutional structures and practices; of globalisation and cultural imperialism; of interactivity and media convergence. The final chapter of this section considers policies and practices: the way in which modern television is regulated by governments; the cultures and working practices of the industry; and the way in which programmes are scheduled and developed. It thus makes a link between the political and institutional history of the medium and the various kinds of broadcast content which form the subject of the next section.

The latter will try to give an adequate impression of the kind and scope of material that television provides. Yet for a number of reasons this is a task which is more difficult than one might expect. First, we have already noted that the material carried by television is highly miscellaneous and, to feed the prodigious demands of numerous channels and round-the-clock transmission, the range of programmes is not only vast but composed of endless conflations and hybrids of older genres which make comprehensive categorisation all but impossible. Second, in what is increasingly an era of themed and streamed channels, 'sequenced' output, and a live coverage of wars and other public events which is often of indefinite duration, the individual programme has become almost as hard to define as the genre.

This section will aim to do two things. It will attempt a broad but flexible characterisation of TV content by locating it along a spectrum which is *factual* at one end and *fictive* at the other – the latter term usefully suggesting both something *constructed* and something which is often, though not always, 'make-believe' or 'untrue'. For programmes at the factual end of the spectrum 'truthfulness' is paramount. Obvious examples are news and current affairs, the more traditional forms of documentary and features, and serious discussion programmes. They are primarily concerned with the communication of facts or ideas, with knowledge and the maintenance of credibility, and in some instances (like weather forecasts or travel bulletins), with being 'functional' in the sense of supplying information which the viewer might wish to act upon.

Programmes at the fictive end of the spectrum do not necessarily deal in make-believe, but the degree of their truthfulness is unimportant: they have a licence to 'rearrange' reality or subject it to artificial rules. They are primarily concerned with entertainment or cultural provision or with forms of 'play'. They are usually more preoccupied than factual programmes with aesthetic considerations and are often 'non-functional' in the sense of serving no *practical*, as distinct from spiritual or psychological, purpose. Obvious examples are dramas, films which originated in the cinema, comedy and light entertainment programmes, variety and game shows. However the distinction between fictive and factual content does not neatly correspond to the distinction between that content which TV creates or adapts and the 'real world' content that it merely reflects or relays. TV relays sports, for instance, and sports are a part of actuality: they are 'real events'. Yet in the sense that they are a kind of theatre which is *played* (a significant word) according to arbitrary rules, they are 'fictions' too – even though they are not fictions that are created by television. Just as the theatre is a metaphor of the real world, competitive sports can be seen as a metaphor of actual fights or battles.

It is also important to recognize that the differences between the factual and the fictive are fully apparent only at each end of the spectrum – that the programming at all points along it is marked by varying degrees of *interpenetration* between the two. For instance, television news contains elements of the fictive in the sense that with an eye to aesthetic matters as well as simple veracity, its bulletins and programmes are carefully constructed and artfully presented. At the other end of the spectrum, quiz shows may deal in matters of fact and information despite their aim to entertain and 'beguile' – while drama often attempts a measure of verisimilitude. Yet the basic distinction would appear to be a useful one. The section begins with the more factual genres and then moves on to those at the fictive end of the spectrum. While it cannot offer an account of all the forms of content to be found on television, it aims to help the student to recognize most of them and identify their characteristics and conventions.

The second aim of the section, and one which will assist in this task of recognition, is as far as possible to trace the origins of the various programme genres in earlier cultural forms such as the theatre and cinema, newspapers and magazines, parlour games and popular fiction, and to suggest the ways in which television has adapted these to its own character and purposes. The section will try to convey the sense in which television is part of a cultural continuum yet also a medium that has initiated forms of its own. But the focus will be on the 'grammar' or typical features of television's genres rather than on specific programmes.

The third and final section – on consumption and culture – is a discursive treatment of the social significance of television. It deals first with audiences in particular: what do they do with television and what does television do to them? It then considers the broader social and cultural impact of the medium: to what extent is TV a means of cultural imperialism on the one hand and of resistance and diversification on the other? Finally it explores the medium's effect on those who are obliged – or who seek – to appear on it. As never before, public behaviour has been rendered by television into a form of theatre. How is the conduct of individuals, institutions and professions modified by the consciousness that they are being observed by unprecedented numbers of people? A summary of what might be perceived as the main strengths and limitations of modern television then brings the book to a close.

Part I
The foundations of modern television

Birth and infancy, 1884–1954

That tuppenny Punch and Judy show.
(Winston Churchill)

Although television appeared many years after the telephone, the search for a device that would send images over distances began just as early as the attempts to send sounds. If ever such a device were to be created, the American inventor Thomas Edison had already coined a name for it in the 1870s: the telephonescope.

No one inventor or country can claim all the credit for television: perhaps the most valuable contributions came from scientists in Germany, the United States, Russia, Japan and Great Britain. The challenge, as explained by the Scotsman A. A. Campbell-Swinton in 1908, was to convert light and shade into electrical signals that could be transmitted from a camera to a receiver on the same airwaves as wireless radio. The first attempt at conversion had been mechanical, when in 1884 the German Paul Nipkow devised a revolving disc with a spiral pattern of perforations. As the disc was turned a beam of light shone through the perforations and thus 'scanned' an image, but with Karl Braun's cathode ray tube in 1897 and the photo-electric cell of Julius Elster and Hans Geitel in 1905, an electronic way of scanning was developed that would prove more fruitful.

Nevertheless, after the interruption of research which had been caused by the First World War another Scotsman, John Logie Baird, elaborated Nipkow's mechanical system to produce a primitive 30-line picture. In 1925 he began public demonstrations of his device at Self-ridges, the London department store, televised moving images in the following year, and in 1928 wired the first intelligible TV signal across the Atlantic.

In order to transform television into a mass medium Baird would have to win the hitherto tepid interest of the BBC, at that time Britain's monopoly broadcaster. However under pressure from the Post Office, the agency by which the government regulated public communications, the BBC agreed to allow Baird to make experimental transmissions in 1930 and 1931 to the 30 or so television sets that had been manufactured. Though it is fair to say that the BBC was not greatly enthused by television in general, a further reason for its indifference towards Baird was a growing awareness that the medium's future lay with the electronic system of scanning. This had been developed from the beginning of the 1920s by a number of American researchers including Vladimir Zworykin, a Russian emigré who worked for the Westinghouse Company, and Philo Farnsworth, a farmer's son from Idaho. Yet despite the achievements of these individuals the development of electronic scanning owed much more to corporate investment than to lone geniuses: while Baird was conducting his primitive trials during the 1930s, the American RCA Company was sinking a much more productive $9 million into research. For this reason the BBC resolved in 1933 to bring Baird's transmissions to an end.

By this time, however, there was no doubt that in one form or another television would become a viable mass medium. Yet because it was radio's younger sibling the philosophical debates about broadcasting had already been conducted, and its institutional foundations established, some ten years earlier. True to its faith in private enterprise the United States had perceived radio as a medium of entertainment and information which could at the same time serve as a valuable means of selling goods and services to the public. The commercial imperative would create competition among broadcasters and choice and variety for the audience and thus seemed to be virtually self-regulating. But during the 1920s an aerial free-for-all rapidly developed when hundreds of radio stations crowded on to the waveband, some seeking to drown out their rivals and some on pirated frequencies. A state regulator – the Federal Radio Commission – was therefore created in 1927 (Turow 1999: 174–5), but what is primarily a commercial system of broadcasting had already been established.

In Britain, a greater scepticism about the benefits of private enterprise combined with technological constraints to produce a rather different system. As the near neighbour of a dozen other European countries speaking a variety of languages and each wanting access to the waveband, it could claim only a small number of frequencies. There was space for little more than a single national radio service, and a feeling that if broadcasting was to be scarce it should not be placed in the hands of a single private company but be treated as a communal resource – a cultural amenity rather like public libraries (Winston 1998: 83). What had bred this squeamishness about private enterprise?

Industrial capitalism had been a dominant fact of life in Britain for longer than in most countries – long enough to create a distrust of unfettered profit-seeking on the one hand and a disquiet about the hardships of mass labour and the miseries of unemployment on the other. Hence during the early years of the twentieth century a concept evolved of the semi-autonomous 'public corporation' which aimed at centralised planning without government bureaucracy, and at commercial initiative without cut-throat competitiveness (Curran and Seaton 1997: 113–15). It seemed the ideal model for broadcasting. The national organisation which was created was, in fact, a private company – the British Broadcasting Company – but it did not operate like one. Formed at the invitation of the Post Office, which sought to avoid what was seen as the 'chaos' created by free enterprise in the United States, it was a consortium of wireless manufacturers who wished to stimulate sales of their products by providing a broadcasting service. Yet it carried no advertising, offered a very modest rate of return to its shareholders, and was funded by a licence fee which the Post Office collected specifically in order to cushion it against the need to maximise its profits.

Under its managing director, John Reith, a Scottish Calvinist who conceived of broadcasting 'in terms of high moral responsibility' (Briggs 1961: 138), the company soon developed its public service philosophy. Its output was intended to be *universal* both in consisting of a comprehensive diet of information, education and entertainment created to the highest possible standard, and in being targeted at everybody in the nation who wished to listen, irrespective of their status or location. It would take the form not of banded or streamed output but of *mixed programming* – a miscellany of genres in which every listener could find his and her particular interests. But by avoiding 'fixed point' scheduling – the transmission of the same or similar programmes at the same time every day – the company also aimed to introduce an element of serendipity and thus *expand* the interests of the individual listener.

In order to underpin the provision of a public service, the company sought to defend two privileges which it already enjoyed. First, it insisted on the need to operate as a *monopoly* because competition from another broadcaster would force it to abandon its 'highbrow' and minority-interest programmes and simply strive to maximise its audience. Second, it extolled the importance of the *licence fee* because the fee ensured that the costs of the programmes were not related to audience size – that if the need arose, good money could be spent even on programmes which attracted a mere minority of listeners. Both as a kind of tax which was raised for a specific purpose and as an alternative to advertising income, the licence fee allowed broadcasting to achieve another aim alongside universality of provision: it gave the company a measure of organisational and editorial *independence* – from continuous political interference on the one hand and commercial pressures on the other. Hence when the wireless manufacturers no longer wished to be involved in the production and transmission of programmes, it was a relatively simple matter to change the BBC from a private company into a public corporation – a change that duly took place on 1 January 1927.

In 1934 the government appointed the Selsdon Committee to consider how a television service might be provided. With the BBC firmly established not only as the nation's sole radio broadcaster but as one which was dedicated to public ideals, it is hardly surprising that the committee proposed that the new medium should also be placed in the corporation's hands. While allowing that an element of sponsorship might be acceptable, Selsdon dismissed the idea that the new service should carry advertising, believing that its costs could be met from the existing licence fee. Selsdon also proposed that the service use both Baird's mechanical system and the American electronic system on a weekly, alternating basis until the superiority of one or the other had been proved. The government accepted these recommendations and the BBC Television Service, the first in the world to provide regular transmissions, opened on 2 November 1936.

The outcome of the technical trials was a foregone conclusion. The greater the number of lines from which the television picture could be composed, the greater its clarity. While pictures were still being created at the level of 60 to 100 lines, Baird's system remained competitive. But even as the Selsdon Report was proposing in 1935 that the regular service be launched to a standard of 240 lines – the uppermost limit for Baird – the EMI system, using all-electronic mobile cameras, could deliver a picture of 405 lines. Working with the Baird system was, said one BBC producer, like having to use Morse Code when you knew that next door there was a telephone. In February 1937 it was dropped.

Even the electronically created pictures were monochrome and not of the utmost clarity. Based at Alexandra Palace in north London, the service covered only the Home Counties and was at first received on about 400 sets. Sales were inhibited not only by their high initial cost but by an awareness that while two transmission systems were being trialled, some sets might soon become obsolete. There was, moreover, little to see: transmission hours were limited and on Sundays there was no service at all. Nevertheless it soon achieved something of that range and variety of content which characterised BBC radio. As well as cartoons and cinema newsreels it broadcast two or three plays a week, some by such major dramatists as Auden and Isherwood, Sean O'Casey and Oscar Wilde (Jacobs 2000: 25–76).

BBC Television was closed for the duration of the Second World War but reopened in 1946 with funding from a new combined radio and TV licence and was rapidly expanded into a national network, a process which was virtually complete by 1952. Yet the service was held back by three factors: embargoes on many sources of programme material, certain attitudes and values prevalent within the BBC itself, and a shortage of money. Throughout history and with varying degrees of justification, those who operate an existing communications medium have been fearful of the threat to their business posed by a new rival: stagecoach owners feared the railway; the railway companies feared the bus; and both rail and bus operators feared the car. The press and various other cultural industries reacted similarly to the launch of radio, and now did their best to strangle the infant television: the cinema industry refused to sell its films, the music halls and theatres withheld their shows and plays, and several sporting bodies denied television access to their major events. Indeed, it would take almost half a century and a degree of imagination to achieve the harmonious relationship of movies and sport with television that now distinguishes BSkyB.

Yet although as the nation's monopoly broadcaster the BBC naturally thought of itself as the body which should assume responsibility for this new medium, there was also a certain distaste for television within its own ranks. Why? As a public service organisation, one of whose aims was to edify its audience, the BBC recruited its creative staff from the educated classes – the products of the public schools and the oldest universities: and to be educated was above all to be literate, to possess 'book-learning'. Though radio was not books, it was mostly a matter of words and in the hands of production staff these often acquired a semi-literary dimension. Television, on the other hand, was pictures – and the pictorial media aroused what would now be regarded as cultural snobbery. They were felt in some circles to make insufficient demands on the audience: pictures were passively absorbed, easily forgotten, and emotive rather than intellectual in their effects. Cinema's very popularity was cited as evidence that it was a lowbrow, inferior medium.

Hence the BBC's initial attitude to television was coloured by a certain ignorance and wariness: it believed that for the more educative purposes of public service its pictures would have to be reined in rather than exploited. Reith despised it. The post-war Director-General William Haley distrusted it. Haley expressed a view which was widely held within the corporation: that if broadcasting could be thought of as a book, radio constituted its text and television existed merely to provide the illustrations. He defined radio and TV as 'complementary expressions within the same medium' (Paulu 1981: 54). Perhaps the most eloquent sign of the failure to think in television terms was that TV programmes were not created within a separate facility but were the added responsibility of the radio production departments.

This was also a consequence of the third factor: money. At a time of severe post-war austerity it was bound to be significant that an hour of television (which would reach only a modest audience) cost 12 times as much to produce as an hour of radio, which would always be heard by several million. Nevertheless, in 1947–8 the BBC devoted less than a tenth of its total expenditure to television (Briggs 1979: 8), and even in 1950 allowed it only half the sum that was lavished on just one of the three radio networks (Curran and Seaton 1997: 165). Yet by the early 1950s the corporation was managing to produce some memorable television, culminating in its extended coverage of the coronation of Elizabeth II in 1953. It was this event, not the launch of commercial television, that prompted the wider public to transfer its allegiance from radio to the newer medium, causing a boom in the sale of TV sets. Over half the nation viewed the ceremony and procession, and by 1955 TV had established an ascendancy which radio would never be able to challenge. While nine million people had acquired television licences by 1958, the average evening audience for radio had shrunk from nearly nine million in 1949 to less than three and a half million (Paulu 1961: 155).

Nevertheless a campaign had begun at the beginning of the 1950s to break the BBC's television monopoly. Its most obvious though not sole cause was the inadequacy of the service, especially in the immediate post-war years. Many people sensed that television had more to offer than the brief and frugal sequence of programmes that passed daily before their eyes. As the *Sunday Mercury* put it, 'If the BBC, for whatever reason, is handling television with a dead hand, then the BBC monopolistic hold must be wrenched away' (quoted in Briggs 1979: 456). There was also something of a reaction against the corporation itself. Though its wartime record had been impressive, a spell of 30 years without serious competition had – in the eyes of many – rendered it arrogant, patronising and smug. And despite some notable acts of editorial independence, it was closely identified with the government. During the war and post-war years of the 1940s, it was a channel of official information not only about events on the battlefields but about ways to conserve fuel and materials and achieve a nourishing diet. There was a suggestion that like mummy and daddy, the government and the BBC always 'knew best'. People now wished to take more control of their lives and perhaps to have a choice of broadcasters just as for so many years they had had a choice of newspapers.

Probably the biggest threat to the monopoly was economic. By the early 1950s austerity was yielding to prosperity. Food rationing would soon end and there was a growing market for new domestic products, especially electrical appliances like refrigerators and washing machines.

Sales not only of TV sets but cars and telephones positively leapt, and the demand to place advertising overwhelmed all the existing outlets. In being visual and animated, and with the domestic, intimate reach of the newspaper, television would make an ideal medium for advertising. A group calling itself the Popular Television Association began a campaign to install a commercial rival to the BBC. The corporation's defenders were neither few nor faint-hearted, but only one outcome was ever likely. Noble as the original idea of public service was, its precondition was monopoly and thus a denial of choice – something which is repugnant to a democratic, consumerist society. If the people could choose their own rulers from a number of political parties, why should they not be allowed to choose their own television programmes from a number of broadcasters? Reith famously denounced commercial television as the cultural equivalent of smallpox and bubonic plague, but the tide would not be stemmed. The Television Act was passed in 1954 and the BBC was about to face competition.

The age of duopoly, 1955–1982

> In particular the idea of competition for audiences but not for revenue seemed increasingly an expression of the British genius for making practical contraptions which then turn into beautiful machines.
> (Colin Seymour-Ure, *The British Press and Broadcasting since 1945*)

Launched on 22 September 1955, the British system of commercial or 'independent' television (ITV) was distinguished by three features. It was a regional system intended to counterbalance what was seen as an essentially London-focused BBC. The whole of the United Kingdom was divided into franchise areas, some of which were allocated on a temporal as well as geographical basis. That is to say that a broadcasting company was assigned to each, except in the three most lucrative areas of London, the Midlands and the Yorkshire/Lancashire industrial belt known misleadingly as 'the North'. In each of these, *two* companies shared the franchise on a weekday/weekend basis, an arrangement which would persist only in London. However, the survival of ITV depended on the ability of those companies in the lucrative franchises to show many of their programmes throughout the entire system. Hence from the beginning, ITV operated largely as an integrated network: with relatively few exceptions, the programmes seen in any one region would be simultaneously seen in all the others.

The second feature of the system was intended to appease the champions of the BBC: ITV was obliged to adhere to the principles of public service broadcasting. The government placed it under the overall control of the Independent Television Authority (ITA), whose duty was to allocate the franchises and ensure that the companies served the entire viewing public by offering programmes of 'quality, range and balance'. Indeed the fact that ITV was a commercial monopoly relieved it of the necessity to target only those sections of the public which would be of interest to advertisers. The third feature of the system was a corollary of this public service requirement: as in the newspapers, there would be a clear distinction between editorial content and advertising. Advertisers would not be allowed to influence programmes: sponsorship of any kind was forbidden and instead spot advertising – 'commercial breaks' – occurred within and between the programmes.

At first available only in London and the south east, ITV was an infant whose survival was in some doubt. The initial costs were unavoidably huge, and because viewers had to convert their TV sets in order to receive it, their numbers were tiny and the advertisers remained coy. An anxious ITA could not hold the companies too rigidly to their public service duties and they hastened to make programmes of proven popularity rather than minority appeal (Sendall 1982: 167). Then suddenly everything changed: viewers embraced it in droves, the advertisers stampeded after them, and as the ITV system was extended across the country (it would be completed by 1962), a patrician BBC watched its audience melt away.

Promoting itself as 'people's television', ITV was much more sensitive than its rival to the nature and needs of popular culture and there were four main programme categories in which it won the war of the ratings. The first was news, where its livelier, more visual approach contrasted with the wordy, radiogenic bulletins of the BBC. In the other categories it embraced the growing Americanisation of British popular culture which had always made the BBC uneasy. First, it screened large numbers of made-for-TV film series – cop shows, westerns, sitcoms – which Hollywood was now churning out in order to profit from a medium that had done so much damage to its cinema audiences. Second, it adopted several kinds of quizzes or 'give-away' shows, so called because they offered big prizes in contrast to the staid parlour-games on the other channel. The competitive and materialistic ethos which underlay the game shows was at once typically American and highly repellent to a BBC whose main aim was to win the public to higher things. Third, it exploited the soap opera much more effectively than its rival. The very name of the genre declares its origins in the commercial broadcasting of America, where the early wireless serials attracted the sponsorship of detergent manufacturers, but while there were long-running soaps on BBC radio, ITV was the first to popularise them on television. During the second half of the 1950s it was estimated that in homes with a choice, ITV was capturing between 60 and 80 per cent of the audience.

These developments had a deeply destabilising effect on the concept of public service, which was still felt to be the cornerstone of British broadcasting. For one thing, successful competition from ITV threatened the licence fee, which was levied on all owners of a television set and was the BBC's only source of income. If audiences spent the whole time watching ITV, why should they be expected to fund the BBC? To justify its income the BBC was therefore obliged to become more competitive, but to do so threatened those programmes for minorities which were at the heart of its public service endeavour. No longer would it be able to boast of providing 'something for everyone'. Moreover, competition had already destroyed the principle of serendipity – of viewers happening on something valuable or interesting which they would not have chosen for themselves. They could now choose alternatives to the programmes they might once have persevered with and ultimately benefited from.

In 1960 the government appointed a committee under Sir Harry Pilkington to review the performance of both BBC and ITV and make recommendations about the future of television broadcasting. These would be crucial because the government also intended to authorise a third TV channel and was likely to give it to whichever of the broadcasters Pilkington favoured. In its dealings with the committee ITV was complacent, believing that the viewing figures spoke for themselves. But the BBC's strategy was to reclaim 50 per cent of the audience by broadening its appeal and then assert its right to the third channel as a place where it could provide programmes for minorities. It argued a skilful case, and the culturally conservative Pilkington Committee was only too ready to listen. Reflecting a widespread anxiety about the debasement of popular taste, Pilkington reminded ITV that it had public service obligations, praised the values and achievements of the BBC, and recommended that the latter be awarded the third channel. The government broadly endorsed these findings, although there was some equivocation about the role of BBC 2, as the third channel was to be called. As well as serving minorities it would be used as a test bed for new technologies that would later become standard: 625 lines/UHF, which would provide better reception and a clearer picture, and colour transmission. But to encourage the adoption of these technologies by the audience as a whole, it was important that the channel should also carry programming of wider appeal. BBC 2 was launched in 1964 and eventually captured about 12 per cent of the viewing public.

British television had begun as a monopoly: the breaking of the monopoly had been attended by unbridled competition: and it was only now, after Pilkington, that it settled into a duopoly. While maintaining its public service duties, the BBC was obliged to stop patronising its audience and widen its appeal; while continuing to attract advertisers, ITV was obliged to provide programmes of quality, range and balance. Competition persisted, but because the broadcasters had separate and virtually assured sources of income, it was not absolute: an audience split of up to 60:40 was acceptable to both.

Hence the duopoly which resulted from Pilkington expressed itself in a kind of *convergence* of programming which on balance was felt to be for the better. The mass audience found that its needs were frequently and handsomely met by the BBC: those with more serious interests in documentary or in dramatisations of classic novels might be equally pleased with ITV. Both broadcasters strove to cater for the public *as a whole*. But the drawback was that they became less distinctive and offered less choice in the sense that while the three networks might be showing three different kinds of programme at any one time, their themes might all be of a similarly serious – or populist – appeal.

For both good and ill, the new technologies of magnetic recording and satellite transmission contributed to this convergence in programming. During the 1940s and 1950s there had been improvements in TV's ability not only to show material which had been recorded for another medium, notably the cinema, but to record its own material, whether prior to or at the time of broadcast. This meant an enormous expansion of television's programme base. It could not only screen old movies but stockpile its own programmes: the resources that were needed to pre-record a whole series were not much greater than those that were needed for a single live show. And recordings could be used not only for delayed or repeated transmission but as goods that could be traded among broadcasters. The movement of content between networks (as well as between media) became much easier and thus eroded, however slightly, the distinctions between them. A made-for-TV series that was shown on ITV might later be acquired by the BBC, and have originated on some American network which was affiliated to neither. Satellite technology had a similar effect. The first satellite to carry live TV pictures was the orbiting Telstar in 1962, but its geostationary successors increased the length of international transmissions. Not surprisingly both BBC and ITV sought to cover the relatively small number of events which were of global significance, such as the funeral of President Kennedy in 1963, the Mexico Olympics of 1968 and the moon landings of 1969, and they often had to rely on the very same pictures.

Soon after the launch of BBC 2, the government announced that it would provide a fourth channel – one which, it was assumed, would be assigned to ITV in order to balance the duopoly. But for a number of reasons – the conversion of the existing networks to 625 lines/UHF and then colour, along with various political and economic crises – almost 20 years would elapse before the channel was launched, and during that time the merits of the duopoly were increasingly called into question. The governments of the 1970s had their own reasons to disapprove of both the BBC and ITV. From time to time each carried programming that embarrassed them – ITV because it did not depend on them for its income, the BBC because it needed to show that financial dependency would not compromise its political independence. But this meant that as criticism of both broadcasters began to be heard from the public, the government was not disposed to do either of them any favours. Though not expressed by the majority, the criticism was strident and came from across the spectrum. The free marketeers on the Right disliked the commercial monopoly which ITV enjoyed, while the anti-marketeers of the Left simply disliked its commercial character, and people of all persuasions deplored what they saw as the arrogance, élitism and lack of accountability of the BBC. But to criticise either broadcaster was in effect to question the duopoly, and what united all critics was a feeling that it was too cosy and needlessly restrictive: television should offer wider access to programme makers and greater choice for the audience.

In 1974, and after many delays, the government appointed a committee under Lord Annan to consider the future of broadcasting, and the committee favoured the replacement of the duopoly by a more pluralistic structure. Among many other recommendations, its report, which was published in 1977, contained the original idea that the fourth channel should go not to ITV but to a new Open Broadcasting Authority which would make no programmes of its own but act as a commissioner and publisher of programmes made by others. However there was a change of government in 1979, and the incoming Conservative administration simply perpetuated the duopoly by handing the fourth channel to the Independent Broadcasting Authority (IBA). This was the name by which the ITA had been known since 1972, when in addition to commercial television it assumed charge of the new system of commercial radio.

Channel 4, as the new service was called, was launched on 2 November 1982. Its role was a public service one: to cater for previously underserved minorities, not all of whom might be attractive to advertisers. The channel would be funded not by the munificence of the licence payers, as the BBC was, but by the regional companies which made up the main ITV network. Channel 4 sold none of the advertising it carried. This was sold for it within their respective regions by the ITV companies, which kept the proceeds but funded the channel with a grant. The beauty of this system was that it broke the bond between programme provision on the one hand and the size or value of the audience on the other, allowing the channel to cater, at least occasionally, for groups of viewers whom advertisers would not necessarily find lucrative enough to target. Moreover the new government accepted one of Annan's key recommendations: although the channel was placed in the hands of the IBA and not an Open Broadcasting Authority, it was to make none of its own programmes but commission them from a number of sources. By the end of its first year it had acquired over half of its content from independent producers. Hence another beauty of the system was that although the channel was part of the BBC–ITV duopoly, it afforded access to a much greater number of programme makers, a large proportion of whom were directly employed by neither the BBC nor ITV.

Yet even before this final component was added to the duopoly, developments in broadcasting technology – home video recording and direct transmission via cable and satellite – were hinting at its obsolescence. These would not only allow viewers to devote their television sets to purposes other than the reception of live content but make broadcasting itself much more abundant and thus challenge the need for a tight and prescriptive system of control. It was reasonable to expect while broadcasting was scarce that it should be publicly regulated to ensure that it would provide a service for everyone and not fall into the hands of sectional interests. But its growing abundance would, it was assumed, lead naturally to a diversification of content and, paradoxically, to a decrease in the strength of its influences in the sense that, as in the press, the political partisanship of one outlet would be balanced by that of a rival. Moreover, it was assumed that the *overall* impact of television would be blunted by its sheer banality – that an audience watching programmes round the clock and on a range of channels would not be too susceptible to any of them. Hence the early 1980s seemed to be on the threshold of an exciting new world of multichannel television which would provide a cornucopia of new material, satisfy a range of interests, and generate its own checks and balances with only a minimal need for public regulation.

Proliferation and deregulation: the 1970s onwards

3

... the duopoly was being undermined by technological developments. Scarcity of available spectrum had previously determined that only a very few channels could be broadcast. But this was changing. It seemed likely that ever higher-frequency parts of the spectrum would be able to be brought into use. Cable television and direct broadcasting by satellite (DBS) also looked likely to transform the possibilities. There was more opportunity for payment – per channel or per programme – by subscription. An entire new world was opening up.

... But this vastly increased potential demand for programmes should not be met from within the existing duopoly. I wanted to see the widest competition among and opportunities for the independent producers – who were themselves virtually a creation of our earlier decision to set up Channel 4 in 1982. I also believed that it would be possible to combine more choice for viewers and more opportunity for producers with standards – both of production and taste – that were as high as, if not higher than, those under the existing duopoly.

(Margaret Thatcher, *The Downing Street Years*)

During the 1970s there were still only three broadcasting channels. Yet television began to grow more abundant in the sense that viewers could use their sets for content other than the live programmes that the broadcasters provided. From 1974 they were able to access *teletext*, a technology which delivered continuously updated news and information, as well as lighter material, in the form of print and graphics. At about the same time the new *video cassette recorders* (VCRs) enabled them to view not only broadcast content which they had recorded earlier but material which had not been originated by the duopoly: cinema films, programmes made especially for the video market, even home movies they could shoot with camcorders. Sales of VCRs were at first inhibited by a struggle between rival formats, but in the early 1980s they began to sell in large numbers and by 1986 were to be found in nearly half of all British households.

Yet even in live broadcasting, the days of scarcity were now numbered. While cable transmission had existed for many years, the arrival of optical fibre or 'broadband' technology at the end of the 1970s hugely increased its channel-carrying capacity. It also increased the potential for two-way or 'interactive' communication and was thus invaluable for telecommunications and 'informatics' – the movement of data between computers. The government's plan was to use the entertainment value of broadcasting, and especially television, as a way of inducing private enterprise to finance a national cable infrastructure. But to make it sufficiently enticing to viewers and thus to any aspiring operators, *cable TV* would have to be allowed to offer many more channels than were currently available under the duopoly. Yet the duopoly still commanded considerable support. By and large, the public seemed satisfied with the quality and range of output it provided. There were many who were unconvinced that more channels would mean more diversity.

Even within the ranks of Mrs Thatcher's Conservative government, there was a certain fear of what deregulated television might bring. Politicians have always believed that the medium exerts a far greater influence on public opinion than radio or even the newspapers – and they would also be aware that, as we shall see shortly, some of the cable channels would originate from abroad. Hence the Hunt Committee, which the government appointed to map out the institutional shape of cable television, was obliged to tread carefully. In its report, which was published in 1982, it insisted that cable television was supplementary and not a rival to the public service duopoly of the BBC and ITV, and would therefore be obliged to carry their networks as part of the package it offered to its subscribers. As with the ITV system, its franchises were to be allocated on a regional basis and several of the operators would come from North America, where the technology was already well established.

Since the launch of cable TV in 1983 was both modest and local, its momentous implications were largely overlooked: for the first time the British public had access to live television which had not been originated from within the BBC–ITV duopoly and which, since it was not obliged to fulfil public service obligations, could be 'themed and streamed' in character rather than providing range and variety. Nevertheless the subsequent progress of cable was disappointing. The establishment of its infrastructure was costly and slow, and the technology was not always reliable. Fewer than 20 per cent of potential customers signed up to it, either because they were satisfied with what was already being provided by the existing BBC and ITV channels or because video cassettes and, after 1989, direct-to-home satellite television gave them easier options.

By 1984 the government was also keen to reappraise the BBC. If 'public service' in the sense of programmes for everyone could be provided by a competitive, market system which was largely 'free' to its viewers, was there any longer a need for a BBC whose costs were a burden on all viewers, even those who seldom or never watched it? The question was particularly pertinent since for a variety of reasons the government had just been obliged to approve a rise of 26 per cent in the licence fee. It therefore appointed a committee under Professor Alan Peacock to consider whether the BBC should take advertising as an alternative or supplement to its licence income, and what impact this would have upon the broadcasting system as a whole. Significantly enough, it was the first parliamentary committee of inquiry into the BBC that was not required to treat the corporation's public service mission as its primary consideration (Scannell 1990: 22): the broadcasting audience were to be thought of simply as 'consumers'.

In its report, which was published in 1986, the Peacock Committee concluded that there were still too few channels to deliver the range of material that licence funding supported and that the BBC's licence income should therefore be retained in the short term. But in the longer term, when the number of channels had increased and conditional access technology had been developed, the corporation should switch to subscription funding, which would oblige it to be much more responsive to the market. Meanwhile in order to help free up the system as a whole, both the BBC and the main ITV network should emulate Channel 4 by commissioning a certain quota of their programmes from outside sources, thus allowing an even greater number of independent producers to gain access to the mass audience. Finally, the link between ITV and Channel 4 should be severed by requiring the latter to sell its own advertising. This would destroy ITV's advertising monopoly and replace their complementary relationship with a competitive one.

While allowing a slimmer and more cost-effective BBC to retain its licence fee for the time being, the government would adopt most of these recommendations in its 1990 Broadcasting Act, and, moreover, authorise the launch of a third commercial network (which eventually appeared as Channel 5 in 1997). This meant, on the face of it, that the duopoly would be dismantled by the middle of the 1990s. Indeed, hard on the heels of the Peacock Report, the external threat to the duopoly which was posed by cable was followed by the much greater threat from *direct broadcasting by satellite* (DBS).

We have already noted that from 1962 both the BBC and ITV used satellite links to relay elements of their programming which originated in distant parts of the globe. However from 1981 a satellite service named Sky Channel began to supply its own programmes to cable television networks in mainland Europe. Two years later it was acquired by Rupert Murdoch's News International, which used it to provide material to the fledgling cable operators in Britain. By this time plans were afoot to achieve the third phase of satellite broadcasting – a multi-channelled subscription service which would be beamed directly into people's homes via a circular aerial or 'dish'.

Before it contemplated privatising the BBC, the government had envisaged the launch of a British version of satellite television from within the duopoly. In 1982 it granted the BBC a licence to provide a DBS service to the United Kingdom using a British-made satellite. However the costs proved prohibitive even when the IBA was brought in to spread them more widely, and the project was abandoned in 1985. The government then instructed the IBA to put the DBS franchise out to tender, and this was duly awarded to British Satellite Broadcasting (BSB) – a consortium whose members included two holders of the regional franchises which made up the main ITV channel. While BSB was slowly preparing to launch its own satellite and searching for sources of programming, Murdoch's Sky TV, already in orbit because it leased transponders on the Luxembourg-based Astra satellite and so did not have to build a satellite of its own, quickly stole a march on its rival. While continuing to act as the major supplier of the cable channels, it launched its own DBS service to the United Kingdom in February 1989. This comprised four channels offering mainly news, sport and movies. By the time BSB began its service in April 1990, Sky had secured the rights to all the Hollywood movies which were available for TV transmission. To the expense of launching its own satellite, BSB therefore had to add the cost of originating most of its own programmes, and after only seven months on air it collapsed into the arms of its rival. In April 1991 Murdoch re-launched his unified DBS service as British Sky Broadcasting (BSkyB).

BSkyB marked a significant step in the 'globalisation' of television broadcasting. For many years there had been a worldwide trade in programmes – most of them exported by the United States – but the conduct of television broadcasting had largely been contained within national boundaries. Now a service was being beamed into Britain by a broadcasting organisation which was partly based abroad and thus partly beyond the reach of British regulators. Moreover since both cable and satellite could provide an unprecedented abundance of channels, these were 'themed and streamed' to target particular interests. This was in contrast to the traditional earth-based or 'terrestrial' networks which mostly reflected the old days of broadcasting scarcity and public service obligation by offering a *mixture* of programming.

During the early 1990s BSkyB secured the rights to blockbuster movies and major sporting events, notably premiership soccer, and thus made slow but steady gains on the television audience. By 1996 over 4 million homes carried satellite dishes and one viewer in five could watch Sky's numerous channels, either directly or via cable. Did this mean the end of the old BBC–ITV duopoly? Not quite. First of all, the retention of the BBC's licence funding ensured that competition between it and the commercial terrestrials was still mitigated by the fact that they drew on separate sources of income. Second, the Independent Television Commission (ITC), the regulator which replaced the IBA after the 1990 Broadcasting Act, continued to exercise a tight control over the commercial sector. The intention had been that it would apply 'a light touch' – for instance, the ITV franchises would be reallocated by a simple cash auction rather than on merit – but a variety of political pressures made it in some ways stricter than its predecessor. The duopoly still had its supporters: not everybody believed that popularity was synonymous with quality; there were many who feared a satellite operator whose power base lay largely overseas; and the government itself had always taken a moralistic stance about the need to monitor television content. Hence when 13 ITV franchises were put up for auction in 1992, the ITC accepted the highest bids for only five of them: the others were assigned to lower bidders on 'quality' grounds. And a year or two later it issued public warnings to those franchise holders who were failing to honour their promises of performance. These measures further mitigated the competition between ITV and the BBC, for the ITV companies were still required to provide a variety of programmes rather than merely chasing the largest audiences. Finally, and despite the challenge of satellite and cable, it was clear that the great majority of viewers were still satisfied with the range and balance of programmes provided by the old duopoly.

This was partly thanks to a strengthened ITV network. It was true that the government was eager to dismantle the duopoly in order to achieve keener competition among broadcasters. But this meant not only allowing newcomers like BSkyB to compete but enabling the incumbents to strengthen their own competitiveness. We have seen that new broadcasting technologies promised vast audiences of a global, not simply national, character but also required a huge investment which would have to be achieved through economies of scale. In other words, broadcasters would have to become fewer and larger. Many of the newer organisations would be consortiums of companies with holdings across a range of media, not to mention a range of businesses. Confronting the threat of a BSkyB with power bases in Australia and the United States and sources of programming in Hollywood, the fragmented regional structure of ITV was an archaism that belonged to the 1950s. The IBA had allowed ITV to adopt a measure of programme sponsorship in 1988. Now, in the early 1990s, the ITC would relax the restrictions on franchise ownership. Consolidation rapidly followed: by the end of the decade the regional franchises were largely in the hands of just two big companies – Carlton Television and Granada – and now they are the virtual monopoly of Granada. Yet given the regulatory framework which was still in place, a strengthened ITV also meant some strengthening of the duopoly. In 1997 more than 75 per cent of British viewing was still of BBCs 1 and 2 and ITV, all three of which had been available at the beginning of the 1980s. Even the 30 per cent of viewers who had home access to multi-channel television still devoted the majority of their viewing to the terrestrial networks (Goodwin 1998: 156–7). With the launch of a fifth terrestrial, Channel 5, in 1997, which also came under the control of the ITC, the duopoly seemed in some respects to have been expanded rather than demolished.

Nevertheless by the middle of the decade the technological threat to the old dispensation had greatly intensified, for after cable and satellite came *digital broadcasting*. Hitherto television had been based on analogue technology, which meant that every channel required its own frequency. By enabling several channels to occupy a single frequency, with each providing a high-quality signal, digital technology made a much more efficient use of scarce spectrum space. To receive digital broadcasts, viewers would need either to buy a new television set or attach a converter or 'digibox' to their old analogue sets. But digitisation would have the capacity to supply hundreds of new channels, many of them likely to be themed. Following on cable technology, it would allow broadcasters control over access to their programmes, thus facilitating subscription and pay-per-view channels, and it would give the audience the opportunity to interact with live transmissions.

The political, economic, institutional and 'artistic' implications of digital technology are enormous and have yet to be fully digested. We will merely observe here that if it allows TV receivers to be used for informatics and telecommunications as well as old-fashioned broadcasting, that if TV receivers will be used to store live broadcasts for later consumption or to access material other than live broadcasts, and that if viewers will be able to respond to and modify live broadcasts or initiate content of their own, then it will become a difficult matter to say what 'television' actually is. At this point we will merely try to adhere to the definition we offered in the Introduction – that television is a medium consisting of sounds and moving images which are transmitted live to a scattered and largely domesticated mass audience – and suggest that a broadcasting system of several hundred channels really would obliterate what remains of the old duopoly and pose the gravest threat yet to the public service character of the BBC.

The organisational framework for digital broadcasting was set out by the Broadcasting Act of 1996. Frequencies were to be bundled into 'multiplexes', and of those that were allocated to terrestrial television, one was given to the BBC, which began digital transmissions in 1998, and the remainder were to be assigned by the ITC to the commercial broadcasters. The biggest of these went to a consortium of companies which included both Granada and Carlton. At first known as British Digital Broadcasting, it was launched in 1998 as ONdigital. For satellite television, BSkyB formed a consortium branded as Sky Digital, which launched in 1998. In broadcasting generally, the multiplicity of channels that digital technology made possible strengthened a tendency which had already been begun by cable: whereas traditional broadcasting organisations transmitted their own channels or networks and nobody else's, many were now becoming *multiplex operators* as well as *programme providers* and carrying the channels of their rivals. This had always been true of the cable operators, which offered very few channels of their own.

In fact, cable television had had a bad couple of decades. Its infrastructure took much time and money to install, and though the cable operators were allowed into the profitable telecoms business from 1990, the system's patchworked, regional structure hindered their efforts to present a single, attractive brand to the public. Takeovers and mergers ensued, the operators took a long time to ensure that their technology would support a digital service, and it was not until 1999 that they began to develop a digital capability of their own. By 2000 only two major players remained on the field, Telewest and NTL: both had huge debt burdens and the former was absorbed by the latter in 2005.

The conversion to digital technology underlined the fact that, though much reviled for its aggressive populism and philistine hatred of the BBC, Rupert Murdoch's BSkyB was the television success story of the end of the millennium. No other broadcasting organisation could match its foresight and predatory opportunism. By using someone else's satellite to launch DBS ahead of BSB, and at the same time securing the rights to all the available material that was worth watching, it strangled its rival at birth. Then it quickly learned from its DBS operation that viewers will not embrace new technology unless it brings new programming – and not even then, if the programmes supplied by the traditional broadcasters are felt to be adequate. It therefore grew its audience base by gaining exclusive rights to premium soccer and blockbuster movies (it would have five million subscribers by 2000), and thus built up a valuable lead in access and encryption technology, the means by which programmes are made available to subscribers and denied to everybody else. It also supplied channels to its programme-starved commercial rivals – at a price. Finally, having acquired a large subscription base, it forced the conversion to digital in as painless a way as possible, a conversion that would otherwise have taken an eternity to happen. Its strategy was to give to each of its subscribers who needed one a free digibox (value £130), and then it switched off its analogue signal in 2001. For every other broadcaster, digitisation is still an issue: for BSkyB, it is history. Moreover the forced conversion helped to destroy another of its rivals. The hapless ONdigital, with tiny audiences and already in thrall to Sky for most of its channels, was obliged to follow suit and give away its own digiboxes. The cost was crippling. The consortium was re-branded as ITV Digital in 2001, but went into liquidation in the following year.

The multiplex it vacated was awarded by the ITC to the BBC in conjunction with BSkyB and the transmission company Crown Castle, and re-launched in 2002 as 'Freeview'. Viewers with analogue TV sets would have to pay for a digibox but then acquired 28 free-to-air channels from the BBC, BSkyB and ITV. Since 1998 the BBC had been steadily enlarging its own portfolio of digital channels. To BBC News 24 and BBC Parliament, along with the digitised transmissions of the old terrestrial networks BBCs 1 and 2, it added the children's channels CBeebies and CBBC in 2001, BBC 4 (arts and documentaries) in 2002, and BBC 3 (entertainment and drama) in 2003. Slowly but surely, the old duopoly of traditional BBC and ITV networks, each containing some range and variety of programming, was losing its dominance. In April 2003, the five traditional networks – BBCs 1 and 2, ITV 1, and Channels 4 and 5 – were overtaken in the ratings for the first time by the combined weight of the smaller, specialist channels, even though fewer than half the country's viewers had access to them. Between them the specialist channels captured 25.1 per cent of the audience, the BBC 23.9 per cent and ITV 1 23.8 per cent.

The changing television landscape revealed other new features. If in future the key players in television broadcasting were multiplex operators rather than individual networks and programme providers, this would mean a virtual merging of the public and private sectors: viewers might find themselves watching BBC channels on the Sky multiplex, or BBC, Sky and ITV channels on Freeview, and not be greatly conscious of the different broadcasting values that underlay them. And digital technology was bringing about a growing convergence of *media* as well as broadcasters: interactive television was not greatly different from networked computers – and both were a form of telecommunication. Hence by the end of 2003, a new Communications Act would replace the ITC as the regulator of independent television with a much larger Office of Communications – Ofcom – which would be responsible for regulating all broadcasting and telecommunications, though with only limited control over the BBC.

We will conclude this brief historical account with a look at just two of the bigger issues raised by the newer broadcasting technologies. The first is that of ownership and control. As we have seen, one effect of satellite and digital transmission is that broadcasting could become a global activity. Without political intervention – and perhaps even despite it – programming originated, let us say, in the United States could be broadcast to a single television audience around the world. Economies of scale are inevitable: national broadcasters will merge and themselves be absorbed by multinationals. There are fears within the United Kingdom that BSkyB has its eyes on Channel 5, while Bertelsmann, Sony and AOL/Time-Warner are just three other organisations with the potential for worldwide operation. But we must also remember that television broadcasting is not the only activity in which the multinationals are engaged. Since they also have interests in newspaper, magazine and book publishing, cinema film production, records, DVDs and computer software, and since all these media make use of a common digital technology, they can easily transfer products from one medium to another. This could lead to a merging or consolidation of *content* as well as *organisations*: despite the number of television channels, the viewer might have not only fewer broadcasters but fewer kinds of programming to choose from. Digital technology also makes it much easier for broadcasters to control the *access* to their programmes, which is likely to mean a growth of television as a subscription or pay-per-view service and a relative reduction in the number of free-to-air channels.

This transformation brings us to the second big issue: the future of the BBC, a body which was conceived to provide a service which was free-to-air, for all viewers, and paid for by a universal subscription in the form of the licence fee. Having launched seven digital channels and helped to establish the Freeview multiplex, it is presently in a powerful position: but its power is always precarious. Though most are streamed, its channels attempt to provide between them a microcosm of everything it is both possible and desirable to broadcast on television, and so justify the continuing imposition of a licence fee on all British viewers. Moreover once the digital receivers or digiboxes have been purchased, the fact that the channels are free-to-air is a strong recommendation to the general public. But the BBC will have to continue to hold a sizeable share of the total audience – which could itself pose a threat to minority content – because if it fails to do so, viewers will resent paying the licence fee for content that they do not watch, especially if the content that they *do* watch requires additional payment. The precariousness of the BBC's position is reflected in the fact that the government has renewed its licence funding only until 2016.

All this leads to larger reflections. When television was a scarce medium, it was possible for broadcasters to address themselves to mere minorities and even seek to expand the interests of the majority. But are adequately funded programmes for minorities deliverable in this era of new broadcasting technology and the economic system that it imposes? Scores of channels mean competition and choice – a market. But can the market offer the range and quality that was paradoxically provided by the old and restrictive licensing system? Would the public as licence holders and voters continue to be willing to *pay* for programmes which they are not, on the whole, willing to *watch*? It might mean, in effect, that they were subsidising the pleasures of those who lack collective spending power because there are few of them, but who are individually affluent – the lovers of fine art and architecture, intellectual discussion, opera, ballet, classical music and drama. And even if the broader public were willing to do this, is it reasonable to *expect* them to – especially when such pleasures are deplored by some as in a sense undemocratic, as instances of 'élitism' and cultural snobbery?

The central issue for television – perhaps 'dilemma' would be a better word – is whether it should be regarded as a national cultural resource rather like the state schools and colleges, museums, art galleries and public libraries – in which case it must be paid for by all viewers, including those who may seldom if ever watch it; or whether it should operate merely as a business, a commercial enterprise – in which case it will ignore those who lack the wealth or numbers to yield profits. Within these overall broadcasting philosophies, we must now look at how the television industry organises itself: at its cultures, policies and working practices, at the pressures it is subjected to by governments and audiences, and at how its schedules and programmes are originated.

Modern television: policies and practices

. . . some form of market failure must lie at the heart of public service broadcasting.

(The Future Funding of the BBC, 1999)

[Public service broadcasting] is a gonner because given the chance at the end of a tiring day viewers don't always choose what's good for them. Many will always pass on the wholesome, healthy and carefully crafted in favour of the easily digestible, pre-packaged and the undemanding. They devour the entertainment, play with the information and leave the education on the side of their plates thank you very much.

(Richard Eyre, 'Public Interest Broadcasting', MacTaggart
Memorial Lecture, 1999)

This chapter will consider three things: the policy of governments towards broadcasting (primarily, of course, television broadcasting); the policy of the broadcasting organisations towards programming; and the values and practices of those within the organisations who are involved in the making of the programmes.

As we saw at the end of the last chapter, broadcasting has been underpinned by two contrasting philosophies. The first is that it is a major cultural and educational resource which should resemble the schools and public libraries in being easily accessible to everyone. Like universal health-care, with which it forms a kind of spiritual parallel, this resource should be a birthright. The second is that broadcasting, notably television, is essentially a purveyor of 'commodities', mostly of entertainment and to a lesser extent information, all of which should be offered for sale in a

market. The former has been characterised as a philosophy of 'commu-
nicative rights', the latter as a philosophy of 'free trade' (Harvey 2002:
227–8). The main organisational embodiments of these philosophies are
the 'public service' model on the one hand and, albeit in rather different
guises, the commercial model on the other. Public service broadcasting is,
of necessity, funded by government, either as a direct grant or – for
instance in the United Kingdom – in the form of a television licence fee,
which is a 'hypothecated' tax, or sum of money raised for a specific
purpose. Commercial models of broadcasting may be located anywhere
along a spectrum which at one extreme charges the consumers the full cost
of the product (as a pure form of subscription television does), and at the
other charges the full cost to the advertiser, as ITV does (Barwise and
Gordon 2002: 200). Since its income is directly related to the number of
viewers it can command, the general aim of the commercial model of
broadcasting is, despite some targeting of 'niche' markets, to maximise its
audiences.

However, in practice the public service and commercial models of
broadcasting are often not very different from each other. Why? The
reason lies partly in the ambivalence which most governments feel
towards broadcasting, especially television. Commercial television
appeals to them because it is not a drain on the public purse, and by
studying majority tastes seeks to give the people what they want – something that strikes a chord with governments in a democracy, since they
depend for their own existence on popular preference. On the other
hand, most governments believe, rightly or wrongly, that television
exerts a great deal of political influence on the electorate, and are therefore happy to maintain the degree of financial control that the public
service model gives them. Of course, governments have a measure of
control over television of all kinds, for both public service and commercial broadcasters lie under a statutory duty to be balanced and impartial
in their coverage of politics. This means that if they cannot be coerced
into presenting the government in its own terms, they are at least
prevented from subjecting it to unmitigated criticism. Indeed, a government must be very cautious in trying to tip the balance in its own favour,
since if it does so it 'interferes with an instrument of its own accountability' (Seymour-Ure 1996: 179) – with the main means by which the
electorate observes and judges it. Nevertheless, the way in which a
public service broadcaster covers politics is always likely to be tempered
by an awareness that the government has a grip on its purse-strings.

Public service broadcasting is also liked by governments who are in
some measure conscious of their duty to provide for minorities, especially
as some may have a disproportionate political influence. Among them, we
might discern those liberal intellectuals sometimes known as 'the intelli-
gentsia' or 'the chattering classes' – a loose socio-cultural network of

academics, professional and business men and women, people involved with the creative arts and, not least, those working in the media: journalists, producers, television personalities. These are the nation's 'opinion leaders' – a group from which many politicians inevitably emerge, grateful for the generous air time they are likely to get from a public service broadcaster which, by its very nature, is not wholly preoccupied with maximising its audience.

Since governments can see advantages in both models, public service and commercial organisations have come to co-exist in many countries. In the United Kingdom, the licence-funded BBC is matched by a commercial sector – ITV, Channels 4 and 5, BSkyB and the cable operators – which has grown considerably over the last 20 years. In theory, however, these models *cannot* co-exist: they are fundamentally inimical to each other. Why?

The logic, indeed the lifeblood, of the public service model is *monopoly*. Its ability to provide a universal service – of a full range of programmes for all viewers – is damaged by the presence of a competitor. As soon as a competitor appears, the public service operator must also compete in order to justify its existence and its source of income, and in the fight for a larger share of the audience, programming for minorities will be sacrificed. The public service operator must, in other words, act commercially and thus lose its public service identity. The logic of the commercial model is, however, *competition*, both internally (one commercial operator must compete for its livelihood against another) and externally – against any other kind of broadcasting, including public service. Its aim is to capture the lion's share of the market, and it will fight all-comers in order to do so. Hence when a commercial model co-exists with a public service model, the former will absorb the latter: the broadcasters of both kinds will have to play the game according to the former's rules, and a public service operator can win only by behaving commercially.

To prevent this from happening, governments typically intervene. The competitive behaviour of the commercial operators is in some measure reined in. They are obliged to offer an amount of news and current affairs which probably exceeds the requirements of the majority audience, and a range of programming which appeals to at least some minorities. Governments will also impose limitations on the amount of advertising that can be shown, as well as on the products that may be advertised. Finally, because the tendency of commercialism is to devour itself – the endgame of competition is an operator who has absorbed or destroyed all rivals and thus acquired a monopoly – a government will also prevent broadcasting from falling into too few hands or into hands which are beyond its jurisdiction.

However, governments will also force public service broadcasters to become in some way more competitive in order to minimise their cost to the public. In countries such as Canada and the Republic of Ireland, they receive only limited public funding which they are required to supplement by carrying advertising. And even where they are fully funded from the public purse, they are usually expected to minimise their dependence on it by practising economic discipline and developing ancillary commercial activities. In the United Kingdom, for instance, the BBC was pressured by the government at the beginning of the 1990s to develop an 'internal market', whereby producers used their tight programme budgets to obtain resources on the best terms available, whether inside or outside the corporation. Through BBC Worldwide (known as 'BBC Enterprises' till 1994), it also sells programmes to rival broadcasters, and books, videos and other merchandise to the general public, and at the political level, it justifies its licence income not so much on the range of its programming as on the size of the audiences it can attract. Consequently most broadcasting organisations, whether public or commercial, are marked by a considerable degree of hybridity and have largely come to resemble each other. It has often been suggested that if the commercial breaks were removed from an evening's programmes on ITV, the viewer would be hard put to distinguish them from those of the BBC.

Both the manner and extent of the government's regulation of broadcasting are primarily the expression of its own ideological position, but it is also forced to take account of the competing policy ambitions of those various pressure groups which represent the interests of the broadcasting industry itself, political activists and audiences (Franklin 2001: 2; Harvey 2002: 220). In Britain, the industry lobby includes the radio and television institutions, advertisers, newspaper owners, telecoms providers and independent producers; the main politically affiliated groups are the right-wing Adam Smith Institute and the left-of-centre Institute for Public Policy Research; and among those representing the broader public interest are the Consumers' Association, the Voice of the Listener and Viewer, and Mediawatch-UK.

How do these broad policy issues influence the cultures and practices of those who work within the television industry? It will be helpful to discuss them from an historical perspective, and mainly in regard to the programme producers, since these are the link between management on the one hand and creative staff (presenters, actors, camera and sound crew and so on) on the other, to some extent combining the characteristics of both. The role of the television producer has multiple origins, harking back not only to the radio and cinema producer, stage director and show-business impresario but, thanks to the idiosyncratic development of British broadcasting, to the civil servant (Tunstall 1996: 103). We will recall that in its pursuit of the public service ideal, the BBC was soon organised along the lines of a public corporation. During the 33 years of its domestic monopoly it was not dissimilar to government departments like the Post Office, which also provided a universal service at a flat rate. Whatever the reality, there was a sense in which its broadcasting function seemed no more partisan or 'ideological' than carrying and delivering the mail or providing health-care, and it was therefore relatively easy for broadcasting staff to think of themselves as public servants. As Tunstall points out (1996: 103), this civil service ethos survived the end of the monopoly for a decade or more, and, indeed, permeated ITV as well as the BBC, partly because it insulated the broadcasters from the advertisers and partly because, insofar as the broadcasters acted as a duopoly rather than as competitors, ITV was also committed to the public service principle.

Nevertheless the competitive aspects of the duopoly – the fact that the two broadcasters were at bottom *different* – meant that the concept of loyalty to one's organisation and the ideals it embodied began to be supplanted by the concept of 'professionalism' or loyalty to one's trade (Burns 1977: 126). Broadcasting employees no longer needed to be bound to one organisation for the whole of their working lives: they could sell their services to the higher bidder – or even choose to freelance. The catalyst to professionalism was the launch of Channel 4 in 1982, for this was a 'publishing' network: it employed no programme makers of its own but commissioned and acquired its material from outside sources. The government saw this system as cost-effective and encouraged the BBC and ITV to follow suit, prompting a significant growth in the number of independent producers. The culmination of this trend was the 1990 Broadcasting Act, which required each of the main broadcasters to take not less than 25 per cent of its programmes from outside suppliers.

Since 1955, broadcasting employees had had the opportunity to transfer their services from one broadcaster to another: now it was increasingly the case that they were not employees at all. A notable civil service feature of the old dispensation had been job security, even though many broadcasters might be freelance by choice. But by the end of the 1980s fixed employment was giving way to casualisation. In 1987–8 ITV employed 17,000 people; in 1993 this number had shrunk to 11,000 (Tunstall 1996: 104, 107). Indeed by this time, the combination of casualisation, channel proliferation and deregulation had created a *further* shift in employment culture – towards entrepreneurialism. Programme production was no longer a *service* nor even a *profession*, but – in the sense that its creative aspects were becoming significantly constrained by the need to survive in the marketplace – a *business*.

To understand this clearly, we need to see how the broadcasting organisations are responding to the new media environment. As Barwise and Gordon (2002: 207–8) point out, they are seeking to cut operating costs – the BBC through internal economies and ITV through mergers – and programme costs by means of new technologies and shortened production schedules. However, the competition to buy scarce talent is keener than ever and forces costs up, as does the purchase of premium movies and the rights to top sporting events. Two further effects of multi-channel competition are a shift from information to entertainment and a growing conformity of programming between broadcasters (Negrine 2002: 240). The increased choice afforded by a plenitude of channels is something of an illusion: viewers may be able to choose between live soccer matches or even between sports, but they are unlikely to have access to as many *kinds* of programme as were broadcast in the old and regulated days of television scarcity (Barwise and Gordon 2002: 207).

Where does all this leave the freelance producer of made-for-TV programmes? With both more and less power: more because there will be an increased demand for material, less because the demand will be for material of a narrower range, and this has serious implications for the future of television as an art form. At this point we should note a further consequence of the new competitive, multi-channel environment: the *schedule* has become much more important than the individual *programmes* that comprise it. As John Ellis (2002: 131) aphoristically remarks, 'Scheduling is none other than editing on an Olympian scale': the scheduler does with programmes what the producer does with their individual elements. However, the balance of power between schedule and programmes has shifted dramatically in recent years. In former times producers made programmes and offered them to the network managers, and the special character of those programmes helped to determine the way in which the schedule was composed (Ellis 2002: 132). The schedule always, of course, contained fixed slots which acknowledged the presumed routines of the audience in needing to be filled by particular types of output such as news or children's programmes, but it also afforded ample room for those unique and irregular artefacts that often result from the creative intelligence of programme makers. Now, thanks to the tyranny of the ratings, network managers begin by devising a fairly rigid and regular schedule and only *then* commission certain types of programmes to fill it.

The artistic implications of this shift from a bottom-up, offer-led to a top-down, demand-led system of broadcasting are twofold. First, the dominance of the schedule inhibits the development of certain kinds of programme which, however important in themselves, are unlikely to find a place in it – programmes which might, perhaps, try to develop new genres or combine old genres in new and interesting ways. Both producers and schedulers tend to be timorous and to stick with tried-and-tested formats that will win commissions for the former and healthy ratings for the latter. Second, *duration* becomes a disproportionate factor in programme making. Programmes are no longer made to a length which is logically suggested by the subject itself or the producer's treatment of it but to the fixed lengths – one hour, half an hour and so on – that are demanded by the schedule. In short, 'individual programmes matter less than the integrity and the identity of the channel' (Ellis 2002: 134). Consequently some relatively serious themes may get only brief and superficial treatment or, more often, slight themes will be eked out over long or serialised programmes. It is against this background of policy and practices that we must now consider some of the better-known television genres.

Part II
Television genres

News and current affairs

5

What is truth? said jesting Pilate; and would not stay for an answer.
(Francis Bacon, *Essays*)

What is news? We can define it simply as information about recent or
contemporary events. But not all news is 'newsworthy' – that is, not all of
it is considered as being of sufficient relevance or interest to its intended
audience. There are, however, certain informal and usually unspoken principles that between them determine which stories will be included in
television news programmes (adapted from Casey *et al* 2002: 144–5):

- a focus on personalities rather than ideas
- a need for long-term developments to be associated with a specific
  event
- a focus on tangible audience concerns (for example traffic and
  travel, weather conditions, or house, transport and fuel prices)
- stories that can be presented in a clear, simple, unambiguous way
- stories that can be predicted from the events diary (anniversaries,
  arts festivals, big sporting occasions)
- stories that are out of the ordinary
- calamities, disasters and tragedies ('bad news is good news')
- stories with an élite orientation – about members of the royal family;
  celebrities in the fields of pop music, film, TV, the arts and sport;
  other public figures such as politicians and tycoons
- 'human interest' stories – of a poignant, humorous, whimsical or
  heart-warming nature
- the availability of audio-visual material – film or at the very least,
  photographs or sound recordings.

Whatever the presence of sounds or pictures, news is mostly a matter of *words*, whether spoken or written; and these words are always *binary* in nature. When conveying a news story they must give as accurate and truthful an account of the facts – the things, people and events that make up the story – as is possible, yet they must also impose an organising principle on them, give them a frame, 'shape' or narrative sequence which reflects the reporter's perception of them and which we might therefore term a 'perspective'. These two elements of news coverage are largely inseparable. It is impossible to report facts without forming them into a sequence and thus creating a perspective of some kind. But in another sense there is an antagonism, or at least a tension, between the two. When recounting facts the reporter must be objective and self-effacing, yet any report is a kind of editorialising – it is always to some extent subjective and value-loaded. The reporter makes a judgement about which parts of the story are more important and which are less so: she chooses one narrative sequence over other possible sequences. The values which inform her judgement will be intellectual but when appropriate they are also likely to be moral. They may be explicit, as when she refers to the 'heroic act' performed by 'a freedom fighter' or the 'atrocity' perpetrated by 'a terrorist', or they may be implicit – declared only in the sequence of her report or in the degree of prominence she accords to its various constituents. Implicit values might, for example, inform a newspaper account of a teachers' strike which covers: 1) where and when the strike took place and its duration; 2) its effects on classes (for example, those which were cancelled and those which were taught by replacement staff); 3) the reaction of the employers; 4) public opinion; 5) the causes of the strike. Partly in order to confirm the status of the report as nothing more than an objective account of the facts, the newspaper might run a separate editorial which expresses an opinion – argues that the strike is or is not justified. But we should be in no doubt that, however subtly, the report itself is *also* value-loaded: in its selection of the facts, the order in which they are treated and the length which is devoted to each of them. The reporter's judgement when dealing with points 4 and 5 is crucial: the perceived nature of public opinion will very much depend on whom she consults and what weight she gives to their views, and the causes of the strike are likely to vary according to individual interpretation. In writing her account, then, we can say that something of the reporter is imposed upon what she reports – a mode of perception or sense of values which is a subjective element – and that the factual raw material of the report is its objective element.

The first attempts to deliver the news were of course entirely verbal, whether spoken by the town crier or written by those creators of the *corantos* and news-sheets of the seventeenth century. To convey the facts accurately and to shape them according to an intellectual or moral vision were both tasks that had to be performed by words. But the transition from spoken to written news was an important one since it was a slight move away from the manifestly subjective nature of speech to the quasi-objective nature of an utterance which was physically separate from its utterer. And this utterance took the form not simply of writing but *technologised* writing – printing – without whose ability to make rapid and numerous copies newspapers would not have been possible at all.

While print technology was available from the end of the fifteenth century, newspapers did not appear for another 150 years and even then took centuries to evolve. Why? Newspapers had to wait upon changes in economic and social conditions – on advances in science and technology which led to the industrial revolution and the birth of modern capitalism. These changes were a result, or a reflection, of developments in philosophy, notably the rise of empiricism with its use of scientific methods of inquiry in pursuit of a knowable objective reality.

The huge growth in demand for news and information was itself based on a belief that it was possible for journalism to be objective (McNair 1998: 66–7), a belief which the already available technology of print clearly helped to foster. As we have just observed, both writing and print achieved the detachment of an utterance from its speaker. Yet unlike handwriting, whose idiosyncrasies reflect those of its creator, print is machine made and so appears to be 'authorless' – to be wholly truthful and impersonal. Of course, printed texts retained many other signs of subjectivity in the stylistic mannerisms of the writer, but what the later news media sought to do was to strengthen the seeming objectivity of print by finding complementary and more vivid ways of presenting the facts. The aim was to use the new technologies of photography, cinema, radio and television to *show* the facts, not merely to report them, and so apparently to reduce the subjective role of human agency. The special contribution of each of these new media was to prove the realness of the things, people and events which were being reported and so confirm the truthfulness of the reports – first in the fixed images of photography, then in the recorded moving images and sounds of the cinema, later in the live sounds of radio, and finally in the live moving images and sounds of television.

Yet we must beware of making simplistic distinctions between the 'objective' world of sounds and images and the merely 'subjective' nature of words. While objectivity and impersonality are ultimately unachievable in language, it is clear that some utterances get nearer to that unachievable end than others. The report of a laboratory experiment, for instance, effaces the writer by such devices as the use of passive verbs: not 'I *heated* the compound to boiling point' but 'the compound *was heated* to boiling point'. Observations are recorded but emotions and opinions are absent or concealed. On the other hand, the sounds and images of 'the real world' can be selectively used, tendentiously edited and even rigged outright. Nevertheless, because words are a human invention and images and sounds originate in external things, we assume (even though in so doing we may tread on the corns of a few philosophers) that images and sounds tend to be more objective, while speaking and writing are more subjective. The former come from the outside world; the latter are always coloured by the persona of the speaker or writer.

The history of the news media can thus be seen as a history of attempts to use technology in order to get closer to the outside world, to the texture and flux of events. Photography provided accurate images but these were fixed; the cinema provided both sounds and moving images but these were merely recorded; and radio provided live sounds but no images. In the competition between media the advantage which one medium held over another was not always clear-cut. As John Ellis (2002: 23) points out, radio's liveness made cinema look dated:

> As radio gave a sense of instantaneity to the news and to the transmission of human speech, cinema newsreels of the 1930s took on a slightly ritualistic quality of showing the people from whom the audience had already heard, and events reports of which they had already read. Cinema stood in much the same relation to news as the photographs of the Crimean or American civil wars stood to the printed reports of them. There was a distance of time involved which emphasised the distance of space.

On the other hand, radio's lack of a visual dimension was clearly seen as a handicap. This explains why in 1940 the BBC devised a programme with the filmic title of *Radio Newsreel*. The hope was that its sound actuality would create such vivid images in the minds of the listener that they would emulate those of the cinema.

When television arrived with both live sounds and live images, it seemed that the truthful and objective presentation of news events had reached endgame. Yet not everybody saw this latest medium as having an unambiguous advantage over radio, nor even radio and television as having such an advantage over the press. Because the broadcast media required a newsreader who would be at least heard, if not seen and heard, the head of BBC news during the 1940s and 1950s, a New Zealander named Tahu Hole, regretted what he saw as their *lack* of objectivity in comparison with the depersonalised medium of print. In this respect radio was less of an offender than television because, though audible, its newsreaders could not be seen. Hence for many years Hole insisted on TV news programmes which hid the newsreader from the camera. Some were cinematic newsreels in which the newsreader's presence was declared only in a voice-over and some were straight re-broadcasts of the radio bulletins during which viewers saw nothing but a photograph of Big Ben. It was not until 1955 that a BBC newsreader was seen on a television screen.

Independent Television News (ITN), which was formed in that year, was the first TV news organisation to play to the medium's strengths. Since the presence of the newsreader could not be eliminated, the ITN producers made a virtue out of necessity by heightening his or her editorial role, transforming the reader into an authoritative 'newscaster'. But they also set out to make a much greater use of actuality in the form of an unprecedented quantity of pictures, whether still or moving: during 1956 ITN provided the only British film coverage of the Hungarian uprising and the Anglo-French invasion of Egypt (Sendall 1982: 285–6).

Of course much television actuality was, and is, no different from that of the cinema in the sense that it was recorded rather than live: but the fact that live actuality was sometimes a possibility and that the cinema could not match the recency of its filmed actuality meant the end of cinema as a news medium. This occurred in 1969 but many years earlier its inadequacies had been ridiculed by the television satire show *That Was the Week That Was*, in which Pathé News was depicted as 'Pathetic News'.

The significance of television's liveness is worth pondering for a few moments. All television is live in the sense that its content is received at the time it is transmitted. (This content may not be *viewed* at the time it is received, but that is another matter.) But though transmitted live, much of it – whether in the form of made-for-TV programmes, old cinema films or items for inclusion in news bulletins – is for obvious economic and logistical reasons pre-recorded. This was not always so. In the early days of television, almost all the programmes were created at the moment they were being broadcast. Yet pre-recording has not blinded us to the essential nature of the medium. Despite all those evening schedules when nothing that is broadcast is in real time – the vintage movies, the cartoons, the commercials, the well-known repeats – and despite the fact that we may have decided to record these things for later consumption, we still think of television as a *live* medium.

Yet what is remarkable is that over half a century after pre-recording became commonplace, television continues to pretend that almost *none* of its content is pre-recorded (Ellis 2002: 31–4) – that it is 'live' just as it was live in its earliest days. Why does it do this? Because recording distracts us from the fact that liveness is television's 'unique selling proposition', the single advantage it enjoys over all the other visual or visible mass media.

Its countless pre-recorded programmes merely mimic the artefacts of the cinema: indeed the old cinema movies which litter its schedules are among the few kinds of programme that television does *not* pretend are live. As Jostein Gripsrud (1998: 19–20) observes, the liveness of television is not just an aesthetic but an ideological principle – and since the term *live* connotes 'life in the raw' and thus 'an inability to lie', it is clear why TV and the news are in a sense made for each other. Television is good for news because the ultimate goal of news is not only to convey the sights and sounds of the real world through 'actuality' but to convey them as soon as possible after they have happened – or better still, *while* they are happening. And news is good for television because it shows television's unique power to its best advantage, recalling the good old days when virtually all its content was live. News bulletins themselves are indisputably 'in real time', and even if their actuality is filmed, it is far more recent than anything the cinema could provide.

This helps to explain a curious fact which we noted at the beginning of this book: that it is not the creative content of drama, comedy and so on which the TV networks regard as central to their identity, but the merely reactive, mirror-like content of the news. It is possible that in the future much of television's liveness will cease to matter. Thanks to DVD players, video cassette recorders and TiVo, viewers will not have to watch content at the time it is broadcast, while video-on-demand will allow them to choose and download their own content rather than having to watch the scheduled programmes of the broadcasters. Yet the demand for news and current affairs, including sports coverage, ensures that television will survive not so much as it is now but as it was in its infancy – as an all-live medium – and so remind us why there was a demand for it in the first place.

Ever since the launch of ITN, the aim of television news has been twofold: to provide more, and better, pictures and sounds of the news, whether live or recorded; and to reduce the time between the occurrence of the news and its appearance on our screens. Indeed a reduction to zero is sometimes possible since news bulletins can incorporate the live coverage of an event. Achieving the first aim has been largely a matter of improving the technology of cameras and sound equipment at one end of the broadcasting process and of domestic receiving equipment at the other; achieving the second, a matter of improving the link between the site of the news and the television newsroom. From the start, ITN used 16mm cameras instead of the 35mm newsreel cameras. The former lacked studio quality but were more flexible and could thus provide more pictures and bigger 'impact' (Davis 1976: 17). In 1958, news film was supplemented by the arrival of Ampex videotape, which in requiring no processing afforded an instant playback facility and so enabled more footage to be shot. For viewers, TV sets with sharper images – 625 lines on UHF – began to replace the 405-line VHF sets from 1964. BBC 2 could be viewed only on 625 lines, but the other networks soon adopted the new standard, and within 20 years VHF transmissions had been discontinued. In 1967, BBC 2 also conducted the first regular broadcasts in colour and was followed by BBC 1 and ITV two years later. The adoption of colour receivers was rapid: from zero to 11 million in ten years (Briggs 1995: 848).

For improving the link between the location of the news and the television newsroom, satellite technology must take most of the credit. Telstar, which was launched in 1962, provided the first live transatlantic transmissions, but for only a short time each day since it was an orbiting satellite. In the following year satellites were launched which were *geostationary* – that is, which orbit at the same speed as the earth and thus maintain a fixed position relative to its surface – and from 1965 the Intelsat series was able to transmit for 18 hours a day. The 1968 Mexico Olympic Games are generally thought of as the first major global TV event, but the live pictures of the American moon landings in 1969 were an astonishing *tour de force*. They attracted 26.5 million viewers in Britain alone – nearly half its population – and a worldwide audience of 600 million. During 1965, a mere 40 channel hours of international television were broadcast in Britain, but by 1970 the figure had soared to 1,214 hours, and by 1980 to 15,000 (Briggs 1995: 846). During the 1980s, the technologies of coverage on the one hand and transmission on the other were combining to achieve an ever shorter time lapse between the occurrence of the news and its appearance on the nation's screens. In 1980, ITN adopted 'electronic newsgathering' (ENG) cameras which used magnetic tape instead of film, and ever smaller widths of tape and the general miniaturisation of components allowed editing and dubbing on location. Four years later, ITN acquired its first transportable ground satellite station which allowed live two-way updates between the newscaster in the studio and the reporter at the scene of the news (Bonner with Aston 1998: 221).

By the end of the 1980s, satellite technology could create live links not only between a TV station and news sites anywhere in the world but between the TV station and its audience. The latter mode of broadcasting was known as DBS – direct broadcasting by satellite – or more generally as 'satellite television', and the satellite channels, along with the cable channels which they largely sustained, answered a need that was now beginning to make itself felt. Television's ultimate goal of contemporaneous or 'real time' news coverage could be frequently achieved but was now faced with what may be termed an institutional impediment in the form of the old-fashioned terrestrial networks. While waiting for the slots they were allocated among the many other kinds of programme that the networks broadcast, news items had to mark time and thus 'grow old'.

The solution was to launch all-news networks, which at that time were within the capacity only of the multi-channelled satellite and cable broadcasters. These networks would aim to provide stories which were not simply 'revolving' or repeated, but continuous and developing – a concept which became known as 'rolling news'. It was pioneered in the United States by Ted Turner's round-the-clock cable channels, which were collectively known as Cable News Network (CNN). As part of CNN's routine coverage, live cameras were present at the launch of the *Challenger* spacecraft in 1986, and thus earned the network its first scoop when the spacecraft exploded a few moments later. But it was during the Gulf War of 1990–1 that CNN came into its own (McNair 1998: 132–3). It soon faced competition from BSkyB, while the BBC responded with its News 24 channel in 1997.

The 'busy screens' of many of the all-news channels, notably Sky News, represent a further stage in television's attempt to convey events in an accurate and truthful way. The dual images, captions, moving text, graphics and invitations to interact are an acknowledgement that news stories develop not as the simple sequence of discrete items that characterise the conventional bulletin but in a simultaneous and disparate way, and therefore that the properly informed viewer must be kept abreast of as many as possible. Consciously or otherwise, the crowded screen of the all-news channels also evokes the visual display unit of a computer – an admission of the challenge the computer poses to television as a multifarious information provider.

Let us summarise the argument we have been making. Over the last five centuries, there has been a general tendency, fostered by the technologies of print, photography, film, sound recording and live broadcasting, to make the presentation of the news as impersonal and 'true to life' as possible. Print introduced into reportage an air of objectivity which now, in the sounds and images of television actuality, seems almost absolute. But we have also asserted that the news is always and unavoidably organised into a narrative or perspective by those who gather it, whether print journalists, camera crews or television reporters, and that this perspective is based on a sense of values – on what they deem to be important or interesting or morally appropriate. We might say that what they do involves a process of *implicit* editorialising.

However, among those who produce television news there has been a growing sense that the actuality it incorporates – some of it live and thus difficult to mediate – is so extensive and its impact so powerful that its editorial elements need strengthening. The audience could become so mesmerised by the images and sounds of events that it loses a sense of the shape and purpose of the stories they form part of, and even, when the bulletin contains lengthy live coverage, forgets that what it is watching *is* the news and not just an outside broadcast.

(At this point it is worth noting that because television is now so much better than newspapers at providing a quasi-objective coverage of events, many of the papers have fallen back on that other ability of words: to make explicit value judgements as well as give objective descriptions. In the past, these judgements were confined to the editorials. But now the news reports themselves – especially in the tabloid press – may openly editorialise, as when an individual convicted of rape or indecent assault is described as a 'sex fiend' or 'sex pest', a philanderer as a 'love rat' and so on. However, the papers are perhaps seeking to have it both ways by hoping that an air of objectivity, of undeniable truthfulness, may still be conferred by the 'authorless', impersonal character of the print medium itself.)

Television news seeks to strengthen our sense of perspective through a number of framing elements, some of which merely serve to declare to us that what we are seeing is indeed the news and not drama or light entertainment, but some of which clarify the narrative approach which is always to some degree present even in 'objective' accounts of the facts. Among the former are the presentational elements, such as the urgent, staccato music and the spectacular graphics and logo by which the news is often introduced. Another is the design of the studio in which the bulletins are read. Though a busy newsroom or bank of monitors may be visible behind it, the studio itself is usually clinical and uncluttered, radiating a calm at the eye of a veritable storm of incoming images, sounds and data. The combined impression is that the news organisation has antennae for everything that happens but is also capable of mediating and ordering it. That such an impression is not fanciful is suggested by the thought and expense which broadcasters devote to design: back in 1993 the BBC spent £650,000 on the creation of a virtual reality news studio (Franklin 1997: 13).

The videographics which now characterise so many news bulletins serve a similar role. Moving diagrams and distinctive script may appear on the screen: the colour tones of the images may be altered and the images themselves twisted, stretched, rotated, shattered and peeled away like the pages of a book. As John Ellis (2002: 97) puts it, 'News graphics play an important role in organizing the incoherent world of news footage into the coherent world of news explanation'. Because of their newsworthiness, images must often be included which are poorly framed and badly lit, with inferior sound and electronic drop-outs: along with the newsreader it is the videographics which help to render them intelligible:

> The bulletins are held together by their direct antithesis: the controlled image of the news anchor-person (whose title here is surely significant), plus the highly contrived graphics that accompany the explanatory material provided by the anchor-person. News has

pushed its image acquisition technology (that is, its cameras plus the means to communicate back to base) towards instantaneity. At the same time it has developed the use of real-time graphics seemingly as a counter-weight, to try to anchor these vivid and unstable images of the near-present. Visually, news is an unresolved dialectic between these two extremes of disorder and control.

(Ellis 2002: 98)

It is in the person of the newsreader that the balance between objectivity and subjectivity, between fidelity to the facts and a sense of perspective, is at its most delicate, and where (as Tahu Hole feared) the editorial element may be overplayed. Notwithstanding the huge and recent shift which has taken place in the news from 'telling' to 'showing', John Corner (1999: 54–5) is right to remind us that television is still much more a matter of speech than illustration. The amount of actuality may be greater than ever before, but its images and sounds need to be explained and their causal or logical links spelt out. In this sense, the newsreader is a powerful presence on our screens. Indeed one factor which may explain Tahu Hole's admittedly rather grudging preference of radio to television news is that, on the former, the subjective character of the newsreader's words is mitigated by the situation of its audience. The blindness of radio means that the newsreader, like the town crier in the olden days, speaks to nobody in particular and offers the news on a take-it-or-leave-it basis. But the television newsreader addresses us directly through the camera and may therefore appear to have a rhetorical design on us.

Yet although the news on television is still largely a matter of telling rather than showing, the language typically used by the reader is as impersonally descriptive as possible: *overt* editorialising in the form of comment, opinion and speculation is largely eschewed. In physical terms she (and he) seems to embody that difficult balancing act which the role demands. Given the aesthetics of the medium, the newsreader is normally pleasant to look at, but – in deference to that anxiety about 'personalisation' which Tahu Hole expressed so many years ago – not in an ostentatious or idiosyncratic way. She must have enough presence to seem authoritative, to promise a sense of perspective, yet she must also retain a degree of self-effacement which implies objectivity.

Nevertheless, there are good reasons why the implicit editorial role of the newsreader is felt to be insufficient. Amid the welter of actuality some measure of *explicit* editorialising is called for, not merely to clarify the values which shape the stories but to transcend the innate limitations of the medium itself, the difficulty it has in conveying those elements of the news that cannot easily be rendered in sounds and images. What the viewers need are not just pictures and brief descriptions of the stories but a proper explanation of their significance – of the factors that prompted them, the trends that underlie them, the context that surrounds them, their implications and possible consequences, and the wisdom or folly of those who are caught up in them. The problem is that because radio and television wavelengths were once scarce and because governments have always thought that sounds and images were more influential than printed words, broadcasting institutions in Britain, as in many other countries, have been forbidden to editorialise in this way.

The solution has been to include within the news bulletins a number of outside reporters or *correspondents*, whose highly paradoxical function we must consider in some detail. The correspondent usually appears in a 'live remote' – that is to say, he delivers from the scene of the news a short report to the camera which is followed by a (not always convincingly) staged interview with the newsreader via a two-way audio-visual link. The first and obvious role of the correspondent is to confirm the truthfulness and accuracy of his report by being where the events have happened and may still be happening. But his second role is to editorialise – to offer perspective and comment on the mass of data, pictures and sounds he has been largely responsible for providing. This role could also be seen as a consequence of the increased choice of news providers which audiences now enjoy:

> In recent years, as the number of broadcast news outlets, and thus competition for each individual organisation, has increased . . . [the prohibition against editorialising] has begun to be relaxed to allow room for opinion and analysis from key journalists. The commercial value of well-founded, authoritative opinion is enhanced in a more competitive broadcast news market, where viewers and listeners have much more choice of provision than ever before. Thus, within the heightened objectivity of the broadcast news form as a whole, senior journalists find an increased freedom to 'intervene' with commentary and analysis, moving closer to the tradition of the print media.
>
> (McNair 1998: 71)

The viewer can hardly fail to notice that the interview between newsreader and correspondent is a highly contrived affair. The newsreader's own account of the news draws largely if not wholly on the material that the correspondent has supplied before the bulletin. Strictly speaking, it is therefore unnecessary to include correspondents *within* the bulletin, as is clear from their absence from the news broadcasts of former times and also from present day summaries. Yet in questioning the correspondent, the newsreader feigns ignorance about the news item, positioning herself as the agent of the viewers by asking what they need to know. This serves to protect the broadcasting organisation against any accusation that it is flouting its statutory obligation to refrain from overt editorialising, for it distances the correspondent from the broadcasting organisation in two ways. First, because the organisation is embodied in the newsreader, the correspondent is treated as in a sense *extraneous* to it, even though he is a news supplier. At the end of the interview, the newsreader never agrees with or comments on the views which the correspondent has proffered: there is, in other words, no endorsement from the broadcasting organisation itself. Second, the interview might go some way to allay the fears once expressed by Tahu Hole in that the correspondent's views are never delivered directly to the viewers: the latter are merely witnesses of a conversation between two other parties whose opinions they may take or leave. Hence the differing strengths and limitations of the written and audiovisual media create an ostensible contrast in the way that they seek to present the news. In newspapers, factual reportage is incorporated within an editorial perspective, whereas in television, an editorial perspective is incorporated within the factual reportage.

In a survey conducted during the mid-1990s, no less than 69 per cent of its respondents cited television as their first and main source of news, thinking it more reliable than newspapers or radio (Abercrombie 1996: 55). Having regard to the innate characteristics of the medium, we must now examine how far their belief is justified. It is easy to see why television news is trusted. Unlike the opaque, human-made, value-loaded medium of words, television's pictures and sounds are transparent. It shows things 'as they really are' and often as they are happening, thus minimising any opportunity for production staff to interfere with them. The pictures and sounds are equally believable whether we are familiar or unfamiliar with what they represent: if familiar, we can check their authenticity against our own experience; if unfamiliar, we credit them precisely because they are our sole source of information. And if there is any risk that we should fail to grasp the point of all these pictures and sounds, there are, as we have just seen, a number of elements by which our perspective on them has been strengthened. Foremost among these are *words*, for words not only make explicit the information contained in the pictures (and in sounds which are not themselves words) and link everything into a sequence, but – largely in the mouths of the correspondents – provide background, context, consequences and comment. The power of television as a rapid or instantaneous news medium is perhaps most obvious in its coverage of isolated and spectacular events whose causes and contexts are relatively straightforward or well-known – for instance, natural disasters such as floods, famines and earthquakes.

However I have argued elsewhere (Crisell 2002: 155–61) that in certain respects television is a rather crude and misleading vehicle for the news – that once the words have performed their descriptive function of identifying and explaining the pictures, they are frequently unequal to the impression conveyed by the pictures even when the words go on to perform their editorial function by seeking to qualify or mitigate them. To put it crudely, there may still be more telling than showing in TV news but once telling has made clear what is being shown, showing tends to prevail.

Let us take a look at its coverage of one of those isolated and spectacular events in which it normally excels. In November 2002, a tanker named *Prestige* foundered in the Atlantic and its cargo of 77,000 tonnes of oil was gradually washed onto the shores of Spain and France. On all the TV channels, the bulletins showed film of the sinking boat and the spillage, and the role of their newsreaders and correspondents was to identify what could be seen in the film and to spell out the significance of the event: in essence, that it would have disastrous ecological consequences. Yet this was not quite the whole of the matter. Despite the undeniable short-term disaster, the marine environment is relatively resilient: in the longer term, the action of the waves will disperse the oil and flush the beaches, enabling fishes and birds to flourish once more. The bulletins failed to mention two other threats to the environment which are much more serious. One is the amount of metal pollution which exists in the form of abandoned batteries, motor vehicles, refrigerators, nuclear submarines and the other technological detritus of modern life. Another is the over-fishing which has occurred off Newfoundland and in the North Sea. Why, then, did the television coverage of the *Prestige* disaster fail to set it in a fuller context? For two closely related reasons. The first is the ratio of words to pictures: a time-based medium such as television, which must rely on speech rather than printed text, simply cannot provide *enough* words. If a news presenter were to read non-stop throughout a 30-minute bulletin she would manage to deliver 3,000 words at the most, whereas each issue of *The Times* contains about 130,000 words. But to allow time for its visual content, a 30-minute TV bulletin actually contains fewer words than the front page of a broadsheet newspaper (Davis 1976: 27). Hence as Brian McNair (1998: 80–1) points out:

> In mainstream television news few stories can claim more than two minutes of coverage, requiring that the complexities and messiness of events be glossed over. If they cannot be, the event may not be reported. The complex histories and processes underlying most events cannot easily be translated into television terms. For the same reason, it is easier for broadcast news journalists to prioritise effects over causes, such as in the case of an industrial dispute. The filming and interviewing of inconvenienced airline passengers at an airport is easier, more televisual, than is narrating the progress of 18 months of negotiations which led up to the dispute taking place.

This means that in spite of the videographics and the explanations and comments of the correspondents, the limited words of a TV news bulletin are hard pressed to fulfil an editorial as well as a descriptive function, thus prompting Pierre Bourdieu's (1998: 6–7) complaint that television news is deracinated: neither the causes nor the consequences of the events it features are apparent.

The second reason why the *Prestige* story was hardly contextualised or qualified was quite simply that once its pictures were identified they would dominate over any further words. In the television world, it is ancient wisdom that when pictures and words are referring to different things the pictures will always win out. Seeing all the footage of the stricken boat, the swathes of discoloured water, the blackened beaches and the tarred and dying seabirds, what viewer would hear any words which suggested that this was a comparatively minor matter – or believe them if she did? For the press, the position is somewhat different. The newspapers covered the event too, but the limited actuality they can carry – still photographs – means that their coverage was less vivid and likely to be more quickly forgotten. Its impact would also have been mitigated by the fact that newspapers can carry far more content than TV bulletins, so this story was just one among many. And finally, the spatial medium of print affords much more scope for contextualisation and qualification even if many papers, notably the tabloids, make little use of it.

Among all the other and more serious threats to the environment which it might have covered why, then, did television home in on the sinking of the *Prestige*? Because it is a specific and highly visual event and not merely an eventless 'issue'. As we noted at the beginning of this chapter, issues without events tend to be ignored by television news because there is no visual 'peg' on which to hang them. What interesting footage can be shown about decaying metal or over-fishing? Given its nature, anyone who expected that television would not make much of the *Prestige* affair would be ludicrously unrealistic: to reject its suitability for TV coverage is almost to reject the medium itself. Yet the affair also illustrates that television can sometimes exaggerate the significance of an event *merely by showing it*. That reality can be reliably inferred from appearances is a dangerous assumption to make, one which leads to stereotyping and 'moral panics'. The violent images of television prompt us to believe that every citizen of Belfast is a rabid sectarian or that urban streets are ruled by the gun, and any words which might qualify these images are either unspoken or go unheard.

But there are, of course, some events which are not spectacular yet whose importance obliges television to cover them. Surely it can deal with these in a fuller, more informative and less distracting way? Let us take a 'non-visual' story – not a specific one, but one that is typical enough for any reader to recognise. In Brussels, a conference of European

Union leaders is convened to discuss economic issues. It is, of course, 'non-visual' not in the sense that it is literally devoid of pictures – television must always have pictures – but that the pictures are not the story. They merely show the EU leaders arriving at the venue and greeting one another, then posing for a 'photo opportunity', and finally sitting in the conference hall. The story itself is an abstract one: it is about what is being discussed at the conference, what are the points of agreement and dispute, and what, if any, are its outcomes. We might therefore expect that in contrast to the *Prestige* story, the pictures will not overwhelm the words but allow us as viewers to concentrate on the essentials. The causes, contexts and issues are explained, mostly by a correspondent who not only speaks to us directly but is interviewed by our representative, the newsreader – and to further assist our understanding, there are videographics: maps and diagrams whose shapes and colours can be manipulated in various ways.

Yet the story is not only abstract but complex, and in relative terms there is time for no more than a few words in which to convey it. Moreover, in a time-based medium not only are the words few, they are *ephemeral*: once seen on the screen or uttered by the newsreader or correspondent, they cease to exist. This means that they are often hard for the viewer to assimilate: unless they risk over-simplifying the story, they can be easily ignored or misunderstood or quickly forgotten. Even the videographics will be unhelpful if we have failed to absorb the words that explain them. What is missing is a visible text which is fixed and also sufficiently extensive to give us a full and intelligible account of the event – the resources, in other words, of the newspaper. Failing this, we would be better off with the wholly unrelated images of the world which we experience while listening to the radio, because this would make us more aware of the words we are hearing – a point I have argued elsewhere (Crisell 2004: 10).

What we get in television's non-visual news stories is, in a sense, neither fish nor fowl. The pictures are not the story, so to that extent we can disattend to what is before our eyes (as we do while listening to the radio) and merely focus on the words. On the other hand, the pictures are not wholly unrelated to the story. Hence we are tempted to look for enlightenment in them, and insofar as we do, they deflect our attention from the scarce and evaporating words we are hearing. Moreover the broadcasters *emphasise* the relatedness of the pictures: as well as the EU leaders in various settings, we are shown the correspondent reporting from the venue itself and being interviewed live at the same location. In the end, the 'non-visual' coverage of the EU conference is not very different from the visual coverage of the *Prestige* disaster, for both attach a disproportionate significance to the epistemological power of sight – to seeing as a means of knowing.

To sum up, then. The combination of large amounts of actuality and limited editorial mediation seems to promote, as it were half inadvertently, a rather simplified version of the news on television and to mislead us about where 'the news' actually lies. Yet we should not perhaps be surprised that the readers of tabloid newspapers place a greater reliance on TV news than broadsheet readers and attach a greater credence to it (Negrine 1994: 1).

In the course of this chapter, I have treated 'current affairs' as broadly synonymous with 'news'. Insofar as it is not, the focus of current affairs seems to be on *issues* rather than the isolated *events* that news is mostly concerned with – and issues are also the province of the documentary. This will be discussed in the following chapter.

Documentary and features

Look and learn.
(Old teaching precept)

When we talk of bridging the gap between the citizen and the community and between the classroom and the world without, we are asking for a kind of educational shorthand which will somehow give people quick and immediate comprehension of the highly complex forces which motivate our complicated society. . . . That is why the documentary film has achieved unique performance in the new world of education. It does not teach the new world by analysing it. Uniquely and for the first time it *communicates* the new world by showing it in its corporate and living nature.
(John Grierson, 'Education and the New Order')

As in the previous chapter, we need to begin with some definitions, and in the shifting sea of semantics the origin of a word may anchor our understanding. 'Documentary' derives ultimately from the Latin *docere* 'to teach', and however tentative and self-effacing some TV documentaries may be, we can still sense this earnest impulse behind them. Their themes are factual and their aim is in some sense and to some degree to enlighten the viewer. 'Features' is an altogether vaguer category and its etymology – from the Latin *factura*, 'an act of making' – is unhelpful and perhaps misleading. We might define features as programmes or programme items which are lighter in tone and seek not so much to impart specific knowledge of the world as to extend our experience of it or to enable us to revisit some of the endearing, admirable or baffling facets of human nature.

For reasons that will hardly surprise us, the documentary owes its existence to the rise of the visual media of cinema and television. Since in their various ways both afford 'a window on the world', and since sight is one of our primary faculties, they hold out that promise which we described in the chapter about the news: 'to see is to know'. Before the rise of the cinema, documentary possibilities could be glimpsed even in still photographs, though without words they lacked the sustained narrative or explanatory power of what came to distinguish the documentary as such. Hence the first documentaries were cinematic films made in the late 1920s and 1930s. Very few were shown on the regular picture-house circuits because these were already the preserve of those fantasy movies typified by the productions of Hollywood. But as a medium, cinema was still young enough to be thought of as having a potential that transcended the mere provision of entertainment, and these documentaries were shown at political, social and cultural gatherings, in schools and organisations such as Miners' Institutes, and in village halls by travelling projection units.

Among the first documentary makers were John Grierson, Robert Flaherty and Paul Rotha, and a notable fact was the extent to which the genre attracted state and corporate sponsorship – from the Empire Marketing Board, the General Post Office and the Shell Company among others (Williams 1998: 114–19). As Grierson (1979: 203–4) points out, '[Britain] was the first country to use the documentary film in an organized way to implement governmental and public purposes (E.M.B., G.P.O., health, slum clearance, town planning, popularization of scientific discovery, Commonwealth relations, international communications, colonial education, etc.)'. In these pre-war years the influence of Grierson and his colleagues extended to radio, encouraging features producers such as A.E. Harding, D.G. Bridson and Olive Shapley to attempt programmes with more contemporary and controversial themes (Scannell 1986: 5–22).

Not surprisingly, however, the main line of development in the documentary remained visual. But by the end of the Second World War the needs of both its state and corporate sponsors had changed. The policies of the new Labour government of 1945 were addressing most of the social and educational problems that the pre-war documentaries had highlighted, and its corporate sponsors were now more interested in direct advertising than oblique public relations (Kilborn and Izod 1997: 64). Under increasing threat from television, cinema willingly surrendered its residual documentary role to its new and domestically based rival: writing at the end of the 1950s Grierson was among those who acknowledged that the best of the genre was now to be found on the latter (Grierson 1979: 208).

For a number of reasons, television has proved to be the most suitable medium for documentary. Not only is it visual, like the cinema, but its domestic character means that documentary has sometimes reached large audiences – in situations where its messages have been difficult to ignore.

Moreover, until recently at least, television was not overwhelmingly associated with entertainment. The BBC and even ITV were also bound by a public service duty to provide information and education – a purpose to which documentary owes its very existence. And thanks to the decline in its cinematic forms, the genre was no longer associated with the vested interests of government or private companies. Its new milieu was not, of course, unproblematic. But since neither of the television broadcasters was permitted to editorialise, the documentaries that were produced under their aegis might seem to be not so much an expression of 'official' or institutional views as the visions of individual programme makers like Paul Watson, Roger Graef and Richard Cawston.

Yet if television is well suited to documentary, documentary is a genre which is very useful to television. In our discussion of television news, we noted that its implicit promise that 'to see is to know' is a deceptive one. The documentary is an opportunity both to provide lots of things to see – copious amounts of actuality – and to strengthen the way in which the actuality is mediated. Its dedication to a single theme means that there is more time for explanation and interpretation. There may also be a visible presenter who will provide a narrative and/or direct our responses to the actuality which the programme contains. There is more opportunity to marry words with pictures – or, where the subject is conceptual, to reduce the distraction of pictures by making use of 'talking heads': interviewees or participants in a studio discussion. For this reason, documentaries have traditionally attempted to treat 'issues' rather than mere 'events'.

In the early years of television, most documentaries incorporated a visible presenter, for which two reasons may be advanced. First, a directly didactic approach was acceptable, even expected, during a post-war period of revived enthusiasm for mass education and self-improvement. The 1944 Education Act had raised the school leaving age from 14 to 15, and it was conceivable that the new medium of television could enhance the role of the teacher – whom it might in some respects even replace. The second and more compelling reason was technological, and even to some extent political. The first TV cameras were expensive, few and cumbersome and unable to cover as much of the world as is now possible, nor did the broadcasting institutions have such extensive reserves of filmed material. Moreover a number of bodies, ranging from theatre impresarios and administrators of professional sports to parliamentary politicians, were able to exclude television from many areas of public life. Hence most of the early documentaries not only made use of a visible presenter in order to describe what could not be shown, but included dramatic reconstructions of actual or supposed events. So essential were these felt to be that in 1946, BBC television established a Dramatised Documentary Unit (Kerr 1990: 77). Inquisitive medium that it is, TV still chafes at its inability to gain access to certain areas of human experience and from time to time broadcasts 'docudra-mas' which attempt to convey those larger moral truths that often elude it. We shall consider docudramas and their sometimes controversial effects in another chapter.

As with the news, however, television's technical ability to cover events more vividly and comprehensively, combined with its admission to more areas of public life, meant that documentary could often replace visible presenters and dramatised reconstructions with filmed actuality. This change coincided nicely with the rising educational standards of the audience, for it is an understandable paradox that those who have bene-fited from teaching soon outgrow a didactic, 'teacherly' approach and prefer more oblique ways of acquiring their knowledge. And aside from enriching the programmes and increasing their appeal to the audience, the growth of available actuality assisted the broadcasting institutions in their dealings with government. Documentary was the means *par excel-lence* by which they could fulfil their public service duty to inform and educate. Yet the genre had been preoccupied above all with social and political issues. The social deprivation and political ferment of the late 1920s and 1930s were what prompted Grierson and his contemporaries to originate it, and the epigraph to this chapter illustrates that he seems to have thought of the genre almost exclusively in socio-political terms. But for broadcast documentary, which without much actuality was necessarily more didactic than its cinematic predecessor, this raised something of a dilemma: it exposed the potential contradiction between the broadcasters' duty to inform and educate and their other statutory duty to refrain from editorialising and political partisanship. The increase of actuality offered something of a solution because it gave broadcasters what looked like incontrovertible evidence with which to rebut any government accusations of editorial bias. What might once have seemed like a mere matter of opinion could now, with the support of sounds and images, appear as a straightforward matter of fact.

In trying to convey the dualistic character of factual television, the vari-ous media theorists tend to find themselves invoking similar sets of polar-ities, some of which will be familiar to us from the previous chapter. They approximate to the following, although the pairings are arbitrary since many of the terms are interchangeable:

Telling	Showing
Art	Reportage
Artifice	Evidence/authenticity
Point of view	'Reality'/'the truth'
Editorial content	Actuality

This terminology presents us with something of an embarrassment of riches. Yet despite the degree of interchangeability, the words in each column are only loosely synonymous. In the left-hand column, it may, for instance, seem strange to associate 'telling' or 'point of view' with 'artifice'. Yet telling is a subjective business, the imposition of a personal perspective on external events, and to that extent a construction or creation – even if out of largely factual materials. Grierson's celebrated definition of documentary as 'the creative treatment of actuality' (1979: 11) is ultimately true of every kind of attempt to represent or reconstruct reality. This inseparability of creativity and truthfulness means that the distinction between all the words of one column and all the words of the other is largely artificial and sometimes almost imperceptible. Why, for instance, is 'telling' on one side yet its virtual synonym 'reportage' on the other? The latter term is an acknowledgement that it is not only the iconic media of TV and radio which strive to present the facts as objectively as possible: so, too, do the newspapers. Their difficulty is that lacking the moving pictures and sounds of the former, they must use words to present the *facts* just as they use words to convey a perspective or impose *values* on the facts – and often the very same words. Yet even in the visual media, 'showing' is partly a matter of 'telling'. We see TV news pictures of heavily armed figures in beards and turbans, but it is only from the accompanying words that we learn whether they are members of Al Quaida or Afghan allies of the Americans.

This means that *all* documentaries contain elements of both telling and showing: all are factual because truthfulness is paramount, yet all are in some degree mediated. Moreover while we might, for instance, expect a narratorless, 'fly-on-the-wall' approach to characterise a showing documentary, and a visibly presented and highly edited approach to typify a telling one, matters are not always this simple. Fly-on-the-wall documentaries may be covertly edited to create a highly selective and tendentious treatment of events, while a visible presenter may attempt an objective and judicial approach in which she balances possibilities and leaves the viewers to draw their own conclusions. Nevertheless the distinction is broadly useful. We shall refer to *telling* documentaries as a shorthand for those which provide an overall perspective and involve a significant degree of artifice and editorial mediation; and to *showing* documentaries as a shorthand for those which convey a vivid sense of reality and involve little artifice or editorial mediation.

There is, however, a sense in which documentary of any kind is at odds with the medium of television. We have noted that in some measure the genre always aims to be instructive or educative, yet much education is a process of *abstraction*: it seeks to elicit from the human and physical worlds a body of principles, rules, axioms or theories that will enable us to make sense of them. Its interest in visible phenomena is largely limited on the one hand to those printed words and numbers (for example in textbooks) which make it easier for us to understand the principles; and on the other to those visual sense-impressions, whether actual experiences or pictorial representations, that will either illustrate the principles or allow us to infer new ones. Television, however, is preoccupied with the *concrete* rather than the abstract. Along with live-ness, moving pictures are what makes it unique. Its impulse to show prioritises what is only the subordinate function of education. As we have seen, the promise of television is that 'to see is to know', or at least, 'to learn': education insists that for the most part seeing can be taken for granted and learning is something else – an abstract, deductive process which seeing may nevertheless assist and confirm.

At its best, television documentary is a synthesis of these conflicting tendencies, usually in the form of what might be termed 'illustrated telling': a great deal of actuality is incorporated within a strong narrative frame. The historical documentaries of Simon Schama (*A History of Britain*, BBC 2, 2000–1) and David Starkey (*Elizabeth I*, 2000 and *The Six Wives of Henry VIII*, 2001, both Channel 4) are good examples, since history is a field in which the student may easily be overwhelmed by a wealth of evidence and fact. As we might expect, both Schama and Starkey make great use of historical locations and artefacts: battlefields, castles, palaces, old portraits and tapestries, weaponry. Yet we are 'told' history rather than 'shown' it. Even the re-enactments of key events are suggestive rather than vividly detailed – more like visual metonyms than full-blooded simulations – and though the presenter always speaks to us *in situ*, he is frequently visible and his manner is reassuringly authoritative.

Many documentaries now avoid making use of a visible presenter. What looks like a sequence of pure actuality accompanied only by a discreet voice-over seems more objective and truthful. Yet we should be clear that most of them are still highly mediated and have a variety of means by which to sustain a narrative or make a point. A typical exam-ple was *Maggie: The First Lady* (ITV 1, 2003), a four-part profile of Margaret Thatcher, Britain's first female prime minister. The series was constructed from six main elements. In Part 1, which dealt with her life up to the point when she became a Member of Parliament, these elements could be classified thus:

- A voice-over delivered by an always invisible presenter. The voice was that of the actor David Suchet and was probably chosen not so much because he is well-known – many viewers may have failed to recognise it – as because it has a mellifluous, quietly authoritative air.
- Talking heads: interviewees (friends, acquaintances and political colleagues of Mrs Thatcher) who addressed an invisible interviewer.

- Present-day film of Mrs Thatcher's former haunts, such as the streets of Grantham and interior and exterior views of her old school and the college where she studied at Oxford.
- Archive photographs and film of Mrs Thatcher as a child, an undergraduate, a young politician and so on.
- Archive photographs and film of key places, people and events in Mrs Thatcher's life-history (images of Grantham, her family, wartime, her husband Denis as a young man and the like).
- The programme's own reconstructions or, perhaps more accurately, oblique evocations of Mrs Thatcher's life-experiences – for example, soft-focus shots of young women studying in an Oxford college; a shot from the neck downwards of a young woman in 1950s dress, apparently canvassing in the streets of Dartford, the first constituency which Mrs Thatcher fought.

The narrative, fictive aspects of the programme consisted not only in the presenter's commentary and in the way the actuality was edited and intercut, but in the apparent actuality of the reconstructions. These were also a reminder that television does not see *everything*: there are always gaps in what it records precisely because some historical significances will be perceived only in retrospect. Moreover, certain other aspects demonstrated that it is by no means a straightforward matter to determine what 'actuality' is. Were the flickering monochrome images of streets those of Grantham, as the presenter allowed us to assume, or merely stock footage of urban Britain in wartime? And while the interviews with Mrs Thatcher's friends and colleagues were 'actuality' in the sense that the interviewees were an integral part of her history and witnesses to it, they were also in another sense detached from it and now seeking to impose a narrative frame on it which might in some respects be less accurate than that of a historian who had never known her personally.

The wildlife series of David Attenborough may be said to mark the apotheosis of the 'telling' documentary. Though hugely popular with television audiences for almost half a century, they have been all but ignored in studies of the genre (Corner 1996; Kilborn and Izod 1997), probably because most media academics are interested only in programmes that carry political significance. Like Schama and Starkey, Attenborough is frequently in vision as well as continuously audible and his manner is frankly if congenially didactic. His programmes do, of course, contain vast amounts of actuality but it is highly mediated: however striking and profuse, the images and sounds exist simply to illustrate the points that the narrator wishes to make. This means that the medium often flaunts its production techniques as well as its ability to gain access to exotic locations. Film is slowed down to focus on the sprint of a cheetah, speeded up to illustrate the migrant trails of wilde-beeste or the growth of protective thorns on a plant. Heat-sensitive and micro cameras show what is normally invisible to the naked eye, such as animals at night-time or in burrows. Addressing the camera directly, Attenborough will sometimes begin a sentence in one part of the world and complete it in another.

Still, what even Attenborough's documentaries illustrate is the power of showing, that 'to see is to know' – whether in the sense of providing immediate knowledge or a reliable guide to it – is a seduc-tive proposition. Why? Partly because it is self-evidently true. For all of us who are not blind, sight is the primary means by which we appre-hend the world. How can I tell that this building is Buckingham Palace and that building is my home, that this woman is my wife and that woman is my daughter? Primarily, if not exclusively, by looking at them: I *recognize* them – a word which carries a suggestion of both seeing and knowing. The proposition is also seductive because seeing is an intrinsically pleasurable and relatively effortless activity. And our 'scopophilia', as this pleasure in seeing is termed, is enhanced when we are looking at something we are not normally able to see.

Yet there is also a sense in which the proposition is not true. As we saw in the last chapter, seeing is sometimes an inadequate and poten-tially misleading guide to the truth. It would be wrong to imply that scopophilia is a merely mindless activity. We might enjoy gazing at the abstract shapes floating across our computer screens without attempting to interpret them, but most of our scopophilia is in some degree bound up with recognising what we see and attaching meanings to it. My pleas-ure in looking out of the window partly derives from understanding that the green shapes in front of me are trees and the red shapes are build-ings. And if a man walks along the street below, it may also be part of my pleasure to wonder who he is and where he is going. But in general, the cognitive power of sight is fairly limited and unreliable. The images of politicians sitting round a conference table will not, of themselves, tell us what the politicians are discussing. We might see a man in tears at a televised press conference, making a moving appeal for information leading to the whereabouts of his missing wife. Yet he is later charged with her murder, and convicted. The more credulous among us would have been deceived by what we saw, taking his tears as a sign of inno-cence: the more sceptical might have dismissed the tears as false. But the only reasonable conclusion is that what we see simply does not provide us with enough evidence. 'There's no art/To find the mind's construction in the face,' laments King Duncan in Shakespeare's *Macbeth*, and then readily entrusts his life to the man who will kill him.

In TV news and documentary, however, we have authoritative *words* to identify, explain and if necessary qualify what we are seeing. Yet as we noted in the last chapter, while we absorb those words that confirm and complement the images, we are resistant to those that modify or contradict them – and this is especially true if we lack personal experience of the things we are watching. Television news might, for instance, bring us horrific pictures of a major train crash, alongside which it will also offer us explanatory words. These will typically give the time and place of the crash, the trains that were involved, the number and nature of the casualties, and some initial speculation as to the cause of the accident. The viewer is likely to absorb these details while succumbing to scopophilia, a fair if disquieting description of an activity which if not exactly pleasurable is certainly irresistible. It is conceivable, though highly unlikely, that in the interests of a fuller truth the words will also *counter* the pictures they accompany. They may tell us that railways are among the safest forms of travel, that accidents are far rarer and involve fewer casualties than those on the roads, and that the huge cost of additional safety measures could not be justified by the tiny number of additional accidents they would prevent. But faced with images of skewed and toppled carriages, twisted rails, covered bodies on stretchers, and dazed and injured survivors, we would be likely to ignore or reject such assertions. They are intellectual propositions for which pictorial representation other than in the form of verbal or numerical symbols is virtually impossible – and they are also very much within the province of teaching and education that the documentary seeks to enter. The images of the crash are undeniably truthful: they are of something that has actually taken place. But they are only a part, and a misleading part, of a much larger truth. Any rational discussion of rail safety (and the obvious place for such a discussion is in a television documentary) would have to take place in the *absence* of such images.

Yet even when there is no conflict between the images and 'the truth', the former may be so plentiful and vivid that we yield to the pleasures of looking without paying much heed to what we are being told – and this may even be true of the 'telling' documentaries of Attenborough and Schama. In other words, despite the educative intentions of the broadcasters, the viewer may treat their work as little more than entertainment at the same time as using her knowledge of those intentions to persuade herself that she is, indeed, learning something significant. Moreover, squeezed as they are between a statutory requirement to include documentary programmes in their schedules and the need to compete for viewers by offering programmes that are pleasurable and entertaining, broadcasters are forced to collude in the notion that to see is to know. One way they do so is to create 'telling' documentaries which recount only as much of the truth as the images will support.

In 2003, BBC 2 broadcast *Cot Death Mothers: The Witch Hunt,* a documentary with a narrative slant that was declared in its very title. Its aim was to challenge the expertise of a leading paediatrician whose testimony had helped to convict certain mothers of the murder of their babies, and in other cases had led to legal decisions to remove children from their parents and place them into care. The presenter John Sweeney seldom addressed the camera directly, but he was visible as the interviewer and provided the 'voice-over' or background commentary. Since the paediatrician declined to appear, the programme relied on dramatised reconstructions of the evidence he had given in court, and these, combined with striking camera-angles, poignant shots of toys and teddy bears, and above all an uninhibited use of background music which raised expectations more appropriate to a Hollywood movie, were a reminder of the entertainment role that documentary must now perform. But the climax of the programme came with a piece of genuine actuality – an interview with a couple whose children had been taken into care, during which the mother broke down and tearfully denounced the man whose unsound evidence, she believed, had destroyed her family.

The programme was of interest in two respects. First it illustrated that the telling–showing distinction is in certain circumstances porous and ultimately untenable. The dramatisation of the paediatrician's evidence was in one sense an obvious fictional intervention (telling), but also 'actuality' (showing) in the sense that it conveyed his words, and his alone. Moreover the programme 'showed' in the sense that Sweeney allowed the tearful mother to speak for herself without any discernible editorial mediation. Yet the effect of this was to privilege a point of view which was not quite equal to all the material facts but which, in the absence of editorial mediation, the programme appeared to endorse. Hence it also seemed to be very much a 'telling' documentary. It is true that in care cases a paediatrician's evidence is likely to carry considerable weight: it is also true that the expertise of this particular paediatrician was later impugned in respect of other cases and even in the Court of Appeal. But there were certain things that Sweeney could not include in *Cot Death Mothers*, since to do so would have weakened the impact of the mother's tears and indeed of the whole programme. One was any account of the reasons why the case had been brought against the couple: we saw things mainly through their eyes because whereas they could speak freely, the paediatrician's refusal to appear was at least partly attributable to the fact that he would have been bound by the rules of professional confidentiality. Another was that care proceedings do not rely *solely* on the evidence of a paediatrician, who is in any case subjected to cross-examination. In the light of later events, the distinction between what the mother was alleging and what was the full truth of the matter was perhaps a fine one: but it is one that we might expect a serious documentary to make.

Another important means by which broadcasters can endorse the idea that seeing is a reliable guide to knowing is the straightforward 'showing' documentary, that adroit pact between learning and entertainment. Looking is both a pleasurable experience and undeniably an educative one in the limited sense that new sights confer new knowledge, even if the precise nature or usefulness of such knowledge is often less certain. Here, the visible and didactic presenter is typically replaced by filmed actuality, whether accompanied by a voiced commentary or in fly-on-the-wall mode, and often too by interviews in which the subjects of the documentary face an off-camera interlocutor and answer questions that are unheard by the viewer. There are, of course, editorial elements but they are subtle and oblique: the commentary may clarify what is before our eyes but there is no authoritative voice to transcend or qualify what the viewer can see, or mediate between the possibly conflicting assertions that the participants make. It is left to us to form any general conclusions.

'Showing' documentaries thus provide weak forms of instruction: they extend experience rather than afford specific intellectual enlightenment, and since in so doing they engage the viewers' emotions and thus provide 'human interest', many of them closely resemble *features* programmes. As the camera follows its subjects around or hovers like a ghost in the background, we learn 'what it is like' to be one of a family of eight or a fire-fighter or a lap-dancer or a cabin steward on an airliner. We may come to admire the diligence and patience of the latter and marvel at how obnoxious the passengers can be, but these are relatively limited lessons – a mere illustration or reinforcement of what we are already capable of imagining, or might already have experienced for ourselves in another context. They are not so much a result of careful deduction as part of our pleasure in watching.

I suggested earlier that documentary and television are somewhat at odds in the sense that the impulse of teaching or instruction is towards abstraction, whereas television is preoccupied with the concrete and visual. I pointed out that teaching is, of course, concerned with the visual world but essentially in order to illustrate principles already inferred or to allow us to infer new ones, and this latter role is evidently what 'showing' documentaries seek to do. But in formal teaching, it is usually the case either that the visual material from which the principles are to be inferred is purged of all redundancy or that the principles themselves are carefully prescribed: 'In these scenes look out for X or Y'; 'What do they tell you about A or B?' and so on. Moreover such teaching assumes motivated, vigilant students rather than a generalist audience watching while at leisure, expecting in some degree to be entertained, and not always knowing where to draw lessons from within the situation they are viewing.

Nevertheless, the broadcasters' confidence in the cognitive power of sight is attested by the number of documentaries – whether 'telling' or 'showing' – which are preoccupied with visual phenomena that most of us are not normally able to see. These are broadly of two kinds: things that are rare or exotic in themselves, and things that are not necessarily rare but which for a variety of reasons are normally withheld from public view. And all such documentaries give the viewer the option of indulging in a scopophilia which requires her to draw very limited inferences rather than absorbing any explicit lessons that they might teach. It also seems to be the case that beyond the visual wonders of nature and the beauties of fine art, sculpture and architecture, many new or rare sights raise problems of a moral nature.

Let us first consider those sights that are rare or exotic in themselves because their causes are infrequent or they occur only in other, remote parts of the world. In the days before television and cinema, those that could be transported made up travelling exhibitions known as 'raree-shows', but television is able to capture many unusual sights either in their original settings or as they casually occur. At the less morally problematic end of the spectrum, we might place alongside David Attenborough's wildlife documentaries programmes about freakish events or mishaps, sometimes of a dangerous and sometimes of a comical nature: police-car pursuits of suspects, meteorological oddities like tornadoes, sporting and show-business gaffes, dramatic rescues of various kinds. Yet there is an element of ghoulishness even here: in Attenborough's programmes we watch animals hunting, killing and devouring their prey, while the programmes about mishaps involve victims – the humiliated, the injured and imperilled. Recognising the scopophilia involved in even the most harrowing and responsibly broadcast images – those of the hijacked planes flying into the twin towers of the World Trade Center in September 2001 – a group of students I was teaching, all of them seasoned viewers, confessed to a sense that they had been 'corrupted' by what they had seen. Like all of us, they had felt compelled to watch over and over again the final agony of hundreds of victims, and were at the same time ashamed of their compulsion.

The intensifying moral problems raised by certain other forms of documentary are implied by the fact that we might think of them as freak-shows rather than raree-shows. In October 2002, Channel 5 broadcast what it termed in its press release for Week 42 'a unique documentary': *Dwarves in Showbiz*. Among others, it featured Ray Griffiths, a male stripper who was part of an act called the Half Monty, and US porn actress Bridget 'the Midget' Powerz, who is quoted:

> I don't want to be an entertainer – I want to be a wife at home, but I got into porn to make a point. By being sexual, I want to show people what a nude little person looks like, so that they won't laugh at us like an elf, or fairy.

The press release adds that the cameras follow Bridget to a test shoot for a British porn director and join her for a date with a German fan – his prize for winning a competition on Bridget's website. The programme's ostensible and intellectually respectable claim is to examine how far disadvantaged people can exploit the opportunities afforded by show-business, and how far show-business exploits them. Moreover it would be perfectly possible to discuss these issues on television, as it is on radio, without using an image of a single dwarf. But the niggling, some-times seedy, promise of television is always to *show*, to be literal, never to trouble the imagination unnecessarily – a faculty whose great virtue is that it can not only compensate for the absence of sight but does so with less blatancy. It is thus hard to resist the conclusion that most people would have watched *Dwarves in Showbiz* for essentially visual rather than intellectual purposes. We do not get to see dwarves very often, or to stare at them with impunity, and the programme's publicity implies that some of them will appear nude. We might therefore get to see whether their sexual characteristics are also dwarfish.

The second common category of 'spectacular' documentary affords sights of things which are not necessarily uncommon in themselves but which, for a variety of reasons, are usually kept from public view. Once again, our interest in some of these may be merely ghoulish, but in others it raises important moral issues. *The Anatomists* (Channel 4, 2002) included the dissection of a corpse which viewers may have found fascinatingly macabre or repulsive, or even educative, but it is unlikely that they felt corrupted by it. That might have been equally true of *BodySnatchers* (BBC1, 2003), a series about parasites that can infest the human body. The first programme showed a woman with a living maggot in her scalp and a man who first grew a three-metre-long tapeworm in his gut – and then evacuated it. But many programmes in this category seem morally questionable because they focus on individuals behaving in ways that are not appropriate to the public domain. For obvious reasons, most such behaviour occurs privately, but even when it occurs in public it is likely to embarrass both those who can observe it and, in the longer term, the individuals themselves. Hence we can say that insofar as they are preoccupied with what people do when they cannot normally be observed, or when they would normally wish not to be observed, such programmes invade the privacy of the individual.

For instances of 'private' behaviour in the public sphere, we might consider those people who are not sufficiently in possession of themselves to be observed, even if for one reason or another they might agree to be. Under the influence of an overwhelming feeling or of drink or drugs, they do not allow themselves to be bound by normal social constraints: they may be angry or passionately affectionate or maudlin or distressed (like the mother whose tears supported *Cot Deaths* in its case against the paediatrician). On the other hand, certain individuals may be freed – or think themselves freed – from normal social constraints simply by being transposed to another environment: a fertile source of documentaries about 'Brits abroad' or holiday company representatives.

The ambivalence of private behaviour in the public sphere creates a corresponding ambivalence in the viewer. We are fascinated by what we can see not only because it may be amusing or affecting in itself but because our circumstances are privileged: we are seeing what we are not generally permitted to see (the justification for terming such programmes 'documentaries'). On the other hand, it is precisely because we have no right to see it that we may feel vicariously uncomfortable for the people involved – embarrassment is often a vicarious emotion – and in that sense both repelled by it and in some measure ashamed of ourselves.

The boundaries between the public and private domains do, of course, vary with time and place. In some societies, people may embrace in public: in others, all physical contact may be frowned upon. Moreover, the legal remedies which famous people seek against those who take pictures of them without their consent – even when these are snapped in the street and of nothing more than a film star at sloppy variance with her public image – are a reminder that the boundaries are constantly being disputed. It may be tenable to argue that anything which is publicly visible, albeit with the help of a telephoto lens, is fair game. But there have been many occasions when television has invaded what is literally the 'private' domain and when the viewer is therefore not so much scopophile as voyeur. We might once again place along a moral spectrum the activities we can observe. At the more innocuous end are washing and dressing; at the opposite extreme is killing as an act of euthanasia or capital punishment; and somewhere in the middle are sexual and excretory acts (all the major channels have carried documentaries on erotica and pornography).

The moral case against showing such things depends absolutely on the notion that there is an entity called the private domain to which everybody has a right: that individuals do, and have done to them, certain things which should not, even with their consent, be transformed into a public spectacle. Hence at this point, the ravenous eye of television ('The viewers must be able to see everything there is to see') comes up against the moral commandment 'Thou shalt not see'; and the only way out of the impasse is if these sights can in some sense be construed as educative or instructive – as enlarging knowledge: 'We have an absolute right to know, and therefore we must be allowed to see'. Hence whatever they tell us, or even if they 'tell' us nothing but merely leave us to draw inferences, those programmes which explore aspects of the private domain can be termed 'documentary' because they are showing us what we have never seen before. They can easily be represented as sociological or psychological investigations or experiments, or as enlarging our knowledge of medicine or anatomy or even, self-reflexively, of ethics. Thus justified, television often blurs the boundaries between the public and private domains. Its ability to bring public events into private living spaces has often been remarked (Dahlgren 1995: 7–8; Scannell 1996: 77–80; Crisell 2002: 9), but television transposes the private experience of a few into the living spaces of so many that it is also, in effect, a public medium.

As we might expect, most documentaries that focus on the private domain tend to show rather than tell, though what ultimately emerges is the artificiality of the distinction. Whether the aim of a particular documentary is to show us something interesting or teach us a lesson, an element of artifice or editorial manipulation will always be involved, even though it may be difficult to detect. Indeed one could argue that at a basic level the very *presence* of cameras is a form of manipulation: people become self-conscious and effectively edit their own behaviour (Corner 1996: 20). Can documentaries with human themes ever show 'the truth' in any absolute sense? Nevertheless, John Corner (2001: 128) speaks of a sliding scale of manipulation or 'fakery'. At the one, acceptable, end are minor interventions by the programme makers: a minimal direction of the participants, the repeat shooting of a scene that has already occurred naturally. At the other and unacceptable end is the wholesale fabrication of events and even persons. And in the middle are the grey areas: the combination of shots from two separate events to suggest a single event; an instruction to the participants to perform actions before the camera which they would not otherwise have performed. There is clearly a difference between enacting for the cameras an event which commonly occurs and one which is unlikely to occur at all.

This issue is of particular relevance to explorations of the private domain because, while much of it is fascinating precisely because we do not normally get to see it, much is also humdrum and uneventful. Television's recent solution has therefore been to *contrive* the private worlds it examines in order to ensure that they will be as eventful as possible. This is the concept of so-called 'reality TV'. In one of the first of these programmes, named *Big Brother* (Channel 4, 2000) after the all-seeing dictator in George Orwell's futuristic novel *Nineteen Eighty-Four*, a number of people were selected for their potentially conflicting if telegenic qualities and placed in a sealed house under the constant observation of TV cameras. In a later variation, *Celebrity Big Brother* (BBC 1 and Channel 4, 2001), viewers acquired the added pleasure of watching the private behaviour of those whose public personas they already knew well. Hence what might have seemed to the viewers to be unmediated actuality was the effect of a comprehensive artifice. And as always, these programmes are readily justified on educational grounds. They are a socio-psychological experiment: they observe the interaction between people of different class backgrounds, different cultural values and different temperaments in order to afford insights into general human behaviour. For many viewers this gives a reassuring respectability to their simple, voyeuristic desire to see what the occupants of the house will look like in various stages of undress and whether they will quarrel or form romantic attachments. There is, in fact, a potentially *inverse* relationship between the educational and entertainment value of these programmes. The more predictable the interaction between the occupants – that is, the more they fight and/or fall in love – the more entertaining and less instructive it will be: but if the occupants confound expectation by adjusting to one another successfully, the effect will be at once illuminating and unentertaining.

In many 'reality TV' shows, the element of contrivance in the service of entertainment is so obvious that their documentary pretensions have been all but abandoned. *Wife Swap* (Channel 4, from 2002) exchanged the female halves of two married or cohabiting couples of contrasting social backgrounds, so that a middle-class woman acquired a working-class 'husband' and vice versa. The exchanges were, of course, for a limited time and on apparently limited terms, and again the documentary pretext was to explore how far people with differing cultural and domestic values could co-exist. But its cruder promise was that the new couples would either have spectacular rows or complain about each other to the camera – or even, as the none-too-subtle title hints, that their domestic collaborations might lead to intimacy of another kind. In similarly titillating vein, *Temptation Island* (Channel 4, 2001) transported a number of couples to an island where attractive men and women sought to lure them apart.

Hence much reality TV could also be seen as the broadcasters' improvised, unscripted attempt to create a kind of real-life soap opera. Moreover the fact that it is at bottom artificial and contrived means that it has always been able to incorporate the arbitrary rules and procedures that characterise games, and so turn itself into something of a competition show. Viewers can vote to expel the participants from many 'reality' programmes until there is a sole, prize-winning survivor. But we have now passed beyond the documentary proper. Indeed, with the decline of the public service ethos in broadcasting, it has been suggested that the future of the genre may increasingly lie in its hybridisation with other genres to create forms of *infotainment* (Casey *et al* 2002: 70). These are the subject of our next chapter.

Let us conclude, however, by summarising our argument about television documentary and venturing some general observations about the issues that underlie it. We suggested that documentary ('teaching') and television are potentially at odds because the primary impulse of teaching or instruction is towards abstraction – the elicitation of principles, rules and theories – and that it is interested in visual phenomena merely to illustrate these principles or to discover new ones. Television, however, is pre-eminently visual: its great promise is to show. Because seeing is our dominant faculty and inherently enjoyable, television seems to imply that to see is to know – or at least that seeing is a reliable guide to knowledge. While at one level this is indisputable (sight enables us to identify things, and new sights extend our understanding in elementary ways), at that less banal level where education and instruction become necessary, seeing is an inadequate and potentially deceptive guide to the truth.

The problem is that even in those many 'telling' documentaries which attempt to elucidate abstract principles, viewers can content themselves with the more banal discoveries that come with the simple pleasure of looking. Moreover under competitive pressures, the documentary makers connive at the idea that seeing is tantamount to knowing. One way they do this is by creating programmes that tell only a partial version of the truth because they can provide a vivid actuality that makes it look like the whole truth. Another is to offer either 'showing' documentaries of weak instructional content that are, in effect, little more than features programmes; or documentaries which, whether 'telling' or 'showing', include sights that most of us do not normally get to see, and which thus allow us to settle for the limited enlightenment that scopophilia brings. Indeed their makers will often contrive the basic settings of these documentaries in order to assure us of a scopophilic experience.

However, what seems to emerge is not simply a potential conflict between the abstract impulses of teaching and the visual promise of television, but a fundamental antipathy between a deeper learning and understanding on the one hand and seeing and enjoying on the other. The instantaneous pleasures of looking tend to pre-empt the slower, laborious business of applying principles and drawing inferences. Since viewers may succumb to mere scopophilia even while watching documentaries whose actuality, however vivid in itself, is included only to illustrate explicit teaching points, there may be a case for reducing the amount of it – for giving greater visual prominence to the presenter and encouraging us to pay more attention to what is being said. In other words, if television is serious about documentary it should not exploit but *restrain* its own visuality – and that, in an age of fierce competition for audiences, is unthinkable.

Forms of infotainment

7

... what I am claiming here is not that television is entertaining but that it has made entertainment itself the natural format for the representation of all experience. Our television set keeps us in constant communion with the world, but it does so with a face whose smiling countenance is unalterable. The problem is not that television presents us with entertaining subject matter but that all subject matter is presented as entertaining, which is another issue altogether.

(Neil Postman, *Amusing Ourselves to Death*)

Introduction

We observed in the last chapter that the pleasure of watching – 'scopophilia' – always provides viewers with an option to be entertained even in news and documentary programmes. Documentary makers may actually feel that it is some part of their function to entertain, to sweeten the didactic pill with pictures that are enjoyable to look at. But the primary aim of the genre is to inform or teach: a documentary that does not, in essence, tell the truth is not a documentary.

In this chapter we move to the middle of the fact–fiction spectrum and explore kinds of programme whose aim is to use factual or informative material primarily in order to *entertain*. To this end, significant liberties may be taken with the facts or 'the truth', even though they are always in some degree crucial to the programmes. However it is worth reminding ourselves, on the one hand, that the pleasures of watching do not wholly exclude an element of learning or understanding, and, on the other, that the entertainment we derive from television transcends the scopophilic and derives from what we can hear as well as what we can see. The programmes in this borderland of fact and fiction are many and miscellaneous – an effect of the way in which producers blend and permutate categories in the unending search for novelty and popularity. They include quasi-documentaries, talk and chat shows, 'reality TV', and some types of drama, and also create a confusing abundance of terms: infotainment, docutainment, edutainment, docusoaps and so on. One could also group these kinds of programme in different ways according to which of the affinities or distinctions between them one wished to focus upon. But in this chapter we shall trace a progression from those whose ostensible aim is informative or educational, even though their actual priority is to entertain, to those that overtly aim to entertain yet will not succeed in doing so without having at least some basis in truth or fact.

We shall begin with *'lifestyle' programmes*. These purport to teach something practical – how to cook, decorate a home, create a garden and so on – but allow the viewer to ignore the lesson, if she wishes, and treat the show as pure entertainment in a way that would not be appropriate to serious documentary. We shall then look at *docudramas*, programmes that seek to tell an historical truth but in an avowedly fictional form. Their impact is usually more intellectual than practical, though they may prompt socio-political changes or the arrest of a crime suspect. But like lifestyle shows, they may be legitimately treated as pure entertainment. Our next genre is *reality TV*, which we have already encountered in the previous chapter. Its undeniable aim is to entertain but it often appends a documentary intention, purporting to be 'a serious experiment in human interaction'. Moreover it deals in 'real people' rather than fictional characters, even though they subserve the cause of entertainment by being placed in an artificial environment and obliged to behave in an artificially competitive way. Finally, there are *talk shows* and *celebrity chat shows*. These also exist primarily to entertain. Yet they, too, deal in 'real people', and we shall see that their popularity is damaged if the audience discovers that the people are not whom they are alleged to be. Nevertheless, in the interests of entertainment, the participants have a certain licence to 'perform' themselves – to turn themselves into semi-fictional characters.

Lifestyle programmes

These consist mostly of 'makeover' shows in which expertise is applied to home improvement (*Changing Rooms*, BBC 1, from 1997), gardens (*Ground Force*, BBC 1, from 1998), the preparation of food (*Ready Steady Cook*, BBC 2, from 1994; celebrity version, BBC 1, from 1998) and personal appearance (*What Not to Wear*, BBC 2, from 1999). But

some shows aim to enhance viewers' lifestyles in other ways – through house buying, holidays and travel, car ownership and motoring, dating, a knowledge of antiques and so on.

In recent years these programmes have experienced a huge growth in popularity which has been ascribed to a general rise in living standards during the 1980s and 1990s. Citing her remark about there being 'no such thing as society', critics assert that Mrs Thatcher transformed the public from citizens into consumers. From the 1980s, council house tenants were given the opportunity to purchase their properties, and the acronym 'yuppie' – a Young, Upwardly-mobile Professional Person – was coined sometime between 1978 and 1980 (Thorne 1991: 579). But it has been observed that spending and consumption are not just economic but cultural matters, and the lifestyle shows represent 'a customization of consumerism to personal identity' (Ellis 2002: 112). Viewers learn how to construct through various acquisitions an image they wish to present to the outside world.

As we might expect of programmes that deal in human aspirations, most lifestyle shows are glossily shot, slickly edited and tightly paced. In recent years, they have become more humorous, or at least whimsical, and have incorporated the game-show elements of surprise and competition – partly, no doubt, in order to win higher ratings, perhaps too as a recognition of the rising educational levels of the audience, who when at leisure prefer gentler, more dilute forms of instruction. But as is so often true of a complex audio-visual medium like television, both the meanings conveyed by the programmes and those that are absorbed by the audience are multiple and unpredictable. From the producer's point of view the message will always contain elements of redundancy, yet some of these may be treated by the viewer as central. The female presenter of a travel show might, for instance, be seen on location in Dubrovnik, extolling the charms of that ancient city; but a female viewer could ignore all of this and instead gain a hint from the presenter's dress about what she might wear on a forthcoming trip to Florida.

Broadly speaking, we can say that the informative or didactic elements of lifestyle shows operate at two levels: the basic level of practical instruction (how to hang wall-paper or make an omelette) and the more elevated if often contentious level of education in matters of taste. Though varying with the subject matter of the programme and the extent to which it deals in common or obscure knowledge, the didactic style is often indirect, intermittent and almost apologetic, especially at the practical level. Racing to finish a garden makeover before its unwitting owner comes home, the presenter of *Ground Force* can spare only a moment to explain to us the right and wrong ways to plant a clematis. And even at the higher level of taste, the lessons may be implied rather than stated, though this is by no means always the case. The presenters of *What Not to Wear*, Trinny Woodall and Susannah Constantine, are famously forthright about what they perceive to be sartorial crimes.

So fragmentary and elusive are the lessons taught by most lifestyle shows that it seems reasonable to assume that their primary purpose is, indeed, to entertain, and their gratifications, though surprisingly various, are all in some degree bound up with the pleasures of looking. First, we enjoy watching expertise in action and its final embodiment in the transformed living room or perfect pasta, even if we can actually acquire little of that expertise for ourselves. This gratification is particularly likely when we are watching the gardening, home improvement and cookery programmes. But at the level of taste, the expertise could be rather more obscure and controversial, in which case the viewer's gratification may lie in questioning or rejecting it: the redecorated living room or newly acquired dress may strike us as aesthetically inferior to the one it has replaced.

A further gratification for the viewer derives from the game-show aspect of many of these programmes, which often takes the form of a race against the clock: Will the meal be ready within a certain time? How will this shambles of a bedroom be transformed into an exquisite boudoir before its unknowing owner gets home? But yet another, and misleading, lesson is implied here. In the real world, gardening, home improvement and cooking all take time and patience and entail a considerable risk of setbacks or outright failure. But the lifestyle shows are fictions in the sense that their slickness belies the lengthy, often humdrum nature of the activities they depict, along with the fact that success is by no means assured. The promise is that 'you too can do it: it's quick and easy, needs no perseverance, involves no trial and error'. In fact, we acknowledge the misleading character of these shows when we wryly echo the cliché of the television cook, 'Here's one I made earlier' – for it signals the moment when she 'cheats', distracting us from the present task, with its uncertain outcome, by taking us straight to a perfect cake or soufflé that seems to have been magicked out of nothing.

A third gratification, mainly afforded by the gardening and home improvement shows, is the moment of revelation, when the householder who has been lured away for a period returns to discover the makeover. Whether she feels delight, horror or distress (and in the presence of cameras she may well feel a duty to exaggerate or alter her reaction), the viewer is provided with a pleasing spectacle. The deception–revelation motif is another way of leavening essentially banal activities with an element of drama and the unexpected, of bringing to a neat and rapid conclusion what normally entails error, reversal and only a gradual coming to fruition.

A fourth and related gratification is voyeuristic, especially when we are watching the home improvement and fashion and beauty shows.

John Ellis (2002: 112) innocuously remarks that such shows are popular for the casual insights they afford into other people's lives: they sharpen our awareness of the subtle social distinctions conveyed in dress, house furnishings and so on. But the pleasures of snobbery and even *schadenfreude* are never far away, especially when, as often happens, an individual's dress sense or choice of décor is openly derided. Safe and distanced, we have a relatively rare opportunity to peer into the private lives of others and witness their humiliation at the hands of those who – supposedly – know better.

It is again worth emphasising that the *informative* elements of lifestyle programmes are largely separate from the *entertainment* they provide, and sometimes even incompatible with it. In our chapter on documentary, we noted the tension that often exists between learning and enjoyment. It may be simplistic to assume that lifestyle shows cater to two quite disparate audiences – one solemnly and assiduously absorbing the lessons, the other merely enjoying the spectacle and either sneering at the guinea-pigs or questioning the expertise of their gurus. But even if there is a composite body of viewers who manage to do both, it is hard to see how they can do so at one and the same time. We cannot find the ignoramus funny if we, too, are ignorant: being amused is one thing and learning is quite another.

Docudramas

On the face of it, there seems to be a surfeit of terminology to describe a genre in which historical fact is presented in the form of a dramatic entertainment: it is variously known as documentary drama (docudrama), drama documentary (dramadoc), dramatised documentary and 'faction' (in this sense a blend of fact and fiction). Yet these different terms do hint at the different ratios of fact to fiction which might exist within the genre, or at the different ways in which they are synthesised, or even at the different perceptions of 'fact' that the genre might embrace. In other words, we are not really dealing with a homogeneous genre at all but with a bundle of similar ones. Nevertheless we shall use 'docudrama' to encompass all these variations: the events, if not the characters, have some basis in fact. Two famous examples are *Death of a Princess* (ITV, 1980), about the actual execution of an Arab princess for adultery, and *The Monocled Mutineer* (BBC, 1986), which aimed to reveal new truths about the First World War. But what *sort* of facts are docudramas based on? These plays made use of actual historical figures: another famous docudrama, however, *Cathy Come Home* (BBC, 1966), used fictitious characters and a fictitious plot yet was based on fact in the sense that it was a composite of the actual experiences of homeless people. In another variation, *The War Game* (BBC, 1965) was a 'preconstruction' from, rather than a reconstruction of, historical fact, extrapolating from Britain's contemporary political and military circumstances to suggest the inevitability of a nuclear conflict.

All these dramas thus differ from conventional drama in the kind of relationship they make with the real world: they claim a significance which is not merely 'artistic' and generalised but historical and specific, seeking in some way to influence our attitude to what has happened or is happening or will happen. John Corner (1996: 31–2) points out that docudrama was originally a mere technique within the documentary genre, a partial compensation for the fact that without the lightweight equipment of later years, it was difficult if not impossible to acquire filmed actuality in certain locations. With improvements in technology, documentaries made less use of drama, while drama itself moved in the direction of documentary. *Emergency – Ward 10* (ITV, 1957–67) and *Coronation Street* (ITV, since 1960), which would today be regarded as soap operas, were both thought of in their early years as drama documentaries (Kerr 1990: 79).

How successful are docudramas in their aim of having an impact on 'the real world'? In programmes such as *Crimewatch UK* (BBC1, since 1984) the re-enactments of robberies, assaults and abductions have had a tangible effect in leading to arrests and convictions. It is claimed that *Cathy Come Home* led to the formation of Shelter, the charity for the homeless, and to a change of government policy on housing (Day-Lewis 1992: 19); likewise that in 1997, the docudrama *Hillsborough* (ITV, 1996) prompted the new Labour government to agree to a fresh inquiry into the stampede at a 1989 FA Cup semi-final, in which 97 people died (Paget 1998: 207). What is certain is that some of the tangible effects of the genre have been damaging for broadcasters and even governments: *Law and Order*, a 1980s docudrama about the penal system, was felt to be so biased that the BBC was denied all further access to prisons, while *Death of a Princess* sparked a diplomatic quarrel between Britain and Saudi Arabia.

There is no denying that docudramas present an intractable critical problem, which is that the viewer can never be sure about what is fact and what is fiction, what is truth and what is dramatic or artistic licence. Let us take as an example *The Deal* (Channel 4, 2003), a docudrama about a power-dividing pact which future prime minister, Tony Blair, and future chancellor of the exchequer, Gordon Brown, were alleged to have made over dinner in a restaurant. For the most part, drama is associated with fiction or make-believe: its characters and situations are invented and the human and moral truths it expresses are thus abstract and generalised. Why, then, does a play like *The Deal* focus on characters whom we know to be real, living people and on actual events? To this 'dramatic' question there can only be a 'documentary' answer: to tell us something about contemporary politics and the characters of our politicians. But then it is clear to us that what we are seeing and hearing cannot be a faithful record of an historical event. Somewhat bizarrely, Blair and Brown, familiar faces from countless press and TV images, are here played by actors whose resemblance to them is only approximate, but in this respect the demarcation between fact and fiction is clear enough. On the other hand, however 'realistic' the dialogue of the play may seem, we are well aware that this is nothing like the elliptical, hesitant, repetitious nature of a real conversation – a fact which lends substance to the objections which have often been raised against docudramas: that they distort the facts and misrepresent the protagonists. But to this 'documentary' objection there can only be a 'dramatic' answer: to make its points and to do so entertainingly, the programme has had to resort to a certain artistic licence, rearrange the known facts in a certain way and use its imagination to supply the unknown ones. It thus conveys a deeper, more abstract truth. Yet this returns us to our original question: why, then, the need to focus on real people and to pretend to be a documentary?

The rationale of the docudrama thus rests on an equivocation, a fact which media theorists have been reluctant to recognise. But it is also interesting to note that when the 'real people' in whom it deals have receded beyond contemporary consciousness – when, in other words, they have 'passed into history' – factual inaccuracy acquires the status of honorary fiction. Our monocled mutineer of the First World War was perhaps on the borderline between the two, but Shakespeare's fundamental misrepresentation of the historical Macbeth, who died in 1057 (Davies 1999: 256–7), has always been regarded as a dramatic work of art because this Scottish king had ceased to have any contemporary relevance in Shakespeare's time, not to mention our own. When actual persons are no longer remembered or influential, for artistic purposes they become every bit as fictional as Mickey Mouse.

We will conclude this section with two further thoughts. The first is that docudrama reminds us that a television genre does not need any kind of theoretical or moral justification in order for it to be popular with broadcasters and viewers. The historical inaccuracy of a number of docudramas, which as we have seen can be defended as artistic licence, has sometimes raised an outcry among those who have been depicted, or who have a material interest in the depiction, but it has never stopped them from being made. The second thought is that however much television might call into question the nature of fact and fiction, or seek to 'reconstruct' or 'negotiate' their relationship (Holmes and Jermyn 2004: 11), the difference between them remains resilient and important.

Reality TV

In 'reality' shows, a group of people are selected by the programme makers to live together in a restricted space – a sealed house, desert island or patch of jungle – and their interactions are televised, or at least filmed, round the clock. A game-show element is also incorporated. This requires the participants to undertake a number of challenging and unpleasant tasks and at different stages allows the viewers to vote to expel a member of the group until there is a single, prize-winning survivor. Programmes such as *Big Brother* (Channel 4, 2000), *Survivor* (ITV, 2001) and *I'm a Celebrity – Get Me Out of Here!* (ITV, 2002) hint not only at the popularity of the genre but at the willingness of both mainstream and minority networks to feature it.

Reality TV is a prime example of the way in which television endlessly combines and recombines older genres, for its antecedents are many, some of them time-worn. The gladiatorial sports of ancient Rome and the festive executions that still occur in some parts of the world are a reminder that those who are enduring hardship, suffering or even death have always made an irresistible public spectacle. In recent times, television viewers have enjoyed the milder pleasure of watching people being humiliated when competing in game shows, but reality TV incorporates certain elements, and offers certain gratifications, that are recognisable from other generic forebears. There is the pleasure of watching those emotional exchanges that occur in fly-on-the-wall documentaries about families or workplaces; the pleasure of identifying with the participants as if they were characters in a soap opera (indeed, reality TV shows could be seen as an unscripted, 'real life' soap opera); and, in those shows which are staged in exotic locations, the pleasure of gazing at the bronzed flesh and beautiful scenery that typify holiday programmes (Fanthome 2004: 162).

The immediate predecessor of reality TV seems to have been those fly-on-the-wall documentaries which focused on the police and other emergency services. Though they might make use of dramatic reconstructions, the development of surveillance technology in the form of closed-circuit television (CCTV) and lightweight video camcorders enabled them to include footage of actual car chases, fights, arrests, accidents and misadventures. These documentaries were soon joined by what might be termed docusoaps, which were more sustained, less intense observations of a single environment and carried self-explanatory titles like *Hotel* (BBC 1, 1997) and *Airport* (BBC 1, 1996). The final ingredients were the performative elements of the game show and similar genres, which are evident in reality TV shows like *Pop Idol* (ITV, from 2001) (Corner 2004: 291–2; Holmes and Jermyn 2004: 3).

Although a fairly new phenomenon, reality TV has attracted a considerable amount of academic attention, and we will look at the three main, largely interrelated, critical issues. First, and notwithstanding its tendentious title, how much of the genre can be accepted as factual and truthful, and how much is fiction and falsehood? In its infancy at least, it wore the serious air of a social experiment. The aim was that 'real people' would be subjected to almost clinical and continuous observation, doing all those things that people do when not obliged to present a public self. The surveillance technology that was involved – webcams gazing hazily into bedrooms and bathrooms – could only confirm the impression of authenticity. Yet there has always been a clear and fundamental sense in which reality TV is a fiction, a contrivance. Tincknell and Raghuram (2004: 259) point out that the *Big Brother* house is effectively a theatrical set, and that its inhabitants – all carefully auditioned and selected by the show's producers – do not form a microcosm of the relationships that typically exist in the real world: those of kinship, friendship or professional solidarity. The principle of corporate coherence that informs a police force or an airport or a university simply does not exist between the inhabitants of the *Big Brother* household or between those of any other artificial environments that the reality shows create.

The inhabitants are, in fact, assembled merely for the purpose of competition – that is to say, of entertainment. But even aside from the specific games they may be forced to play, they are unlikely, under the constant gaze of cameras, to behave authentically: the temptation will be to modify their behaviour, to 'act up' in order either to stay on the show or be voted off. Moreover, the conventional transmissions of the shows, as distinct from the continuous coverage of web TV, are invariably edited, one consequence of which has been that the producers of some of them have been sued by the participants for misrepresentation.

But the issue of truth and falsehood, of fact and fiction, is more complicated than this. First, it is worth remembering that fact and fiction are deeply intertwined in our everyday existence. Clothes and grooming create what is, in a sense, a fictional presentation of our real selves. Arbitrary rules and conventions also constrain the way we behave, especially in the public sphere. Social interaction obliges us to suppress our indifference or antipathy to others and behave towards them with the 'artifice' of politeness or courtesy. Indeed, when this artificial behaviour is taken to extremes, we often condemn it as insincerity or hypocrisy.

With respect to certain television genres, the degrees of artifice might be arranged along a kind of spectrum. At one end is the behaviour of those who take part in reality shows. The continuous presence of cameras and the element of competition with an unknown outcome mean that it is always constrained and, conceivably, wholly artificial, yet much of it seems naturalistic and spontaneous.

In the middle lies sport, in which the behaviour of the participants is also constrained (by rules even more than by cameras) and which will also produce an unknown outcome. Yet its artifice is at once more obvious and more limited than that of reality TV. The rules that govern conduct are more overt, the participants wear special attire, its environments have been purpose-built, and each contest has a fixed duration: sport exists outside 'normal' existence rather than pretending to be coextensive with it in the way that the reality shows do.

At the other end of the spectrum we might place drama. Its elements of artifice are every bit as obvious as those of sport, but by means of a script, behaviour is constrained to the further extent of achieving an invariable, predetermined outcome which is known to the participants and, quite often, to the audience. The sharp separation from ordinary existence that characterises both sport and drama is attested by the fact that the participants in both can be termed players: they are not 'for real'.

So are the participants in reality shows 'people' or 'players'? The comprehensiveness of the artifice suggests they are the latter. Nevertheless it has been argued that an artificiality of behaviour cannot be sustained throughout, that sooner or later the participants will reveal their real selves. Hence the paradox of reality TV is that the artifice eventually exposes the real (Liddiment 2003: 3).

The question of personal honesty and authenticity leads us to the second area of critical interest created by the genre: notions of 'celebrity' and 'ordinariness' and the relationship between them. We might define celebrities as those who are literally 'celebrated' for some perceived talent (musical, comedic, theatrical, sporting and so on) or attribute (beauty, sex appeal, lack of inhibition, engaging foolishness and so on) which sets them apart from the crowd and which results in extended or frequent exposure on any of the mass media – pre-eminently television, but also cinema, radio, newspapers and magazines, records and even books. Conventionally, then, celebrity depends on a degree of distinctiveness, rarity, egregiousness.

Reality TV is fascinating in the way that it plays with and challenges this notion of celebrity. In its non-celebrity versions, people who are *not* especially distinguished are viewed repeatedly if not continuously, and acquire celebrity because of the audience's opportunity to develop an empathy with or hostility towards them. This growth of celebrity through ordinariness or familiarity is reminiscent of that which attaches to actors in soap opera, whose plot dynamics the reality shows often seek to mimic by means of the collaborations and betrayals that their competitive element entails (Persaud 2000: 7; Dovey 2001: 136). It is only through the continuous, domestic and banal media of broadcasting, and especially television, that such genres as soaps and reality TV, and with them a demystified notion of celebrity, could develop. As its presenter Davina McCall points out, the *Big Brother* contestants are 'the most famous non-famous people' (quoted in Holmes 2004: 117). The caveat is, of course, that without some accompanying talent the fame is unlikely to last, and some of the *Big Brother* contestants have already returned to suitable obscurity.

In 'celebrity' forms of reality TV (that is, those which draw on the more conventional notion of celebrity) the participants conceivably have one of two contrasting motives for appearing on the show: they see it either as an opportunity to enhance their fame or as an antidote to it (Branigan 2004: 7). The first motive rests on the conventional, traditional notion of celebrity – the celebration of *extraordinariness*: their aim is to revive their careers. (Those celebrities whose careers are in no need of revival seldom appear on reality shows.) The second motive draws on that newer notion of celebrity fostered by television in general and reality TV in particular: the celebration of *ordinariness*. Through continuous, banal coverage, the celebrities seek to reveal themselves as the (likeable) people they really are and not as the two-dimensional creatures that fame has made of them. Since the conventional depiction of celebrity focuses on the individual's uniqueness, a degree of distortion or exaggeration is not only almost unavoidable but something in which the individual has had to collude: she must perform to expectation and can thus project only a partial, 'fictional' version of herself. But the newer form of celebrity that the conventionally famous seek is based on David Liddiment's paradoxical premise that the artifice of reality TV reveals the real (Liddiment 2003: 3). The programme makers' calculation is that the difficulty of maintaining a facade through-out continuous coverage, and especially during the performance of fright-ening or undignified tasks, means that the participants are bound to show themselves in their true colours. From the celebrities' point of view, the reality shows are a chance to 'put the record straight'.

For the viewers, the ironies that are generated by this situation, and particularly by a participant's combined self-consciousness and lack of self-knowledge, can be among the keenest pleasures the genre provides. On the one hand, she may be unaware that her 'real' personality is less attractive than her public one: on the other, her 'real' personality may never be fully apparent because whatever the circumstances she can never quite forget the cameras. An element of performance or artifice is ever present in her behaviour – or to put it another way, the viewers are aware that she always has a design on them.

Celebrity shows bring into clearer focus a range of gratifications that are also present in other kinds of reality TV, some of which we have already noted. There is the over-arching pleasure of voyeurism, of watch-ing what is normally private and 'forbidden' (we might see not just anybody in states of disarray or undress but *famous people*), and there is a possible empathy with the participants as well as an ironic detachment from them. We may feel sadness or amusement, or some mixture of both, as has-beens struggle to revive their flagging careers or the talentless and unremarkable strive to ensure that their fame will last.

These gratifications bring us to the third main area of critical interest: the sense in which reality TV democratises television by providing its audiences with various forms of *empowerment*. First, the genre holds out the possibility that the 'ordinary' viewer can become a celebrity. It is not simply that she can empathise with a participant who is similarly ordinary: there is a real possibility that she, too, can appear, and gain a more sustained exposure than she would get from a conventional game show. Second, and as we have already seen, there is the pleasure of voyeurism – of being able to observe what is normally an area of private experience. We can see the participants in states of undress and dishevelment and also hope to watch intimate encounters: squabbles or sexual activities.

Reality TV owes its existence to recent developments in surveillance technology, among them the ubiquity of CCTV and video cameras (Dovey 2001: 136). The abundance of CCTV and video footage across the whole range of factual television is based on its acceptance as reliable evidence, especially as much of it is machine-operated and hence seemingly 'authorless' and objective. The ostensible lack of human agency can add to our voyeuristic pleasure by seeming to reduce the element of human collusion and personal responsibility: we have not been invited to watch forbidden images by someone, we are merely viewing what has come within the undiscriminating scope of technology. Moreover, within the surveillance culture that has prevailed for the last half century, reality TV has helped to tip the balance of power away from 'the authorities' and towards the ordinary people.

The growth of surveillance coincided with the beginning of the Cold War, that hostility between the western allies and the Soviet Union which prevailed from the late 1940s to the end of the 1980s and which expressed itself not in open warfare but in propaganda, mutual espionage and an attendant atmosphere of suspicion, accusation and witch-hunting. In the United States, Senator Joseph McCarthy launched a massive campaign to root out Communist sympathisers, and from time to time spy trials took place both there and in Britain. Since traitors were evidently in our midst, it was expected that the authorities would practise widespread vigilance (Clissold 2004: 33–8). Yet vigilance creates paranoia as well as a sense of security: on whose behalf were the authorities watching – ours or their own? George Orwell's novel *Nineteen Eighty Four* (1949) captured the anxieties of the Cold War by inventing the original 'Big Brother' as the all-seeing ruler of a totalitarian state.

By the 1980s these anxieties were being fuelled by another political issue: Mrs Thatcher's government was keen to reaffirm 'law and order' in the face of what was perceived to be a rise in crime and in civil, especially industrial, unrest. But she was also bent on rolling back what she saw as the 'nanny state' – in part by encouraging self-policing. It was the new surveillance technologies of CCTV and video cameras that made these aims compatible (Jermyn 2004: 75). They also produced enough authentic footage to inspire programmes like *Crimewatch*, which launched in 1984 and, in providing the opportunity to survey as well as be surveyed, shifted power from the authorities towards the public and lent moral legitimacy to the pleasure of covert watching. Surveillance has always raised issues about the individual's right to privacy, but these seem to be outweighed by the public's right to protect itself against crime. Historically, our ghoulish delight in watching floggings, executions and the like has been able to borrow moral respectability by presenting itself as a desire to see justice being done; but thanks to *Crimewatch*, the moralistic pleasure we once took in watching the *punishment* of crime has now been transferred to watching the *performance* of it (Jermyn 2004: 81).

While reality shows can in no sense share the moralistic aims of *Crimewatch*, they offer even greater empowerment to the viewer – we can see more things and see them more often – and can avoid at least some moral censure because they occur with the knowledge and consent of the surveyed. In this respect they hark back to the early Cold War programme *Candid Camera*, which was a kind of cheerful inversion of surveillance culture in the sense that it could not show film of those on whom it spied without first gaining their permission (Clissold 2004: 42). Hence reality TV empowers the participants as well as the audience, and what the latter stand to gain is a voyeuristic view of unguarded, instinctual and thus 'private' behaviour, but with just enough knowingness in the participants to remind them that they have to be worth watching.

The third form of empowerment lies in the fact that the viewers are able to influence the outcomes of reality shows. While their ability to vote for the expulsion of the participants has been technically possible since the birth of television (telephones being an even older technology), and could thus be seen as no more than a gimmick to stimulate audience interest, there is no doubt that it has been greatly boosted by the arrival of new, more convenient media. Indeed reality shows are probably the first instance of significant interactivity on the part of the television audience: in 2002, *Big Brother* attracted no less than 22 million votes – half of them by phone (including mobiles), but 49 per cent by interactive TV or text messages (Fanthome 2004: 162). Viewers also have the option of mobilising responses through Internet chat rooms and the creation of websites. The fundamental debate about all these forms of audience empowerment is whether they are transient and illusory or enduring and real (Tincknell and Raghuram 2004: 267).

Talk shows and celebrity chat shows

There are, of course, many forms of 'talk television', ranging from three or four people in a discreetly lit studio – critics discussing the latest film or intellectuals debating some moral or political problem – to forums like the *Oprah Winfrey Show* (Channel 4 and others, from 1988), in which a personality presenter, with or without a panel of key speakers, moves through a studio audience inviting opinions on some issue of public concern. But the genre is of interest in bringing into focus that incipient enmity between the visual and the intellectual which is so often a feature of television. As the broadcaster and critic Jonathan Miller once put it:

> the idea of the talking head is anathema to most television people. It seems to me that the talking head is the best sort of head there is, and the head, in general, is the most interesting thing we have really, and it is best to talk through it. . . . I do not believe this violates some platonic ideal of television.
>
> (quoted in Bakewell and Garnham 1970: 131)

In a media environment that is now much more competitive than at the time of Miller's remarks, the talking head is anathema to most television people for two closely related reasons. First, talking heads form a large part of our ordinary daily experience – when we meet somebody, we are likely to listen to what she has to say and to look at her face while she says it – and there is a belief among television people that television should, as far as possible, provide us with images that lie outside that experience. If few would go so far as to claim that it is television's *raison d'être* to show us something new, or at least out of the ordinary, most would allow that the channel that does so is likely to gain an advantage over its rivals.

The second reason is that there is a sense in which 'talk' is a non-televisual pleasure. It is not simply that we do not need a television set in order to see people talking: the talk show is a genre in which, for the most part, the cameras are pointing at something other than its essential subject matter. Talk shows tend to deal in opinions about, or reactions to, something that exists elsewhere: politicians expound or argue about a measure that has been, or will be, passed in Parliament; even the two-timers and victims of the *Jerry Springer Show* (ITV, from 1998) appear in connection with events that have already happened. In fact, the more completely and dispassionately the discussion focuses on its subject, the less (tele)visual the discussion becomes. Certain visible paralinguistic factors may illuminate it – gestures to imply emphasis or concession, facial expressions to signal agreement, irony or dissent – but the fact

remains that the main object of interest is off-camera, and this makes
television jealous. The medium can reassert itself only if a visual irrele-
vancy is introduced, if it can replace distant issues with present theatre,
perhaps by putting distracting graphics behind the studio speakers, or by
selecting subjects and speakers to ensure that passions rise and produce
visible effects, or by eschewing any thematic continuity in a discussion
in order (as in studio forums) to show as many fresh faces as possible.
Most of the studio forums are simply incoherent: a sort of intellectual
stockpot into which discordant assertions are thrown, with little scope
for either justification or refutation.

Among the distinctive characteristics of the talk show are the moral
authority of the host and, on occasions, the invited expert; the central-
ity of audience participation; and a focus on social issues that have a
personal and emotive relevance (Shattuc 2001: 84). In other words, the
shows are less likely to focus on income-tax returns or home improvement than on rape, marital infidelity, drug use and sex changes – matters
that promise to yield something to look at in the form of people who are
not fully in command of their feelings. It is at this televisual end of the
spectrum that talk shows can be regarded as infotainment, but even this
is perhaps too dignified a word for programmes like Jerry Springer's,
which incorporate the triggers of confession and confrontation. Yet if
they are nothing more than entertainment, they have a darker side:

> Contemporary daytime talk show discourse on television is not
> organised around the slow payoff of working through an issue or
> controversy inclusively and over the long term. Instead a kind of
> discursive virginity is preferred, in which something is disclosed or
> done or someone is confronted, preferably for the first time, live.
> Far from allowing truth to surface, such a performance elicited by
> the camera is designed to create a spectacle that otherwise may not
> have happened or might never have been such an exaggerated, or
> on occasion, deceitful way to provoke the emotional reaction of the
> parties involved. Then the participants are left on their own to sort
> out the aftermath of this intervention in their lives.
>
> (Morse 2004: 214)

Jerry Springer takes the talk genre to the limit, showing, in the forbearing
words of John Ellis (2002: 107–8), 'what happens when talking can no
longer contain conflict'. This border zone is evidently where television and
talk can best do business with each other. Yet although the priority of these
shows is to entertain, an element of authenticity in the participants and
veracity in their accounts is still vital: the revelations that some of the
participants on the Jerry Springer Show were actors and that their brawls
were staged, not spontaneous, did serious damage to its popularity.

The celebrity chat show forms a rather different category. Here, there is less disjunction between the speakers and their subject matter because they are often talking about themselves: but even when they are referring to biographical matters that are not presently visible, we viewers have the further pleasure of comparing the private individual who is presently before us (for again an element of authenticity is crucial) with the public performer – the actor, pop star or sports personality – we are already familiar with. The relationship between these two personas is complex, for they are never wholly congruent nor wholly distinguishable. If the celebrities are actors, they normally play other people: Sir Anthony Hopkins, for instance, becomes Hannibal Lecter. If they are celebrities of other kinds, they 'play' themselves in the sense that they are constrained by the particular role for which they have become celebrated: Mick Jagger becomes a rock singer, David Beckham a soccer player. On the chat show, however, celebrities of whatever kind are liberated from their performative roles and free – encouraged – to behave 'as they really are'.

There is, of course, an element of performance and artifice even here. One forerunner of the celebrity chat show, and a variation on the theme of actors who become well known by playing others, is the situation comedy in which the actors 'play' themselves: on television, celebrities like George Burns and Gracie Allen and Lucille Ball and Desi Arnaz began the trend over half a century ago (Gillan 2004: 55). In chat shows, however, there is no script and no role, so how do we know that the celebrities are only 'playing' rather than 'being' themselves? The simple and obvious answer is that in the public sphere the self is always in some sense performed or constructed: you are obliged, in T.S. Eliot's words, 'to prepare a face' as soon as you encounter another person, however much your intimate. But in the case of the chat show guest, there also remains the priority to entertain, which takes precedence even over the requirement to be truthful. As viewers, we expect a measure of honesty on the guest's part and hope for some personal revelations; but for the sake of being entertained we will accept some elements of fiction from her – usually an invented or exaggerated account of her experiences – and pretend to regard them as the whole truth (Tolson 1996: 194–5). We are ready to overlook the distinction between public performer and private individual, and accept the logic that if somebody is a great actor or brilliant athlete she must be a fascinating person in her own right.

We must now consider television's coverage of another phenomenon which combines the actual and the artificial, which is both a significant feature of real life and a kind of playful fiction: sport.

Sport

8

Diversion, entertainment, fun: an activity providing this, a pastime.
  (Definition of 'sport' in the *Shorter Oxford English Dictionary*)

Some people think football is a matter of life and death . . . . I can
assure them it is much more serious than that.
  (Bill Shankly, Manager of Liverpool Football Club, 1959–1974)

Sport is of particular significance to television. Its major events are
uniquely able to disrupt TV's schedules and displace even the news, and
it can draw vast audiences and hold them even outside peak viewing
times. BSkyB swiftly exploited sport as its major attraction, because it
recognised that in a predominantly free-to-air market there are only
three kinds of programming that viewers are willing to subscribe to:
movies, pornography and sport (Horsman 1997: 90). Moreover sport is
much more likely than other forms of television to attract old-fashioned
communal viewing, whether at home or in public places like bars and
hotel lounges (Whannel 1992: 93, 197–8). Sport and television are made
for each other: theirs is a marriage like that of music and radio. Why?
  Sport illustrates more vividly than most kinds of content the unique
and overlapping strengths that television possesses: *spectacle*, the
primary source of its ability to provide entertainment; and *liveness*, the
presentation of something which is happening now and will have an
unknown outcome, and which thus makes an important contribution
to its power as a news medium. Even the use of recording in television's coverage of sport is paradoxically intended to get closer to and
illustrate this liveness in a way that other kinds of recording are not.
Television's taping of a play or a concert or a cookery programme is

intended to capture the event, as it were, 'in the round' and save it for a transmission which could take place weeks, months, in some instances years, after the time of recording. But recording at a sporting event has two rather different functions. First it is used to play back even *within* the live coverage of the event. This is the 'instant replay', whose aim is to enable the viewer to better understand the dynamism of the moment – to recapture what was too quick and intricate for the naked eye to follow. And the second function of recording is to recover, as far as possible, the 'nowness' of the whole event through recency. At most only hours after the event has ended, television will often broadcast edited highlights, and at the beginning of them, withhold the result from the viewer. Unlike its other recordings, then, television's recording of sport has a short shelf-life: there is 'a "zone of liveness", after which the liveness effect will have expired' (Kavka and West 2004: 140). Sport on television thus approximates to news, though we shall see shortly that the two are not quite identical.

The aim of this chapter is first to explore the ambiguous nature of much sport, which television brings into sharper focus and which presents a challenge to the medium. It will then consider the ways in which watching sport on television transcends the experience of the conventional spectator, and lastly the extent to which television has succeeded in promoting various sports and in modifying their character.

Sport is indelibly associated with play and leisure. It is not in any ultimate sense important or serious: that is its whole point. Sport seems to stand in a kind of vicarious or figurative relationship to ordinary life. The structures of individual games create a parallel world to the real one. Their arbitrary rules are intended to generate a competitiveness which is a kind of metaphor, and sometimes a rehearsal, for actual conflict. In various guises, team games simulate battles while individual games simulate single combat. To assert this is uncontroversial, even self-evident, yet it does not quite do justice to our modern experience of sport. There is now a sense that sport transcends the merely recreational. Why? A paradox is introduced when the pursuit of a sport becomes of such interest to spectators that many of them are willing to pay to watch it, and in some instances to wager sums of money on its outcomes. Ironically for television, sport was not *conceived* as a spectacle at all, but merely for the benefit of its participants: the players. But the economic consequence of spectatorship is that at least some levels of a sport will become professionalised – that those who play it with a fair degree of skill and success will command payment for so doing.

It is worth emphasising that those sports that cannot attract spectators in consistently large numbers will never become professionalised and will thus remain 'sports' in an unproblematical sense. But those that do become professionalised also become a contradiction in terms:

their participants acquire a salaried hobby, a pastime for which they are paid. A young man who plays soccer for fun, perhaps at weekends, discovers by being spotted by a talent scout working for a major club that he is good – so good that people will pay to watch him, along with certain other players. His mode of recreation then becomes his work: however much he continues to enjoy it, it will no longer just be fun. This situation is not peculiar to sport: it characterised the theatre for several centuries before organised games developed. A young actor, singer or dancer may likewise discover that people will pay to watch him exercise his talents. But the important difference between theatre and sport is that the former exists *wholly* to attract spectators: the unobserved exercise of theatrical skills provides limited satisfaction. Sport, in the strict sense of the word, exists primarily – indeed entirely – for the participants: their enjoyment of it does not depend on the presence of a single spectator.

Hence much modern sport is characterised by a kind of bifurcation. There is sport in its pristine sense of a hobby, the pub soccer match or game of badminton between friends at the local leisure centre, which is of interest only to the participants. These are known as 'amateurs', a word which originally meant *lovers* of a certain activity and which also carries the suggestion that they do not get paid for performing it. Then there is sport which is of interest to significant numbers of paying spectators, and which is therefore adopted as a profession and run as an industry.

This bifurcation is vividly illustrated by our ambivalent reactions to the notion of 'sporting conduct', the discretionary courtesy that a player might extend to an opponent in recognition of the fact that what they are contesting is *only* a game and not of real-life significance. It is claimed, for instance, that in the early days of soccer, the taker of a penalty kick would often stroke the ball directly to the opposing goalkeeper rather than attempt to score. This was to affirm the belief that the foul which had occasioned the penalty had not been malicious, and therefore the team to whom the kick had been awarded would not exploit the advantage it gave them. While we might feel a kind of abstract regret at the disappearance of such conduct, we should be clear that it would be unthinkable in the game's present ethos. Professional soccer is, in effect, the creation of spectators who pay their players to win. Hence the players' failure to take any advantage that the rules afford them amounts to a dereliction of duty: 'sporting' conduct is literally *unprofessional* conduct. Moreover the 'real life' consequences of such failure may well extend beyond a few baffled and angry spectators: it could change the result of a match, which in turn could determine whether the team wins or loses a competition or is promoted or relegated to another league. And these things in turn affect the fortunes, if not the very livelihoods, of players, managers, trainers, players' agents, administrators, commercial sponsors, manufacturers and retailers of sports equipment and merchandise, even television channels. They may not quite be 'a matter of life and death', but neither are they trivial.

It might be useful to see the dualism within professionalised sport – self-contained pastime on the one hand, major industry on the other – in the light of the general distinctions we have been making between fiction and artifice on the one hand and fact and 'real life' on the other. We observed in the last chapter that sport is 'fictional' somewhat in the way that theatre is. In its use of arenas, its need of special costumes and equipment and its imposition of rules on the behaviour of the partici-pants, sport is sharply demarcated from ordinary life. Each match or game or contest is in some sense neatly concluded, if not by the victory/defeat that occurs within it, then by a time limit. And there are no immediate and obvious consequences: the losers are not, for instance, imprisoned. Afterwards, and as with the theatre, real life is resumed. Also, as in the theatre, the very presence of spectators – people who have sufficient leisure to sit and watch something – reinforces the notion of sport as a fiction, in some sense separate from the world of work. The money they pay at the turnstiles is in exchange for a kind of escape: it is not the 'functional' payment they make for fuel or groceries.

Yet sport is in some ways less neat and more lifelike than theatre. Though its events have firm conclusions, they are, at the beginning, unknowable to players and spectators alike. Theatre is a wholly collaborative enterprise with a predetermined outcome. But while sporting opponents collaborate in the sense that they agree to abide by the rules, their activities are essentially adversarial and competitive, assuming something of the rivalry and indeterminacy of everyday life. This also means that spectators take more of a gamble when they attend sporting events than theatrical audiences do – and they do so knowingly. As Garry Whannel (1992: 84) points out, '[A sporting event] does not offer the same guarantee of quality as a theatrical or variety performance. It can be argued that traditionally spectators have accepted that some matches will be good and some dull'. The unpredictability of the event and the unknowableness of its outcome are inherent and lifelike features; and in professional sport, the outcome will, as we have just seen, have 'real world' consequences of varying but never negligible significance.

The unknowableness of the outcome is what enables sport to acquire the status of *news*. Yet not all sport is news: those sports that do not attract a large spectatorship – lacrosse games or bowls tournaments, for instance – do not make the headlines. Sport is news *only* insofar as it is entertainment, and as we have just seen, it typifies much entertainment in being of fixed duration, reaching a firm conclusion and then allowing a return to 'the real world'. Yet sport differs from other kinds of news in being *intentionally* theatrical and entertaining: it is a form of play, a fiction – in some sense not real, not serious, despite its palpable economic and social consequences. At this point, then, we can perhaps trace a series of connections, however loose or variable, between the 'amateur–professional' dualism of sport, the distinction between 'fiction' and 'real life' that we have used with respect to general television content, and the 'entertainment–news' dichotomy that we can discern in both sport and television. Sport provides both the spectacle which is at the heart of television's power to entertain and the uncertainty of outcome, and thus newsworthiness, which television can exploit through its liveness. Yet for television, sport's potential as both news and entertainment can create something of a dilemma.

As is implied in its very name, 'news' deals in both novelty and recency: ideally, events and outcomes must be made public as soon as they are known. But sport's function as entertainment entails a contrasting need to *withhold* information: the pleasurably suspenseful nature of television's spectacle may challenge the newsworthy potential of its liveness. In other words, because it is entertainment, sport is not of *paramount* importance as news. This conflict is often apparent in news bulletins which are to be followed immediately by the recorded highlights of a particular match. The newsreader warns the audience 'If you don't want to know the result, look away now', and the result is silently posted on the screen.

It is interesting to explore how television seeks to reconcile a journalistic concern for fact and truth with the need to keep its viewers entertained (Whannel 1992: 26, 66). The journalistic imperative is to reveal the result as soon as possible: the entertainment imperative is to create suspense and a narrative. The journalistic preference is for the live and full transmission of an event, accompanied by a transparent, objective commentary. The entertainment option is to transmit recorded highlights (a term which intentionally implies that all the humdrum parts – the 'lowlights' – have been edited out) within a mixed package of previews, interviews and post-match analysis. As Gary Whannel (1992: 190) also points out, this is because, unlike theatre, sport is a commodity whose quality and satisfaction cannot be guaranteed, and an artful TV package can make an entertaining programme out of a poor game. Yet even when the game is broadcast live and in full and the commentary is being provided by trained journalists, their instinct is to impose a 'mood' or 'narrative' on what they see (Whannel 1992: 114–15).

Thus we have already broached the second theme of this chapter: the ways in which television's coverage of sport, whether as news or entertainment, differs from the experience of the conventional spectator. Since television is interested only in sports that large numbers of people wish to watch, and will thus pay to watch, whether by means of a licence fee or subscription or through the hidden costs of advertising and sponsorship, it is almost invariably concerned with sports that are – or could become – professional. Indeed, merely by turning them into something that can be more widely seen, television has been instrumental in professionalising certain sports that were once only or mainly amateur, such as darts and snooker. But TV does not merely make available to many more pairs of eyes in faraway places what those in the sporting arena can see for themselves: it *transforms* what they can see. Quite aside from abridging it or embedding it in a context of studio discussion and film clips from other matches, it makes the spectacle of the sporting event itself far better than anything that could be beheld with the naked eye. This, of course, explains the frequent provision of television technology within the stadiums – giant screens to compensate the spectators for the paradox that an unmediated presence at a sporting event can seem paltry in comparison with a mediated absence from it (Whannel 1992: 98). Hence the alteration that television makes is both quantitative (more spectators) and qualitative (the spectators see better).

Not surprisingly, television has quickened the trend towards professionalism in many sports, either by raising the pay and status of professionals beyond anything they could have aspired to in the age of press and radio coverage, or by professionalising sports that in former times were partly or wholly amateur. Indeed, by 1995, with rugby union the last to fall into line, the top players of all the most frequently televised sports were professional (Williams 2004: 223). It is also not surprising that the rise of television, followed by its attendant refinements of instant replay, slow motion, colour, micro-cameras and videographics, and latterly the launch of dedicated channels by BSkyB, has made sport much more central to the national consciousness. A country's achievements in global competitions like the World Cup or the Olympic Games will often have a palpable effect on the morale of its people. One might even regard televised sport as an equally fierce and colourful, yet bloodless, alternative to more traditional forms of international conflict – one in which the effects of victory and defeat are felt almost as keenly but are happily less lasting.

In what ways, then, is television's coverage of sport better than the actual observation of it? Whether live or recorded, it offers not the fixed standpoint of the single spectator but a range of standpoints, each affording both close-up and distant views, together with action replays, slow-motion sequences and freezes. These can be located not just within an arena but over the extended terrain used by sports like horse-racing, golf, rally-driving and cross-country running. Some of the pictures come from helicopters or blimps, the backs of trucks or the jibs of cranes; some from micro-cameras in the cockpits of racing cars; some from humanly inaccessible places such as cricket stumps and goal stanchions. Superimposed on the pictures are periodical read-outs of current match statistics. Computer technology combines with video recording to enhance not only the spectacle but our analysis and understanding of it by providing, in addition to the replays, graphic illustrations of a ball's trajectory or, within a virtual image of the cricket field, the distribution of shots by which a batsman has gained his runs. All this is incorporated into the comment, analysis and predictions of studio experts, and within its overall need to entertain, illustrates television's abiding wish to teach. We also noted earlier that television's recorded coverage of games edits out all the delays and uninteresting bits. Finally, we can view televised sport of any kind from the comfort of our own home or personal space.

The pleasures of being present at a sporting event should not, of course, be forgotten. The greatest of these is the sheer sense of atmosphere that television can only partly capture. The spectator who is a supporter also has the pleasure of paying physical homage to his team and often of ensuring that his approval or disapproval of the players is audible to them; and he has a much greater degree of autonomy than the TV viewer in being able to look outside the images that are framed by the cameras, however multifarious and exciting these may be. But there can be no doubt that, on balance, television's coverage of sport far exceeds anything that can be seen by the naked eye, and provides a much more enlightening and varied experience than is available to the spectator in the grandstand.

We can discern two respects in which television has transformed sport. First it has popularised sports that were previously of limited interest, either because they were not spectacular until television made them so or they were for one reason or another little known. But in addition, television has prompted a number of sports, whether or not they were already popular, to alter the ways in which they are played in order to enhance their attractiveness to the medium. Of those that were not spectacular until television made them so, darts and snooker are two prime examples. For the first time, the cameras enabled large numbers of spectators of both games to get close to the participants and the scene of the action – the dart board and the snooker table – and in snooker, a bird's eye view also became possible. However, with its variously coloured balls that have to be potted in a particular sequence, the game had to wait until the advent of colour technology before television could take an interest in it. Previously, it was not only of limited appeal as a spectacle but largely unknown outside working men's clubs (Hodgson 1995: 22).

Another sport that has always been spectacular but was not well known before it caught television's eye was showjumping, though as sumo wrestling illustrates, if a spectacular sport is unknown this is usually because it has hitherto been played in another part of the globe. The recent penetration of American satellite television has been identified as the cause not only of a growing enthusiasm for basketball in the Caribbean but of a loss of interest in cricket (Casey *et al* 2002: 228–9). However, sumo and showjumping also illustrate that the popularity of certain televised sports is sometimes short-lived. Indeed sport on television reveals that there can be unexpected limits to the medium's influence – that if a sport's cultural roots run deep, it will not be easily supplanted by newer rivals that appear on the screen, however exciting these may be. Games like American football, baseball, ice hockey and basketball are hugely popular across the Atlantic and undeniably spectacular, but despite considerable television exposure, they have not achieved lasting popularity in Britain. Conversely, soccer and cricket have spectacular potential but American television has hardly bothered to take them up – all of which suggests that the 'cultural roots' that seem to be the prerequisite of a sport's *sustained* popularity on television lie in the extent to which the sport has been played rather than simply watched. In other words, much sport on television – which is almost by definition *professional* sport – will not enjoy sustained success on the medium unless it has first been *amateur*. Soccer has a better prospect of becoming popular on American TV since it began to be played at grassroots level by large numbers of children.

But in order to win the attention of television, many sports have changed the ways in which they are played by making themselves either more interesting to watch or easier to fit into its schedules and thus, presumably, better suited to the habits and tastes of the viewers. The most obvious changes have been presentational. In pre-televisual times, soccer teams wore jerseys of a certain colour merely to distinguish themselves from their opponents, while since there is less physical interaction in cricket, the players of both teams simply wore all-whites. Now, sporting strips are designed with much more attention to their aesthetic appeal: cricketers wear different coloured pyjamas (whites are retained only for certain major matches) and players of almost all televised sports display sponsors' names on their kit – a small instance of the advertising that has proliferated around stadiums and along race tracks.

Boxing – one of the few legalised forms of violence, and holding out a promise of blood and knock-outs – has always been hugely telegenic, but it, too, has undergone presentational changes. Title fights are often preceded by light-shows, thumping music, and processions of the boxers and their retinues into the ring, which is itself plastered with logos and sponsors' names. Between rounds, the violence is made sexy by scantily-clad women who circle the ring, holding up placards that display the number of the next round. Nor is it fanciful or cynical to suggest that theatricality has extended even to the behaviour of the participants, for instance those soccer players who clutch their heads in chagrin when they miss an easy opportunity to score. In the days before television, the chagrin would have been just as keenly felt but could be safely internalised. Now, it is only prudent that a player being watched in close up by the millions who are making him rich should show how keenly he regrets his failures.

Presentational changes in a sport will not, of themselves, always succeed in recommending it to television, whose interest can of course make the difference between amateur and professional status. In this respect, two racket games – tennis and squash – have had contrasting fortunes. Neither tennis nor athletics have ever needed to make presentational adjustments to gain the attention of television, and thanks to the latter's coverage, Wimbledon tennis became professional in 1968 (Whannel 1992: 80). But squash, though exciting to play, is simply too fast to make easy viewing. It therefore introduced a transparent, multi-coloured court to enable spectators to make better sense of the action, but its failure to capture the interest of television means that unlike tennis, it remains a largely amateur sport.

Sports may also seek to make themselves more attractive to television – or to be more precise, to its schedules and hence the presumed lifestyles of its viewers – by changing the times and seasons during which they are played. Cricket is traditionally a daytime sport that is played in natural light. But in 1977, the Australian tycoon Kerry Packer sought to feed his Channel 9 TV station by launching 'World Series' cricket, a game that, as well as introducing coloured kit, was played in the evening – and under floodlights – in order to capture the biggest audience. For a similar reason, many matches in the 1994 soccer World Cup, which was staged in the United States, took place in sweltering midday heat. They were of scant interest to the local audience, but could thus be seen at peak viewing times in soccer-besotted Europe. Conversely, the world title boxing match between Lennox Lewis and Oliver McCall was staged in Britain at 2 a.m. because it could command a huge evening audience in the United States. As part of an £87 million deal to televise British rugby league, BSkyB required that from 1996 the game should not only re-brand itself as the Super League but switch from a winter to a summer season (Hadfield 1995: 24). The reason, presumably, was that BSkyB's winter schedules had already been filled with other sports.

It is hardly surprising that many sports have sought to increase their exposure on television (and thus to attract commercial sponsors) by devising new competitions to replace or run alongside the traditional ones. It is safe to say that, without television, cricket would never have launched a Gillette Cup or its variously branded successors; that cricket and rugby union would not have devised their world cup competitions; and that athletics would not have thought up its World Championship. Indeed it is felt by some that television has fostered too many competitions: these can become meaningless in themselves and exhaust the more talented players by committing them to an excessive number of games per season. In soccer, an élite club will no longer maintain a team with just two or three reserve players but a 'squad', which is about double the size of the team, and within which various players, every one of whom may be a star in his own right, will be 'rotated' in order to cope with fixture congestion.

Since television can see far better than the naked eye, it has inevitably brought changes in sporting adjudication. Rugby Super League uses a 'video referee' to make difficult try decisions, while many cricket matches use a third umpire, who sits off the field with a replay monitor. If an on-field umpire is unsure whether a player has been stumped or run out, or whether a ball has reached the boundary-rope, he may seek the help of the third umpire – and if the latter feels able to make a ruling, it will override his own. Though the umpires do not use other televisual facilities, it may only be a matter of time before they do. Channel 4's videographic 'hawk-eye' device would appear to remove much of the doubt from lbw decisions by tracing what the line of the ball would have been, and its 'snickometer' eases one of the umpire's hardest tasks: to discern whether the ball has clipped the bat or part of the batsman on its way to the wicket-keeper.

By now it will be apparent that cricket has made more concessions to television than most other sports. This is perhaps because although in many respects highly watchable, its matches are too sedate and protracted for many viewers, and Kerry Packer's World Series cricket was an early paradigm of almost all the televisually induced changes that we are discussing – in presentation, competitive structure, new times of play, and most crucially of all, in the rules. Rule changes go to the heart of a sport and can sometimes make it difficult to determine whether we are dealing with two versions of a sport or two different sports. One-day and other limited-over versions of cricket were prompted by the needs of television for more excitement and a quick, decisive result (Whannel 1992: 79–80). The number of overs has usually been 50 per side, but 'twenty20' cricket – a game lasting only two or three hours and played under floodlights – is a further attempt to hold television's attention. Some cricket enthusiasts would even claim that the traditional game and limited-over games require very different skills and are beginning to produce two different kinds of cricketer.

Other sports have changed their rules to accommodate television, often in ways that reduce their satisfaction for the players even as they increase the interest for the spectator. Snooker invented shorter matches than most professionals thought was a fair test of their skills; figure skating competitions dropped certain compulsory figures when television lost interest in them; and squash changed some of its rules, but was still too fast to make comfortable viewing (Whannel 1992: 81). Soccer's traditional means of settling drawn cup matches was to require them to be replayed, but in televised games this has increasingly given way to the penalty shoot-out. Many players deplore the shoot-out as little better than throwing dice – a test of nerve rather than skill – but there is no doubt that it makes better television than a repeat of the entire match.

Finally, television has wrought contrasting changes in the autonomy of sportspeople, and these have also had effects, albeit indirect, on how matches are played. TV did not cause economic individualism among players, but it has certainly strengthened it – to the extent that the conduct of team games can be undermined (Whannel 1992: 191). In soccer, for instance, the top performers within a team are competing against each other, as well as against their opponents, in earning power and for star status. Their allegiance to the team can thus be weakened, although the player who admits as much will paradoxically reduce his marketability. Moreover, because professional team players are individual mercenaries who are bought and sold within an oligarchy of clubs, most do not share the largely local origins of their club's supporters. This has been a fact of life for well over a century, but the sums of money generated by television have increased its magnitude. In premiership soccer, for instance, it is not merely the case that most players in a club will not come from its locality; many will not even share its nationality. There are now numerous leading English clubs in which British, let alone English, players are in a minority.

It should be added however that the TV paymasters of certain sportspeople will sometimes seek to *reduce* their autonomy. BSkyB's bid to screen rugby league included the condition that it could veto player transfers (O'Hagan 1995: 24). The aim was to preserve a balance of power between the clubs of the new Super League and thus ensure that it remained competitive and a source of exciting television. But it is clear that too little autonomy among players can have just as damaging an effect on team spirit as too much of it.

We have so far considered the ways in which television has covered existing sports, but we must conclude with a brief look at how television has invented sports of its own. These are sometimes known as 'para-sports', and some have their origins in game shows such as 'Beat the Clock', a segment of *Sunday Night at the London Palladium* (ITV, 1955–67 and 1973–4), and *It's a Knockout*, which ran on the BBC from 1966 until 1982. Since ITV launched *Gladiators* in 1992, para-sports have begun to take themselves rather more seriously, using vast and lavish sets and setting challenges that are ever more demanding and spectacular. But even those made-for-TV events that more closely resemble traditional sports, like log rolling and truck derbies, have had difficulty in establishing themselves as 'the real thing' (Blain and Boyle 2002:

417). The reason is evidently that para-sports have no cultural roots – no tradition of having been *played* in the original, amateur sense of the word. They have been devised purely as entertainment for (television) spectators and are only incidentally of amusement or interest to the participants. Nor is there much likelihood that they will be taken up by their spectators, since they mostly involve the use of bizarre studio sets and unique and unpurchasable equipment.

Among para-sports we might include professional wrestling, since it differs so much from amateur wrestling as to be less an adaptation of it than a child of television. Amateur wrestling is not very telegenic, but professional wrestling is carefully choreographed fakery. It may be entertaining to watch and is especially popular in the United States, but for many British viewers it is fatally compromised by not being genuinely competitive. The outcome of its bouts is predetermined, which means that it is theatre *par excellence* but falls outside the definition of sport. In fact, professional wrestling is of interest in illustrating a risk that attends all professional sport. We have already noted that sport is primarily, originally, designed for the gratification of its players and not for the spectators. The moves of the game are not 'scripted' and its outcome is uncertain: that is its essence. But this means that its entertainment value to the spectators cannot be guaranteed. Nevertheless, because the income from the spectators provides the livelihood of the players and ensures the general prosperity of the game, there is always a risk that the tail of entertainment will wag the dog of sport – that legitimate attempts to ensure the quality of the spectacle by buying and training the best athletes will spill over into a collusion between opposing sides. It is the global stadium of television which reminds us most vividly that the aims of sportspeople and the interests of their spectators do not always coincide.

Drama and film

I am not yet convinced that television drama is sure of its target. Does it aim to be more than a photographed stage play? Does it dream of competition with film? Or should its principal aim be that of *illustrated broadcasting*?

(Val Gielgud, *The BBC Quarterly*, 1947)

It is probably fair to say that, of all the genres of television, drama has received the largest share of critical attention, and the purpose of this chapter is to identify, as far as possible, its distinctive characteristics. Critics point out that it began as something essentially theatrical and progressed towards something essentially cinematic: our aim will be to see how, in itself and in the art forms it has generated, television drama differs from both theatre and cinema.

When television first sought to screen drama, it looked, logically enough, to the traditional stage, either by re-creating theatrical sets in its own studios and pointing a fixed camera at them or by taking a fixed camera into actual theatres and showing plays as live outside broadcasts (Caughie 2000: 39–40). Yet as Charles Barr (1996: 58) illustrates in his lucid account of its progress towards the cinematic, television drama began to differ from stage drama almost at the outset. By the mid-1940s it could cut between several cameras, whether on one set or several, and thus switch between close-up and long-shot:

The best of live television drama brought its viewers into extreme proximity with outpourings of emotions, or the visible marks of emotional repression. . . . It was unlike theatre because viewers and performers were not in the same space, and because viewers had a mobility of viewpoint, produced by the use of multiple cameras and the ability to give extreme close-up.

(Ellis 2002: 32–3)

But as well as creating a kind of mobility by cutting between static cameras, television could soon deploy cameras that provided pictures while they were being moved and thus reduce for the viewers that sense of 'frontality' that was created by the fixed contemplation of box-sets.

These more flexible forms of live transmission were followed in the late 1940s by the ability to record the television image. Live plays could be filmed from a studio monitor in a process known as 'telerecording' (Cooke 2003: 7), and from the early 1950s television material could also be pre-recorded. The landmark BBC drama, *Nineteen Eighty Four* (1954), an adaptation of the famous novel by George Orwell, was associated with both developments. The play was transmitted and repeated as live performances but contained filmed inserts and was also telerecorded while being performed (Cooke 2003: 24–5). The practice of broadcasting television plays as generally live performances but with the inclusion of filmed sequences continued well into the 1960s. From the end of the 1950s, however, the tape-recording of the television image also became possible, and early in the following decade, tape-editing. At first, plays were electronically recorded in the studio, but later they were filmed on location and gradually acquired a more cinematic style. Cooke (2003: 86) identifies a light-hearted crime series, *The Avengers* (ITV, 1961–9), as encompassing all the main technological developments of the time: it began as a live studio drama, then was recorded on videotape in the studio before switching to film in 1965 and colour in 1967.

We can trace how the technological shift from the theatrical to the cinematic was matched by a shift in content and production. Like many other new media, television was at first unsure of itself and paid homage to the media that had preceded it by adopting their cultural forms with a minimum of alteration. In its dramatic repertory, it did not presume to create but merely to relay or reflect. At first, all television plays were theatrical adaptations, then later, most of them were: it was not until the late 1950s that plays that were written for the medium began to outnumber those that were adapted for it (Jacobs 2000: 76). In Britain, this deference to the theatre, and also to the literary canon of which so much theatrical drama formed a part, was reinforced by the public service philosophy that underpinned broadcasting in general. The BBC had a duty to provide not just a universality of content but to the highest possible standard, and the best way for television to gain cultural prestige was to ground its dramatic repertory in that of the classical theatre (Cooke 2003: 10). And just as the theatre was live, so should television be. Hence even when recording on tape became possible, the tapes were routinely wiped and re-used (Jacobs 2000: 11).

In contrast, television was inclined to play down its resemblance to the cinema because the latter was widely regarded as a lowbrow, inferior medium. In the 1940s television broadcast very few cinema films for two reasons. First it had a technical difficulty in screening them: its electronic image consisted of 25 frames per second, while cinema's was only 24, the discrepancy appearing as a series of black bars on the TV screen (Winston 1998: 268). Secondly the Cinema Exhibitors' Association refused to sell its movies to a medium that had taken such a bite out of its revenues. But from the late 1950s, the networks were able to acquire and show cinema films, while at the same time television's own technological advances were pushing it in the direction of a more cinematic aesthetic. As the medium grew in strength and confidence, why should it not create dramas of its own, as the cinema did? So the 1960s saw the rise of the authored television play. Among those who were eager to reach the new mass audience, and to do so without the tight constraints of the commercial theatre, were David Mercer, Dennis Potter, John Hopkins, Alan Plater, Allan Prior, Jack Rosenthal and Fay Weldon (Cooke 2003: 77).

However the ascendancy of the television playwright was a mere transitional stage in the medium's development – one, moreover, which looked back to the theatre quite as much as it looked forward to the originality of most cinema films. Why? Many of the latter are multi-authored and entail a creative process in which dialogue is only one, and sometimes a subordinate, element. But the television play of the 1960s and 1970s drew on the older, theatrical concept of an artefact whose dialogue is more important than all else and almost always the work of a single author. Nevertheless, the technological, largely cinematic, developments that were taking place in television were turning the making of TV plays into an increasingly collective matter – what we have elsewhere termed an 'industrial' process that involved camera crews, lighting and sound engineers, film editors, a producer/director and so on. This meant that the primacy of the writer was being challenged by the producer/director, since it was the latter who was obliged to take overall responsibility for the televised artefact. (I am using the terms 'producer' and 'director' interchangeably here since different broadcasters favour different titles.)

Charles Barr (1996: 67) sees the 1970s as the period in which television plays occupied a halfway point between the theatre and the cinema. They were 'shot on 16mm, on very tight schedules, respectful of their scripts, publicized on the writer's name more than the director's, and a prey to "ephemerality"'. Nevertheless, the playwright Trevor Griffiths, who was writing for television during that period, lamented that

Any writing, notes for a character, notes for a sequence, images, jottings, draft treatments, sub-structures, all characters created, all language used on a page, including dialogue, stage directions and so on . . . belong to the producer. They don't belong at any point . . . to the person creating them

(quoted in Tulloch 1990: 129)

And in the same period, TV directors like Richard Eyre, Stephen Frears, Jack Gold, Roland Joffe and Ken Loach, all of whom went on to work in the cinema, were becoming every bit as well known as the playwrights (Cooke 2003: 95). Television's progress from the theatrical to the cinematic was also reflected in the change of titles of its series of single plays. Between the 1960s and the 1980s, 'Armchair Theatre' (ITV), 'Play for Today' (BBC 1), 'The Wednesday Play' (BBC 1) and 'Theatre 625' (BBC 2) were superseded by 'Screenplay' (BBC 2), 'Screen on One' (BBC 1), 'Screen Two' (BBC 2) and 'Film on Four' (Channel 4) (Nelson 1997: 19).

While television drama evinced certain cinematic characteristics even when it was wholly live, such as the intercutting of images and use of close-up, there is no doubt that the most significant element in its shift from the theatrical to the cinematic was *recording*, and we need to wrestle for a moment with the paradox of the medium's liveness and recordedness. If liveness – instantaneous transmission – is television's great and indeed unique strength (radio has no pictures), what is the point of compromising that strength by transmitting material that has been made days, weeks, perhaps even years before the moment of transmission? In this respect, exchanging the liveness of theatre for the recordedness of cinema seems a retrograde step, especially since television likes to pretend that it is totally live even when it is not (Ellis 2002: 33–4). The answer is, of course, that television must satisfy other and contrasting needs that are of equal or almost equal importance. The first is the need for interesting pictures, especially in news, current affairs, documentaries and sport. Sometimes, as we have seen, these pictures can be live, but if the choice is between live pictures of a mere presenter or reporter and recorded pictures of an event which are recent enough to be topical, television will adopt the latter. Hence in much factual or informative television, we can say that recording underpins its liveness, or that it is a *quasi*-liveness.

But as a medium broadcasting daily if not round the clock, television must satisfy another need: for programming in enormous quantities. Recording enables programmes to be created well in advance of transmission, to be stockpiled and repeated – especially fictional programmes, where liveness and topicality are much less important. In this respect, recording forms the basis of television's claim not only to reflect the world but to be creative, to originate its own works of art. By emulating the artefacts of the cinema, it can thus claim that its drama is an improvement on the live, hence merely ephemeral, character of theatrical drama. Indeed, in showing cinema films, it effectively passes them off as artefacts of its own. We can thus see a loose correlation between the 'liveness–recordedness' duality of television and its alternation between a passive, factual role on the one hand and a creative, fictional role on the other. The correlation is only loose because some factual programmes, for example wildlife documentaries, do not have to be topical and can thus be recorded well in advance of transmission; and in any case, there is, as we have already noted, a measure of overlap between the factual and the fictional. But the duality helps to explain why television is such a difficult medium to pin down – why at one moment, it seems to be a self-contained medium originating material across a range of genres, yet at another to be self-effacingly preoccupied with things outside itself; why its essential liveness is at times overwhelming, and why at others the viewer is not greatly aware that it is a broadcast she is watching and not the tape or disc in her video recorder.

But pre-recording as a way of satisfying television's unending demand for content has not simply been applied to single plays: it has introduced *mass production* by encouraging the creation of drama that is broken into episodes, whether in the form of finite series and serials or in open-ended soap operas, and to all of which the term 'serial drama' can be applied. It is true that serial programmes, including serial drama, existed on television before the advent of recording, but there can be no doubt that recording has provided the real economic impetus to their growth. And it is of particular significance to drama, since drama is among the costliest forms of television programming, requiring at least one scriptwriter, a director, actors, make-up and technical staff, sets or locations, and costumes. By encouraging the growth of serials, pre-recording allows these resources to be used for several programmes instead of just one, and during the extended period of their transmission there is also an opportunity to build and retain large audiences.

Yet while it is true that pre-recording introduced into television the mass production of drama that has long been a feature of the cinema, the analogy between the two media is not straightforward. Cinematic mass production is the creation of separate recorded products – feature films – though these can be turned out at frequent intervals. The purpose of such production is to tempt people to make repeated journeys to the cinema. But because – unlike both cinema and theatre – television is domestic, because switching it on involves no journey greater than the breadth of the living-room carpet, demand for its content does not have to be stimulated in this way; it is already huge, unceasing and hard to satisfy. Hence we can say that whereas in cinematic drama the techniques of mass production are geared to *repetition*, the creation of recurrent artefacts, those of television drama (and many of its other genres) are also geared to *seriality*, the creation of continuous artefacts. The daily soap opera, with its relays of scriptwriters, not to mention all the other resources it commands, is the classic instance of industrialised drama, of the application of the techniques of mass production to artistic creativity.

Between the late 1970s and the late 1990s, series increased from 47 per cent to 63 per cent of all British TV drama, and soaps from 10 per cent to 29 per cent (Cooke 2003: 191). This growth of serial drama has thus been achieved at the expense of the single play, whose decline has been mourned by the critics. They point to the economy of its exposition and narrative development, to the critical alertness it demands of an audience otherwise stupefied by an anodyne profusion of output, and to its ability to make the theatrical classics more widely known. In contrast they often condemn series, and some serials too, as banal and formulaic, and observe that the range of drama has now narrowed to crime and hospital sagas, soaps, sitcoms and historical serials, many of which are mere adaptations of famous novels (Casey *et al* 2002: 74). Be that as it may, one could also claim that the serial drama is a genuinely new art form in the sense that it is seldom found in the theatre nor, other than as separately conceived sequels or 'prequels', in the cinema. Seriality has long been a feature of novels, magazines and of course radio, but in the form of a dramatic spectacle it is largely telegenic. (I have been using 'telegenic' more or less synonymously with 'televisual' to mean 'to do with the character of television', but there are shades of difference. Whereas *televisual* means 'that which happens to be on television – which is capable of being exploited or shown by television', *telegenic* has the further sense of 'that which is *especially suited* to television – that is part of, or illustrates, the distinctive character of the medium'.)

Lez Cooke (2003: 20–1) sees the screening of *The Quatermass Experiment* (BBC, 1953) as the point at which television drama became telegenic, because it was a) a serial and not a single play; b) made especially for the medium and not adapted from the theatre; and c) though broadcast live, partly telerecorded. As soon as pre-recording could be used to produce television drama, the cinema industry joined the rival it could not beat by making films-for-TV – but filmed *series*, not individual cinematic films. Warner Brothers was the first major studio to do so, agreeing in 1954 to supply the American network ABC with three westerns: *Cheyenne*, *Sugarfoot* and *Maverick* (Turow 1999: 237).

We need to begin our discussion of seriality by reminding ourselves that it characterises many other types of programming than drama: but drama is perhaps the most interesting, and much of what we say about it will be applicable to the others. We can divide serial drama into two kinds – *series*, collections of discrete, self-contained episodes that focus on a single character, theme or situation and may be screened and viewed in no particular order; and *serials*, episodes that are sequentially linked and may or may not reach a narrative conclusion. Of the two, serials are perhaps of the greater formal interest, though certain things we observe about them will also be true of series. Because television differs from theatre and cinema in being viewed by a remote, dispersed audience, most of whom are at home, we can claim not only that it achieves the domestication of drama in general, but that in serial form it often resembles that other domestically and even privately consumed genre from which it is said to be descended: the Victorian novel (Allen 2004: 242).

In the nineteenth century the novel, as embodied in the works of Dickens, George Eliot, Thackeray and Trollope, was at the height of its power and popularity. Typically, it embraced a vast social panorama, carried both main and subordinate plots that were skilfully intertwined, and just as significantly, was often written – and read – in numerous and lengthy instalments that were published in magazines. The critic Henry James famously referred to Victorian novels as 'loose, baggy monsters'. It is hardly surprising that many of them have been adapted for television, but even in serials of its own, the medium creates a world in which the audience can immerse itself over a period of time, inhabit the minds of the characters, and ponder their motivation and behaviour. In soaps especially, the characters build up a personal history, and their internal consistency is very important to the viewers (Abercrombie 1996: 49). Critics have fairly objected that the subtleties of literary fiction, in which the writer can talk *about* his characters as well as *through* them, are not easily matched by television, which tends to focus on aesthetics at the expense of social and moral complexities (Cooke 2003: 167). Nevertheless we often overlook the fact that most serials, let alone series, are many times longer than the average cinema feature film, and that in a medium which cannot, in general, afford the spectacular action, locations and technical effects of the cinema, dialogue will be prominent, and well-crafted dialogue especially evocative. Hence television drama remains more of a writers' genre than is the cinema, even if its words are likely to make less impact than in the limited spectacle and brief duration of a stage play.

The originality of serial drama manifests itself not only in dialogue and characterisation but in its plots and themes, and in the timescale over which its action commonly unfolds. Soaps and soap-like serials, in particular, are characterised by what has been termed flexi-narrative (Nelson 1997: 30–1). They lack a single, unifying perspective and instead carry a number of co-equal storylines, constantly switching between them. Soaps can contain up to 40 characters, none of them 'heroes' in the old sense of being central or pivotal characters. Some of the storylines end in a neat, conventional way but others simply peter out – and the soaps themselves, along with many series, never achieve formal closure. Indeed it has been argued that their formal 'untidiness' encourages the viewer to believe in a future as yet unwritten and incapable of neat resolution (Geraghty 1996: 363). Nevertheless, many soaps and serials adroitly combine a masculine preference for action and narrative momentum with a feminine predilection for fluidity, open-endedness and human interest (Nelson 1997: 39).

Television serials often differ from traditional drama in two further respects. First, their themes are not especially exotic or remote from the experience of their audience: they focus on domestic existence or the life of the workplace. Second, their timescale is not elliptical – that is to say, they do not omit intervening occurrences in order to leap from one 'significant' event to the next. Many adopt a 'real time' chronology in the sense that their action advances roughly in parallel with the lives of their viewers, and the implication is that it continues to do so whether or not we (or the cameras) are watching (Fiske 1987: 179). In both their preoccupations and treatment of time, then, many continuous serials are broadly congruent with the lives of their viewers, just as is the domestic and unending character of television itself, and for this reason the scholar Charlotte Brunsdon has described soap opera as 'in some ways the paradigmatic television genre (domestic, continuous, contemporary, episodic, repetitive, fragmented and aural)' (quoted in Mumford 1998: 125). We can conclude, then, by claiming that serial drama is truly telegenic – very different from both traditional, theatrical plays and cinematic feature films, and a classic instance of the way in which technological and economic exigencies can inspire, indeed require, the development of new art forms.

But where does all this leave the single play? Occasionally, television wishes to mark the fact that it is not, or ought not to be, always viewed routinely or distractedly but as an event, and it does so in an idiom that is cinematic rather than theatrical. We have seen that this is attributable to recording technology. Recorded artefacts are usually of high quality since they are assembled from a number of 'takes': errors and redundancies have been eliminated and the recording thus represents the best performance that the actors are capable of. Moreover, such artefacts are reusable and saleable, whether to other broadcasters or, as commercial videos, to audiences. The single television play is thus closer in character to the feature film than to the stage play.

Television's ability to incorporate the technology of the cinema means that it can not only transmit the latter's artefacts as well as its own but create dramatic productions for cinema exhibition as well as for broadcasting. This close, partly cooperative, partly antagonistic, relationship between TV and cinema allows us to make a crude but useful generalisation about television in Western Europe – that it has been the beneficiary of the American film industry but the benefactor of the European one. In Britain, Channel 4, which was launched in 1982, pioneered the notion of making feature films for its 'Film on Four' series that would be both broadcast on television and exhibited in cinemas. This certainly benefited television because the promise of cinema exhibition allowed the dramas to be made on higher budgets and gave its writers and directors the opportunity to create what would gain more than a single TV screening (Cooke 2003: 139). But television benefited European cinema even more. Between 1980 and 1990, European film production was overwhelmed by the American cinema industry and found an important new source of revenue in television. By June 1994, 51 per cent of European films in production were being backed by TV money (Hill 1996: 152). In Britain, nearly 7 per cent of Channel 4's total budget was at one stage going on 'Film on Four' and helping to finance almost half the British films being made (Williams 1998: 209).

Nevertheless there can be no doubt that over its entire history, television has gained much more from the cinema, especially American cinema, than it has given. Indeed television passes off cinema films as if they were part of its own repertory: not only are channels such as Sky Movies, Sky Box Office and FilmFour wholly given over to cinema films, but even on a traditional mixed-programme network, the highlight of an evening's viewing is quite likely to be the TV premiere of what has been a cinema blockbuster – an interesting example of proudly proclaimed *déjà vu* by a medium whose unique strength is its liveness, the transmission of something that is occurring now and has not occurred before! We might sum up by saying that as the descendant of that live and static art form, the theatre, the single television play is all but dead, but as a filmed, cinematic artefact, it is alive and well. The problem is that we have been looking for it in the wrong guise.

Comedy and light entertainment

Of all forms of communication there are only two that evoke a physical response from the audience. One is comedy, the other pornography . . . . The audience has to change its physical posture. In a sense you could say that the laughtermakers and the pornographers are the most neurotic because they are the most power-hungry . . . . From there you can go into all sorts of Cloud-cuckoo-land about sexuality and power. The life and soul of the party who is effecting physical changes on everybody around him is practising a sort of rape, a kind of assault.

(Denis Norden, quoted in David Nathan, *The Laughtermakers: A Quest for Comedy*)

Between them, comedy and light entertainment occupy a huge, almost illimitable field. Quite aside from the argument advanced by Neil Postman (1986) that many kinds of television adopt a posture of entertainment in order to hold the viewer, I have suggested in this book that even serious or educative content can be treated as 'mere' entertainment simply because it affords scopophilic gratifications. However, the focus of this chapter will be on designated forms of comedy, with a few observations on two other light entertainment formats: game shows and 'music television' in the guise of pop videos.

Within the electronic media of film, radio and television, even 'pure' comedy displays an astonishing formal diversity: the variety show, the short, the sketch, the narrative feature, the cartoon, the sitcom, stand-up routines (Mills 2001: 61; Neale and Krutnik 1990: 10) – to which we could add the wisecracks and improvisations of the celebrity panel game. Moreover, comedy can pervade genres that are conventionally serious, giving us tragi-comedy, the comic western, the comedy-thriller and the comic horror film (Neale and Krutnik 1990: 17–18). This seems to be because, as a 'sense of humour', our perception of the comic is instinctive, sudden and spontaneous before it is ever worked up into a consistent and self-conscious work of art. In other words, while we might develop plays or films or novels whose attempt to elicit laughter is sustained enough for them to be labelled 'comedies', things can immediately strike us as absurd and thus risible within *any* area of our experience, no matter how tragic or solemn or frightening it may generally be.

Why do these things so strike us? Why do we need to laugh, even to the extent of inventing comedy over and above that which we can discern within ordinary life? The answer to these questions is by no means clear, and in their incisive study of film and television comedy Neale and Krutnik (1990: 62–82) review some psychological theories of humour. Freud is, of course, their main authority. He argues that the creation of humour affords relief from social inhibitions and from the oppressive need to think rationally and distinguish truth from falsehood (Freud 1976: 146–7, 175). He then provides a sharp insight into the *mechanics* of humour – the way in which jokes operate:

> The two fixed points in what determines the nature of jokes – their purpose of continuing pleasurable play and their effort to protect it from the criticism of reason – immediately explain why an individual joke, though it may seem senseless from one point of view, must appear sensible, or at least allowable, from another.
>
> (Freud 1976: 181)

This insight is developed by Neale and Krutnik (1990: 67): 'There must . . . be a degree of normality in the abnormal, a degree of the appropriate in the inappropriate, a degree of the logical in the illogical, and a degree of sense in the otherwise nonsensical.' We might therefore venture the generalisation that any act or utterance that aims to be comic, or any event that strikes us as comic or amusing, will contain elements of skill, rationality, plausibility and aptness on the one hand, and clumsiness, foolishness, absurdity and ineptitude on the other. At the crude, physical extreme, the clown's pratfall is a clever perfection of human fallibility, making the subjection to the law of gravity of that intellectual and spiritual animal, a human being, seem funny rather than painful or embarrassing. At the sophisticated, intellectual extreme, the pun or play on words rests precisely on the logic/illogic of assuming that identical or similar sounds imply identical or similar meanings: 'Two girls went for a tramp. The tramp died'.

However, it is not our purpose here to go deeply into theories of comedy: we will content ourselves with the definition of comedy as that which, for whatever reason, makes – and aims to make – people laugh. Yet although frequently illuminating, most studies of broadcast comedy (for example, Foster and Furst 1996; Nathan 1971; Neale and Krutnik 1990; Took 1976) seem uncertain as to whether they are studies of the phenomenon of comedy which just happens to be on radio and/or television or studies of the way in which comedy is *mediated* by radio and/or television. This chapter will try to focus on the way in which television has mediated comedy. What are the origins of its comic formats? What formats has it stimulated, if not originated? And what difference has it made to the way in which comedy is enjoyed? We can say of almost all television comedy that its immediate origins lie in either radio or cinema, or both, and that its ultimate origins are theatrical, whether in the conventional stage or in the variety and music hall. The exception is the animated cartoon, which originated wholly in the cinema.

Probably the most popular comic format on television, and the one which attracts the most critical attention, is the situation comedy or 'sitcom', and these two factors suggest that there is something especially telegenic about it. Sitcom has its roots, by way of radio, in the variety hall sketch (Neale and Krutnik 1990: 227; Williams 2004: 201, 203) – of which it is a kind of narrative expansion. British radio was rich in sitcoms even before the Second World War (Took 1976: 112), and critics have discerned in them a number of common structural features (Casey *et al* 2002: 30–3), as well as a range of themes and preoccupations. First, the sitcom is seldom an isolated programme but takes the form of a series with a certain number of episodes, each of which normally lasts for half an hour. It also contains an established core of characters and settings. The latter were originally domestic, but since the 1970s, with shows like *Are You Being Served?* (BBC 1, 1973–85), *The Office* (BBC 2, 2001–2) and *Extras* (BBC 2, 2005), workplace settings have become increasingly popular (Bowes 1990: 129). There has also been a tendency to use settings in which disparate people are thrown together by chance or force of circumstance: the armed forces (*Dad's Army* (BBC1, 1968–77)), prison (*Porridge* (BBC 1, 1974–77)), a lodging house (*Rising Damp* (ITV, 1975–8)), a pub (*Early Doors* (BBC 1, 2003–4)). Within these settings, sitcoms have been classified according to the way in which the characters operate: in some, there is an interplay of two main characters (*Steptoe and Son* (BBC 1, 1962–74)); in others, a character is alone (*Hancock* (BBC, 1961)); and in yet others, there is an ensemble cast (*Absolutely Fabulous* (BBC 2 and 1, 1992–2003), *The Royle Family* (BBC 2 and 1, 1998–2000), *Absolute Power* (BBC 2, 2003–5)) (Selby and Cowdery 1995: 120).

Another commonly observed feature of the sitcom is the cyclical nature of its narrative: the end of each episode returns to its beginning in the sense that after half an hour of dialogue and incident, the characters typically find themselves 'back where they started' (Neale and Krutnik 1990: 234).

Hence, as John Ellis (2002: 119) points out, there is no character development and no cumulative memory: each episode is a self-contained event that 'forgets' all its predecessors. In a few sitcoms, the plots and settings have evolved somewhat (Neale and Krutnik 1990: 235–6; Ellis 2002: 120), but the evolution is usually marked by a separate series: *The Likely Lads* (BBC 2, 1965–6), for instance, was superseded by *Whatever Happened to the Likely Lads?* (BBC 1, 1973–4). This relative lack of narrative and character development gives rise to some interesting features and audience gratifications. There is scope for jokes and comic business which are extraneous to the development of the story – a phenomenon that has been described as 'narrative excess' (Adams 1993: 69, 70) – and since the viewers, unlike the characters, can anticipate the outcome of each episode, their anticipation is amused rather than suspenseful. By understanding the implications of the situation in a way that the characters do not, they thus savour that phenomenon known as dramatic irony.

A third common feature of the sitcom is its characters' frequent recourse to catch-phrases. This is a concise way of revealing their idiosyncrasies, which the audience will need to appreciate as swiftly as possible within the brief duration of each episode. The catch-phrase is thus a means of *stereotyping*, of establishing the domineering mother-in-law, the middle-aged 'queen', and so on (Bowes 1990: 134). In recent years stereotyping has been so frowned upon that we should perhaps remind ourselves of its usefulness. We are told that it encourages simplistic and misleading judgements about people, and that it can be used by dominant groups to impose their ideologies on the rest of society (Woollacott 1996: 175). But this not only perceives stereotyping as the making of definitive judgements when they often aim only to be provisional but overlooks the fact that in certain circumstances it is something we all instinctively and necessarily do. If, while walking alone down a dark alley, we are approached by a young man in a baseball cap and hooded jacket, we can hardly avoid invoking our knowledge of stereotypes and feeling more wary than if he were bare-headed and formally dressed – though none of this is to deny that subsequent events could prove us wrong. In sitcom, of course, the stereotyping is usually well-founded since we need to form an early and reliable impression of the characters, and we do not object to its reductive effect since they have to be relatively simplistic in order for us to find them consistently funny.

Critics have also discerned a number of recurrent themes and preoccupations in sitcom. Domestic sitcoms frequently focus on the aberrations of family life, either by featuring unconventional families or families who are conventional but dysfunctional, while workplace sitcoms are often concerned with sexual exploration (Hartley 2001: 66). Other workplace themes are the self-delusion and ineptitude of the managers (*The Office*) or the interaction between a pompous, ineffectual or incompetent superior and a shrewd, capable or wily subordinate (*Yes, Minister* (BBC 2, 1980–2), *Fawlty Towers* (BBC 2, 1975–9)) (Selby and Cowdery 1995: 105–6). It has also been observed that the circularity of the sitcom's narrative structure commonly supports the theme of the characters' *entrapment* in their circumstances (Bowes 1990: 129). They cannot escape their class or their jobs or their gender or their marital status – or, ultimately, themselves (Selby and Cowdery 1995: 119–20) – and are thus studies in failure, ineptitude and frustration (Adams 1993: 69). Many sitcoms – for instance, *Steptoe and Son, Open All Hours* (BBC 2, 1973–82), *Only Fools and Horses* (BBC 1, 1981–96) and *Minder* (ITV, 1979–94) – have also been seen as ridiculing the overweening ambitions of small businessmen (Williams 2004: 61). But a recent critic has preferred to characterise the format in the more abstract terms of an interaction between binary opposites: masculinity–femininity; work–domesticity; rationality–emotionalism; intolerance–tolerance (Bignell 2004: 92).

We have seen that sitcom originated not in television but radio, and that its essence is the comic sketch that had been a staple of the theatre. Why, then, is it especially popular on television? What has TV brought to it that the other media could not? Television has certainly made a technical difference, just as radio did. It can incorporate a range of naturalistic locations, and within them, shifting viewpoints that embrace close-up as well as long-shot. Whether live or recorded, it can intercut events, remarks and reactions. Tony Hancock was a sitcom performer who had been reared in radio, but his performance was greatly enhanced by television's use of close-up and reaction shots (Goddard 1991: 82). In these and other ways, watching sitcom on the television transcends the experience of watching comic drama in the theatre. Indeed the way in which the audience is conceptualised by television, whether in sitcom or any other form of comedy, is worth dwelling on for a few moments.

Two interesting aspects of comedy are the relationship that exists between performer and audience and that which exists between the individual members of the audience. The performer requires a reaction from those who are watching and listening, not simply as a sign that the jokes are both understood and enjoyed, but in order to be able to judge the timing, mode of delivery, and sometimes even the selection and sequence, of the jokes that will follow. But a relationship also exists between the members of the audience, since laughter is pre-eminently a gregarious activity. It takes a very good joke to make us laugh aloud when we are alone: our laughter mainly imitates and feeds off that of others. In live theatre, both relationships are clearly established. In the cinema, the remoteness of the audience from the performers means that the only relationship that is established is between the members of the audience, though this is enough to trigger audible laughter. But neither relationship exists in radio or television. Not only are there considerable distances between performers on the one hand and their invisible audiences on the other, but the latter are dispersed, listening and viewing in their own environments, often alone and seldom in more than twos or threes. Hence the phenomenon of the surrogate, audible audience, which so conspicuously marks the difference between broadcasting and the more traditional comic media of stage and cinema.

The surrogate audience is of two kinds. The first exists merely in the form of recorded reactions – as 'canned laughter' – and serves as a prompt for the viewers and listeners. The second and more interesting is the studio audience, which prompts the viewers and listeners on the one hand and cues the performers on the other. When the *broadcast* audience hears canned laughter, its members are aware that it is occurring outside their own environment and are thus reminded that the comedy is 'mediated' – that what they are experiencing is not theatre but television (or radio). This is also true when they hear a studio audience, but the latter means that the comedy show has in a sense become a conventional theatrical event: performers are confronted by live spectators in a relationship at which the members of the broadcast audience, though the target audience, are merely bystanders. This points up the ambivalence which runs through so much television and makes it hard for students of the medium to keep their conceptual footing. Should it – does it – relay an 'outside' world or create a world of its own? When witnessed by cameras, do theatrical shows and soccer matches remain autonomous events or do they become creatures of television? It was observed many years ago that 'producers seem seldom able to make up their minds whether television is simply a means of broadcasting other material or is an artistic medium in its own right' (Dyer 1973: 13). In terms of television comedy, the ambivalence is reflected in the contrasting views of two well-known performers, Benny Hill and John Cleese. Yet each view is of interest in showing a rather disingenuous awareness of its counterpart. Benny Hill affirms that:

> To a great extent I'm guided by the studio audience. You can say you are doing it for the people at home, but you are swayed a lot by the people in the studio. If you get coach parties who go 'who-hoo' when you say 'knickers' and who don't laugh at something a little more subtle, you find you are going that way.
>
> (quoted in Nathan 1971: 166)

Hill is thus willing to regard the studio audience as a reliable representative of the broadcast audience. The implication is that there is a single auditorium – that hearing studio laughter, whether live or canned, is, even for the solitary, domestic viewer, not that different from hearing

people laughing around her in the theatre. Yet he also shows an awareness that the studio audience and 'the people at home' are not necessarily one and the same. Speaking of *Monty Python's Flying Circus* (BBC 1
and 2, 1969–74), John Cleese claims that:

> We had a studio audience and were polite to it, but it was ignored.
> The incredible thing about a lot of television shows is that the direc-
> tors are more concerned about the three hundred people in the
> studio than the ten million people watching. It stems from a lack of
> confidence and the belief that if you can make the studio audience
> laugh it is a successful show, no matter if it looks absolute rubbish
> on the box.
>
> (quoted in Nathan 1971: 186)

Hence Cleese insists that telegenic comedy is something quite different
from theatrical comedy. But he, too, is being a shade disingenuous. If
Python included an audible audience merely in order to prompt the
broadcast audience, a 'canned' one would have sufficed. But the studio
audience whom Cleese claims to have ignored must have been used to
reproduce at least one of the conditions of theatrical comedy: to cue
the performers. Thus Hill and Cleese agree, in effect, that although the
surrogate audience is telegenic in the sense that it proclaims the presence of television (and radio), and by extension the existence of a
remote and dispersed audience, it is much more a sign of the *theatricality* of broadcast comedy than of its televisuality. Of course, neither
The Benny Hill Show (BBC, 1955–68; ITV, 1967, 1969–89) nor
Monty Python were sitcoms in the accepted sense, but while the surrogate audience may be heard in any form of TV comedy it is almost
invariably present in sitcom.

    We are perhaps inclined to feel that there is nothing *inherently*
telegenic about sitcom. Such shifts of location as it employs would be
largely manageable through scene changes in the conventional theatre,
and those technical mediations that create changes of viewpoint largely
replicate, albeit more effectively, the way that the live spectator's gaze
moves around the stage, switching between those who speak and those
who react, taking in any physical business, and glancing at the costumes
and the set. The laughs that are produced by theatrical comedy would
appear to yield nothing in frequency or intensity to those that are generated by television sitcom, nor do the latter's jokes seem to stem from
anything that is peculiar to the medium.

    Nevertheless, we have observed that despite its theatrical origins and
essence, sitcom is not in itself a theatrical form. It is longer than the
dramatised sketch of the stage revue and, quite aside from the fact that
it normally forms part of a series, shorter than the comic plays that lure

audiences out of their homes and into costly theatre seats. Indeed its duration suggests that the popularity and distinctiveness of sitcom on television are attributable not so much to the inherent nature of the medium as to what may be termed cultural and organisational factors. Since its themes extend to the domestic, social and professional spheres, one or other is likely to find favour with the various segments of television's large and heterogeneous audience. Sitcoms feature characters, or at least stereotypes, that most of us can recognise, and their cyclical, non-evolutionary structure means that we can be drawn into them at any stage in a series. Each episode injects only a modicum of novelty into a scenario that is reassuringly familiar. Finally, their popularity with audiences ensures their popularity with broadcasters. Because they are easily accessed and their content is innocuous, they are likely to be durable. And this, along with other factors such as a small cast of actors and a limited number of settings and sets, means that they will probably be cost-effective (Adams 1993: 68).

In a search for more telegenic forms of comedy, we might turn to self-conscious, experimental shows like the legendary *Monty Python's Flying Circus*. But in some respects the difference between *Python* and conventional sitcom is less than we might suppose. We have seen that the sitcom contains elements such as close-ups, edits and shifts of perspective and location that proclaim the mediating presence of television. To these, *Python* adds only cartoons and graphics, which were originated by cinema, not television. On the other hand, *Python* is basically a sketch show, and the sketch, like the sitcom, has its roots in the traditional theatre. Indeed, versions of the show not only appeared as cinema films but were successfully presented on the stage.

Why, then, do we feel that *Python* is especially telegenic? Partly, of course, because it draws much of its subject matter from television itself. Not all of it, however: the famous 'Dead Parrot' sketch would have been perfectly intelligible to an Edwardian music hall audience. On the other hand, TV comedies of all kinds, including sitcom, often take television as their subject, satirising serious programmes as well as 'media people' (Ellis 2002: 118). *Drop the Dead Donkey* (Channel 4, 1990–8), for instance, is set in a TV newsroom. The obvious reason for this self-preoccupation is that much of our knowledge of the cultural and political worlds is itself mediated by television. But while most shows explore television within a conventional format and confine their attention to a single genre – the news bulletin or documentary or quiz – *Python* intercuts sketches and graphics to parody not only a range of TV genres but the modes and conventions of the medium itself (Neale and Krutnik 1990: 196–208). In other words, it offers a series of *formal* as well as *material* parodies.

Let us begin with the material parodies. In 'Philosophers' Match of the Day' we see some of the great thinkers of history dressed in period costumes and striking contemplative poses on a soccer pitch, with Karl Marx warming up on the touchline. Great thinkers feature in another sketch, a general knowledge quiz in which the participants, Marx again among them, compete for the prize of a three-piece suite. And a studio debate between a prelate and a philosopher about the existence of God suddenly takes the form of a wrestling match, in which God's existence is proved beyond doubt by the fact that the prelate wins. All three sketches rely on an old and effective device: they generate bathos by pulling together wholly disparate aspects of culture and experience. The habitués of intellectual and spiritual life are defined by the tough physical laws of soccer and wrestling matches; the world's great exponent of the internal contradictions of dialectical materialism mutters an obscenity when he fails to win the three-piece suite. The *forms* that these sketches assume – the sports programme, the game show and the studio debate – are made to some degree ludicrous because they have been put to an inappropriate use; but the primary focus of the humour is on the *content*, on what these otherwise perfectly acceptable genres have been filled with.

Yet *Python* attempts formal as well as material parody: the conventions and clichés of television continuity are comically laid bare. Seated at desks in fields or ponds, presenters appear at inappropriate moments, announcing, in response to the viewers' presumed craving for visual novelty, 'And now for something completely different'. The BBC logo pops up at arbitrary points in the programme; gratuitous official apologies are issued; and the sketch, that staple of so much TV comedy, is deconstructed. The conventional distinction between the introductions to the sketches and the sketches themselves is removed. Some sketches end without a punch-line, some change course and merge into other sketches. Yet others are interrupted or partly repeated in order to link further and disparate sketches. The notion of the sketch as a single and climactic entity is also ridiculed by using a figure of authority, a policeman or broadcasting executive, to step in and halt it – the executive also serving to deride what is often perceived as the bureaucratic and restrictive culture of the BBC. In sum, *Monty Python* is telegenic not just in its content but in its preoccupation with television *form* – in the way it constructs (or perhaps deconstructs) its content. Yet even though it can call upon many of the same technical resources, we have not suggested that television has transformed comedy to the extent that it has transformed sport. Why?

For audiences, it would seem that whereas sport is pure spectacle, the basis of much comedy – which we earlier defined as the creation of laughter – is *verbal*, even in the theatre and the cinema. There are numerous and glaring exceptions: the entire art of theatrical mime, circus clowning and pantomime slapstick, the *oeuvre* of the silent cinema (Charlie Chaplin, Buster Keaton, Harold Lloyd and others), even modern television in the form of *Mr Bean* (ITV, 1990–5). But much comedy, even that which we think of as mainly visual, has at least *some* verbal content that is not only amusing in itself but helps to explain the visual business. Moreover, because most parts of a theatre auditorium are nearer to the stage than most parts of a stadium are to the field of play, the magnifications that television brings to comedy are much less than those it brings to sport. Nor can television comedy rival the high technical standards and lavish production values of comedy in the cinema. Notwithstanding *Mr Bean*, television's main claim as a comic medium rests on the quality of its *dialogue*: it is this that provides the basis of its characterisation and the context for much of the visual humour it attempts, as well as being amusing in its own right.

We will conclude this chapter with a look at two other categories of light entertainment.

Quiz and game shows

These shows have their ultimate origins in party and parlour games (McQueen 1998: 71), and their immediate ones in radio:

> The quiz show genre is a highly diverse one, ranging from straight contests of knowledge, to audience-participation games featuring outlandish and sometimes humiliating stunts, to programmes built around stumping a panel of celebrities. . . . Contests of knowledge range between 'official' and vernacular knowledge, from arcane facts of history or science to the prices of everyday commodities.
>
> (Boddy 2001: 80)

To this miscellany we could add those celebrity game shows like *Have I Got News for You* (BBC 2, 1990–2000; BBC 1, since 2000), *Never Mind the Buzzcocks* (BBC 2, since 1996) and *They Think It's All Over* (BBC 1, since 1995), which although ostensible tests of knowledge are really a pretext for wisecracking and comic improvisation, and whose gratifications for the viewer lie not so much in being enlightened as watching conventional comedy. With respect to quiz shows, one systematic approach is to divide them into celebrity shows, tests of specialised knowledge (of film, sport and so on), intellectual and 'brain-teasing' shows like *Mastermind* (BBC 1 and 2, since 1972) and *Countdown* (Channel 4, since 1982), and mass-audience shows (McQueen 1998: 69–70). The latter may test the competitors' knowledge of popular culture, or, like *Who Wants to be a Millionaire?* (ITV 1, since 1998), celebrate the pleasures of acquisitiveness and audience participation. Yet despite their popularity and the challenges they present to both competitors and viewers, quiz shows suffer from low cultural status because they are cheap to produce; they are thought to encourage envy, competitiveness and material greed; and they legitimate social inequalities (Casey *et al* 2002: 100).

Nevertheless, there have been attempts to identify the gratifications that quiz and game shows generally provide. They are marked by a progression of 'ritual–competition–ritual' (McQueen 1998: 72; Casey *et al* 2002: 100–1). At the beginning, they establish a sense of social cohesion: various but similar people are drawn together and, in a friendly spirit, agree to abide by the rules of the game. For the viewer, there is the opportunity of identifying with the competitors yet at the same time competing against them. The second, competitive stage takes these similar people and makes them unequal: there are winners and losers. And in the third and final stage, ritual is reaffirmed: competition can be harsh, yet it is fair. All competitors begin on equal terms, but we acquiesce in a meritocracy that is based on the possession of skill or knowledge and in which ordinary folk can show their potential and achieve distinction. This plausible interpretation of quiz and game shows is not very different from the way in which we saw sport in the previous chapter, and we can perhaps regard these, too, as embodying a kind of metaphor for the often conflictual nature of real life.

Music television

Music videos can be seen as an attempt to make what seems to be a logical marriage between the most popular art form of the era – pop music – and its most popular medium: television. Yet it is a task that has proved unexpectedly difficult. How can the acoustic essence of music be given visual expression? The most obvious means, which the music videos frequently adopt, is either to show the artists performing their songs or dancers dancing to them. But this entails two problems: such images are often of relatively limited interest in themselves, and they cannot disguise the fact that the real focus of attention – the music – exists, as it were, elsewhere. Like ideas, music is an abstraction that television struggles with, and music videos have often been criticised for privileging the visual over the aural (Casey *et al* 2002: 136).

Another way of conveying the music is to create a short visual sequence that expresses the mood or meaning of the music or its lyrics. If, for instance, the song is a woman's lament for her lost lover, the video might show pictures of a tear trickling down her cheek, melancholy shots of falling leaves and dead trees, and blurred, slow-motion images of a retreating male. But this approach can also create problems. The inherent 'meaning' of music is not always so easy to pinpoint, and is certainly of a different order to the representational meaning of words and pictures. Perhaps music has *no* meaning outside its form or structure. We may assume that the lyrics of a song express the meaning of its melody, but these, too, are often cryptic and can sometimes seem at odds with it: for generations, soldiers and schoolchildren have taken the solemn tunes of hymns and put new and bawdy lyrics to them.

A further solution that music videos commonly attempt is to express a song symbolically – in a visual sequence that is ostensibly unrelated to it and may or may not include images of the performer. This confers on the viewer an almost overwhelming latitude of interpretation because the meaning of images is much less specific than that of words. Words can be ambiguous, too, but their ambiguity is normally more contained: or to put it another way, the interpretative options of the audience are fewer. When the poet Alexander Pope refers to someone who fished 'In troubled waters, but now sleeps in port', one meaning is that this person, like a formerly busy fishing boat that has now been laid up in harbour, used to live a full and rewarding life (fish bite better in rough seas) but has since retired; and the other meaning is that he no longer tries to exploit the quarrels of others because he is in a permanent drunken stupor. Yet in order for us to understand Pope's joke, there has to be a *limit* to the ambiguity that his words contain – the literal and figurative senses of fishing in troubled waters and the two definitions of 'port'. The words cannot mean whatever we make them mean.

The images of many music videos, on the other hand, seem almost devoid of intentionality. They are so unprescriptive – so vastly ambiguous – that the viewer has a free hand to attach her own meanings to them, or, an infinitely easier option, to attach no meaning at all but surrender to that virtually passive scopophilia which we have suggested can be an unintended effect of all television output. Indeed, music videos perhaps give fuller rein than any other TV genre to our simple love of looking. They could almost be regarded as a celebration of the difficulty, if not impossibility, of making meaning out of pictures that lack a verbal context: they exist, quite literally, as something to keep our eyes occupied while we indulge in the primary business of listening. Nor is it surprising that they have been discussed in terms of that much-analysed intellectual and cultural movement of the late twentieth century, postmodernism (Kaplan 1987): 'where modernism was concerned with questioning the relationship that exists between reality and its representation, postmodernism focuses on surfaces, styles and appearances, and questions or ignores the very existence of a "knowable", external reality' (Casey *et al* 2002: 171).

It is tempting to attribute much of the rise of postmodernism to the universal popularity of television, since to watch it is to be immersed in a stream of disparate yet vivid pictures that are full of semiotic redundancy; where news footage of an atrocity slides within moments into a game show or commercial for soft furnishings; and in which factual and fictional images seem to be indistinguishable from each other, and thus of equal truth-status. The medium itself seems to occupy a position of moral and ontological neutrality: in admitting everything, it declines to take a stance. It has thus been seen as an important locus of postmodern culture (Abercrombie 1996: 37–40). Of course, not all television genres are as ambiguous or as semantically reticent as music videos, but the latter serve to legitimate that scopophilic option which, as we have seen, exists even in the most 'meaningful' television.

Part III
Television culture

Television: audience uses and effects

Belief in television's influence is rather like the belief in life after death. Most of us would like to be able to prove it, but the evidence is inconclusive.

(Peter Black, former television critic of the *Daily Mail*)

The situation of the television viewer is paradoxical. The medium is self-evidently private: he watches it in his domestic environment, typically alone or with, at most, two or three others. But there is also a sense in which he is living in two places, and sometimes two times, at once – in the world in which he is physically situated and the world that television presents to him (Scannell 1996: 91). And though watching privately, he is also aware that he is part of a wider viewing public, especially, perhaps, when television is covering a ceremonial or sporting event at which spectators are visibly, or at least audibly, present. Thus, because television domesticates communal experience on the one hand and makes private experience communal on the other, it is neither public nor private in the traditional sense (Dahlgren 1995: 123).

Television is undeniably popular. The average viewer watches for about 27 hours a week (Bignell 2004: 254) – an amount that suggests that watching is, above all else, a leisure or recreational activity (Seymour-Ure 1996: 12–13). It is possible to devise a typology of viewing pleasures, among them visual enjoyment, para-sociality (the pseudo-relationships we form with those whom we see on television), the dramatic satisfaction of witnessing a performance and events with an unforeseeable outcome, the gratification of gaining knowledge and so on (Corner 1999: 94–9). Moreover, the fact that in 1999 more people lived in households with three or more sets than in those with just one

(Williams 2004: 14) suggests that television is not only a domestic medium but becoming one that is individually owned.

It is only reasonable that something whose programmes cost so much money, time and effort to produce and are so avidly consumed, yet which are also momentary and soon forgotten, should prompt a great deal of interest in its viewers and the ways in which it influences them. We can broadly divide this interest into four kinds: industrial, political, popular and academic. Embracing broadcasting professionals, the institutions, independent producers, advertisers and market researchers, the media industry is primarily interested in how popular television programmes are. Viewing figures tell the programme makers how well they are doing and offer clues as to what might be popular in future, and they tell the advertisers and market researchers how useful television is as a medium for selling goods and services. It would be fair to say that while the professionals are interested in what viewers think of the programmes, their primary concern is with the audience's size and social composition.

Political pressure groups like the right-wing Adam Smith Institute and the left-of-centre Institute for Public Policy Research also take an interest in audiences, but one that we might describe as abstract rather than empirical. With the welfare of the viewing public only implicitly in mind, they are primarily concerned with the ownership and conduct of television institutions: the structure of public service broadcasting on the one hand and commercial broadcasting on the other, the extent to which they should compete with and complement one another, the problem of satellite transmissions that may originate in another country – in essence, with how television should be paid for and regulated.

The third kind of interest in audiences can be described as 'popular', though only in the strict sense of 'originating and belonging within the public sphere': it is not necessarily an interest that is shared by large numbers of the public, although groups like the Voice of the Listener and Viewer (VLV) and Mediawatch-UK would probably wish to claim that they command widespread support. It seems fair to say that they are not greatly concerned to investigate the opinions or behaviour of the television audience but start from the premise that these are self-evident. While the VLV is interested in enhancing and maintaining the general quality of British television, the focus of Mediawatch-UK is more moralistic – on what it perceives as violence, bad language, the high incidence of sex and nudity, and a negative representation of minority groups and beliefs. Its assumption is not only that these things are abundant in television but that they give widespread offence and are harmful. Finally, the Campaign for Press and Broadcasting Freedom is of interest in spanning all three of these categories: it consists mostly of media professionals, members of the journalism and broadcasting trade unions; it has connections with the Labour Party and the political aim of breaking up media concentration and promoting broadcasting diversity; and it also claims to represent the public interest and be 'an independent voice for media reform'.

Although it extends to the industrial, the political and the popular, the academic concern with television audiences is supposedly 'disinterested' – that is to say, it has, or should have, no particular axe to grind but focuses on audiences and effects *per se*. How do television viewers behave and what influences, if any, does the medium have on them? While it is well known that influences and effects are almost impossible to gauge, it may be less apparent that the very identity of the audience is hard to pin down. What constitutes a viewer? How do we define the business of watching and listening? Shaun Moores (1993: 2) illustrates the problem by comparing the television audience with theatregoers. The latter make a special journey to a place that is separate from their normal environments, and so since – in the jargon of the market researchers – 'consumption necessitates footfall', they are easy to identify and count. But television viewers are not only geographically dispersed but embedded in a domestic context, with all the competing demands and distractions that it involves. Moores goes on to argue that within such a context, the *motives* of the viewers should be explored – that viewing could, for instance, be a form of indirect intimacy between two people, or a way of precluding conversation or deterring visitors, or, in disputes over what to watch, an occasion for family power struggles (Moores 1993: 34–5).

What is clear, however, is that there are degrees of attentiveness within the audience: at one extreme, television can be virtually ignored – treated as a 'background' medium – and at the other viewed raptly, and given varying amounts of attention in between. If viewers are prepared to subscribe to pay-per-view and even pay surcharges for particular programmes, it is logical to assume that they watch television attentively for at least some of the time (Barwise and Gordon 2002: 208). The relatively new phenomenon of interactivity could be seen as an attentive use of television *par excellence*: digital TV provides electronic programme guides from which viewers can compile their own schedules; Sky News Active allows them to access text and images that expand news bulletins and particular news stories; and Sky Sports Active enables them to choose their own camera angles and supporting textual information (Bignell 2004: 267). Yet interactivity raises as many problems about the audience as it solves (McQuail 2000: 407). Some of its manifestations, such as websites, bulletin boards, e-mails and MP3s, are outside the television medium itself (Brooker 2004: 569), so those who contribute to them may or may not have viewed the programmes under discussion, and their reactions may or may not be coloured by what they take to be those of the other contributors. Moreover, interactivity, even within the medium, is not necessarily the same thing as attentiveness. The 'channel surfer' with a remote control in his hand is in one sense an alert and busy viewer, yet in another absorbing little of what he is watching.

But if we can agree about how attentive one needs to be in order to count as part of the audience, empirical research does throw light on viewing behaviour and tastes and on the social impact of television. It has been noted, for instance, that men and women approach television in characteristically different ways (Morley 1992: 146–55). In general, men are more systematic: they pre-plan their viewing and off-air recording and watch more attentively. When families view together, the father usually determines what will be watched – a fact that is humorously illustrated by Jim Royle in the sitcom, *The Royle Family* (BBC 2 and 1, 1998–2000). He is the custodian of the remote control, clutching it to his belly throughout each episode and changing channels on a whim and without reference to the others. For women, on the other hand, home is a place of work as well as leisure, and their use of television is more *ad hoc*, desultory and even afflicted by a sense of guilt. Without as much opportunity to plan their viewing, they use the video-recorder less often and may even not have bothered to learn how to operate it. Male programme preferences are for news and current affairs, scientific and other documentaries, action and adventure movies and sport. Women prefer sitcoms, soap operas, dramas, romantic movies and quiz shows.

Television has also had observable effects on family life, especially as the multiple ownership of sets has increased. It has clearly contributed to a decline in communal meals, which once provided families with the opportunity for sustained conversation. Now it is often the case that hastily improvised meals or convenience foods are individually prepared and eaten silently in front of the television set – or sets. Yet even observable facts like these can too easily result in questionable conclusions. Because people spend so much time watching TV, poor diet, obesity and lack of exercise, the decline of literacy, and attention deficit disorder are among the ills that have been laid at its door.

Poor diet and the lack of properly prepared and communally eaten meals are, however, also attributable to other aspects of modern living. Aside from the general pressure to 'beat the clock' and fit as much into the day as possible, the different schooling and work routines within families may mean that its members are never at home together for long enough to eat a communal meal. Obesity and lack of exercise may be the effect not of watching television but of the more sedentary, less physical, nature of modern jobs – and also of driving to work rather than walking or cycling. Attention deficit disorder, an inability among the young to concentrate on anything for more than a few moments, has been blamed on the restless, noisy and vivid styles of children's television, while the decline of literacy has been ascribed to 'the obvious fact' that children are now spending time watching TV and not reading. But 'junk food' has also been blamed for the inability to concentrate, and the fact that those who watch a lot read less than those who watch little could reflect the existing differences between people rather than the effect of television (Cumberbatch 1998: 271).

It has been observed that academic theories of media effects tend to oscillate between 'powerful messages' and 'powerful audiences' (Livingstone 1990: 8; Abercrombie 1996: 201–4) – between stressing the dominance of the television 'text' and, like John Fiske (1987: 62–83), insisting on the autonomy and critical alertness of the viewer. A dominant text implies an audience that is relatively passive and easily influenced, and a dominant audience implies a relatively weak and ambiguous text – though as we shall see, matters are not quite so straightforward. We can chart the full range of possible audience effects by saying that at one extreme, dominant texts produce powerful, irresistible meanings – they evoke 'intended' or 'preferred' readings from the viewers – and that at the other, dominant audiences produce 'oppositional' readings; while somewhere in between are a range of 'negotiated' readings. These embrace degrees of acceptance of the message, qualified by degrees of rejection. Finally, we might mention 'aberrant' readings – those that are not intended by the programme makers but which the television text can nevertheless support.

As a simplified illustration, we can take a police drama whose aim is to persuade the viewer that 'crime does not pay'. It may succeed in its aim, establishing its *intended* or *preferred* meaning. But it may have an *oppositional* effect in that the viewer rejects the message and persists in his view that crime does pay; or while accepting that crime does not pay, he may adopt a *resistant* reading in believing that it is a truth that the drama has failed to demonstrate convincingly. But in addition, or alternatively to any of these readings, he may take an *aberrant* interest in the speech style or dress sense of one of the characters or in the décor of one of the settings. Finally, the drama may make no impact on him whatsoever: perhaps he does not register its message, or is not affected by it in one way or the other and instantly forgets what he has been watching.

However, a number of problems are raised by classifying texts and audiences in this way. First, it fails to tell us much about the possible variations in viewing behaviour. It implies that the text is 'dominant' and powerful only if the audience declines to reject its meaning – or, put the other way round, that the audience is powerful only if it opposes the message. But sometimes at least, an alert and powerful audience may *accept* the message of a text, albeit after subjecting it to critical scrutiny. Indeed a powerful text is more likely to make an impact on such an audience than on those 'couch potatoes' who are gazing in a state of mindless scopophilia. In a kind of semantic somersault, we could even describe *the latter* as the powerful and dominant audience because they are almost impervious to television's messages! Discussing radio, I have argued that there is no simple correlation between the way in which a person attends to the medium and the degree of its influence on him (Crisell 1994: 221–3) – and this may be equally true of television. But it seems fair to suggest that almost all viewers are to some extent influenced by television's messages, since even to reject or misread them displays an influence of sorts. In sum, it is misleading to see powerful texts and powerful audiences as in an oppositional, see-saw relationship: they often collaborate, and there is also a sense in which even 'inert' and uncritical viewers are powerful because proof against television's influences.

Another problem with this classification of texts and audiences is that it seems to involve an oversimplified view of television's messages – a problem that is hinted at in the term 'aberrant' reading. Because television is visual, there is a sense in which it always says *more* than the message: the latter is submerged in copious, redundant data – or perhaps it is more accurate to say that the limits of the message are almost impossible to determine. The weather forecaster is on our screens merely to forecast the weather. But we notice his cheerful smile, his choice of shirt and tie and the cut of his suit, and in so doing we fail to catch all the details of the forecast. There is a sense in which the message has been sabotaged by the messenger, yet one could also argue that the things we have been admiring are *not* extraneous – that they lend authority and 'eloquence' to the message. The forecaster is obliged to appear in one guise or another, and it is hard to think of an alternative that would not be even more distracting. But television's messages plainly raise difficulties that are not encountered in the more abstract media of print and radio.

A third problem that arises when we talk about intended or preferred meanings is that these seem much less characteristic of some genres, for instance drama or sport, than of others, such as news or documentary (Moores 1993: 29). Indeed it often seems to be true that the better the drama, the more multiple or ambivalent its meanings: they are not reducible to a simple message. And what sense does it make to talk about the 'message' of a soccer match or display of gymnastics?

Finally, it seems likely that the influence of television content will vary not only from genre to genre but from programme to programme within the same genre; from viewer to viewer, and from time to time within a single viewer – we are likely to be more receptive at certain times than at others. We are often aware, for instance, that the second viewing of a programme may make much more, or less, impact on us than the first viewing did. In all this surmise, the old semi-facetious conclusion seems the only appropriate one: that in some circumstances and under some conditions, some messages have some effects on some people. But the difficulties of identifying these effects are well-nigh insuperable. Here are just a few of them.

First, because there is so much sharing and reinforcement of content among the mass media – they often 'feed off' one another – it is hard to isolate the particular effects of television: indeed, it probably makes more sense to speak of 'media' rather than 'television' effects. But it is equally hard to distinguish media effects from those of other social phenomena such as personal relationships, education and general life experiences. It is not just the case that media influences are one thing and other influences are another, even though they are hard to disentangle from each other: the social phenomena themselves may be irradiated by media influences. In other words, the latter are not confined to TV viewers or radio listeners but may be experienced at second hand (Thompson 1995: 110). I might, for instance, wish to buy a certain brand of trainers only because I have seen and liked my friend's pair: but he might have bought his as a result of seeing them advertised on television.

The sheer difficulty of discerning any specific media effects may tempt us to conclude that the media are not very influential. Throughout history, each new medium has tended to provoke fears that it will have harmful effects (Cumberbatch 2002: 259) – above all, that it will incite people to commit crimes, especially of a violent nature. Yet the evidence of such effects is scant and broadly unpersuasive (Cumberbatch 2002: 262–8). Not only is it difficult to separate the effects of television from those of the other media, but many that seem to originate in the media do not actually do so: they originate in society and are merely reflected back at it by the media (McQuail 2000: 416). But perhaps the most convincing indication that the media are not very influential is subjective – within each of us. We are inclined to feel that our critical powers are mostly sufficient to withstand any thing, or any one, with rhetorical designs on us, and this feeling is perhaps strongest when watching commercials or party political broadcasts. We feel indifferent towards a great deal of television content and sometimes contemptuous even of what we like ('I enjoy it but I know it's rubbish'). We are also aware that we have forgotten even content which made a big impression on us at the time we watched it. The prime example is content that has prompted so-called moral panics: the export of veal calves, the threat posed to children by aggressive breeds of dog, the availability of firearms following the mass killings at Hungerford and Dunblane, the incipient spread of vCJD, the human form of 'mad cow disease' – these are just a few of the anxieties that have now receded from the public consciousness. After all, television is not like the theatre and cinema, which require us to make a journey to experience an isolated event. It bombards us domestically and daily, and its individual items, swiftly succeeded by countless others, are soon half-forgotten.

Yet it could also be argued that all these television experiences remain with us at a subliminal level. And coexisting with our confidence that we are proof against the medium's influences is a contradictory yet equally common-sensical feeling that 'television simply must do something to viewers' (Cumberbatch and Howitt 1989: 12). Few of us, for instance, would believe that small children can be exposed to hard-core pornography or scenes of extreme violence without being harmed. And even though we may regard *ourselves* as proof against television effects, in a curious mental paradox that might merit the old-fashioned term 'hypocrisy', we are very ready to believe that commercials or porn films have strong effects on others.

In fact there is a body of evidence, however unscientific, to suggest that in one way or another television has strong effects on all of us. We may regard ourselves as immune from the patter of politicians or advertisers but there is no doubt that TV advertising increases the sales of products. It may be true that we are not greatly influenced by television content that deals in matters that are familiar to us: on the other hand, '[m]edia . . . have been shown to be more influential on matters outside immediate personal experience' (McQuail 2000: 422). A classic instance of this was the coverage of the tsunami which occurred in the Indian Ocean at the end of 2004, causing widespread death and destruction in several countries. Such a disaster and its consequences were unimaginable to people living in Britain and most other countries, and the appeals for aid raised many millions of pounds. (In a short digression it is, however, worth reminding ourselves of a fact that we noticed in our discussions of news and documentary: that television's tendency to focus on what is visually interesting can have a distorting effect. Its preoccupation with the tsunami brought relief to the 2 million people whose lives had been wrecked, but somewhat at the expense of the 22 million in Africa who were suffering less spectacularly from famine, disease, civil war, persecution and poverty.)

Though reports of events outside our personal experience may have the greatest impact, it is clear that even familiar television content is often highly influential. In response to the weather forecast we wear more or fewer clothes, we react to the stock market reports by buying or selling shares, and at the news of another oil crisis we drive in our thousands to the filling stations. But television must also have helped cinema to establish the cultural conformism that in recent decades has become truly international. So many of us seem to be eating the same food, singing the same pop songs, wearing the same designer clothes, watching the same films, reading the same books. Certain speech patterns and even physical mannerisms, apparently copied from American sitcoms, are universally

adopted: within days, or at most weeks, new fads and fashions are ubiquitous. It is hard to believe that television has not played a major part in this global homogenisation.

It might still be objected that while these influences are palpable they are also superficial and short-lived. But as is so often the case in audience studies, the evidence is ambivalent. We have suggested that many moral panics are ephemeral, but not all of them are – and in any case, the way in which each of them can subtly readjust our sensibilities may eventually amount to a transformation in attitudes. It has been observed that the influence of television is probably patchy – often long term, and usually elusive, gradual and diffuse (Lewis 1990: 156). But over recent decades a revolution has come about in values relating to the environment (climate change, the need to conserve natural resources and tackle pollution); to economics (the gulf between rich and poor nations); to diet and exercise; to women and sexual orientation; and to questions of ethnicity and racial difference. It is once again hard to believe that television has not been instrumental in bringing about this revolution – though we can still debate whether the medium originated it or merely acted as a catalyst for what originated elsewhere.

In an attempt to push audience and effects studies in a new direction, John Hartley has suggested that television's most important and influential role has been to teach 'cultural citizenship'. He observes that participation in public decision making is largely conducted through the media, with television foremost among them (Hartley 1999: 157). It 'reports' social groups to one another and in so doing creates an interesting paradox: 'Television, the medium that is often seen as most "mass", least sensitive to identity, presided over the era of identity politics; taught *cultural citizenship* equally to those whose identity made them subject to assimilationist and liberationist rhetorics alike' (Hartley 1999: 172). Such citizenship may have been inculcated not simply by the content of television but by the experience of watching it that we described at the beginning of this chapter: viewing is a separate and often idiosyncratic activity, yet one which we are aware of sharing with the wider community.

Globalisation
and localism

12

Perhaps the most striking characteristic of the end of the twentieth century is the tension between [the] accelerating process of globalization and the inability of both public institutions and the collective behaviour of human beings to come to terms with it. Curiously enough, private behaviour has had less trouble in adjusting to the world of satellite communication, E-mail, holidays in the Seychelles and trans-oceanic commuting.

(Eric Hobsbawm, The Age of Extremes)

The convergence of technological possibilities and economic practicalities has meant that for most of its history, television has been a *national* medium: we might describe this as its 'default status'. However, the technological developments of the last quarter century – satellite, cable and digital broadcasting and a consequent increase of spectrum – have made it possible for television to move both 'up' to the global level and, more abundantly than has yet been the case, 'down' to the local one. Our main focus in this chapter will be on the global, but we will first dwell on the local for a few moments.

Perhaps because the 'tele-' in 'television' comes from a Greek word meaning 'far away', there seems to be a lingering sense that television exists primarily to bring images and sounds over great distances – that the further they have to travel, the more the medium is doing its job. But it is, of course, doing its job if it conveys any images and sounds that are beyond the mere compass of our own sensory faculties. In his study of radio in the global age, David Hendy (2000: 21–3) makes the interesting point that while radio differed from television in having global potential from its very beginnings, it seems to have assumed especial importance as a local

medium. This was largely a consequence of its relative cheapness, but now television could assume a similar importance. Yet conflicting forces are at work. New technologies could make local television abundant, but economies of scale also become possible. Though they have hitherto been checked by strong state regulation, the impulse of global media operators like Sky is towards networking and consolidation, which explains why they have shown little interest in local television (Sparks 2004: 145). But deregulation could end the duty of the bigger broadcasters to maintain relatively expensive variations and could result in local provision that is at best underfunded and inferior, and at worst non-existent. The 'tele-' in 'television' would then be entirely apposite.

In this chapter I shall use 'localism' in the sense not of a neighbourhood or locality of just a few miles' radius but a region of any size that could be contrasted with 'the global' or 'worldwide': it might be an individual nation state or embrace a group of nation states that are not necessarily contiguous but have identical or closely related languages and cultures.

Over the past 30 years or so, globalisation has been accelerated by improvements in the technology of transport and communications on the one hand, and on the other, by rising living standards in such areas as South America and Asia (Hesmondhalgh 2002: 173). But the phenomenon is not, of course, new. Its pre-history was the expansion of trade between the late fifteenth and early sixteenth centuries followed by the colonialism and industrialisation of the seventeenth, eighteenth and nineteenth centuries (Thompson 1995: 150). The first viable telegraph systems were established in the 1840s (Thompson 1995: 78) and led to the development of international news agencies, such as Reuters. By 1900, approximately 190,000 miles of submarine cable girded the world (Thompson 1995: 153). These improvements in communication conferred great general benefits, but because they were also the sinews of colonial expansion they led, rather later, to anxieties about *cultural* as well as media globalisation – to the development of the 'cultural imperialism' thesis. This is, in essence, that worldwide patterns of communication-flow mirror those of economic and political domination; and specifically, that the advanced western nations, with the United States foremost among them, have swamped most of the other nations of the world with their cultural values and products (Hesmondhalgh 2002: 174; Bignell 2004: 62).

This is another phenomenon that is not new. The artefacts of Greek and Latin culture, the Bible in particular and Christianity more generally, and the works of William Shakespeare were being exported round the world before the United States had been born (Casey *et al* 2002: 51). But thanks largely to the electronic mass media, the present scale of the phenomenon is without precedent, and as we hinted in the previous chapter, the threat is of a worldwide cultural homogeneity. We now need to look more closely at this notion of cultural imperialism and see how far it is valid.

The evidence seems compelling. Since early in the last century, the American export of cultural artefacts – cinema films, television programmes and formats, pop music recordings – has been huge and irresistible. Television is, of course, pivotal because it not only generates its own content but subsumes that of the cinema and music industries and gives them yet wider currency. Moreover, because cinema and television are representational media, they promote the commercial products and characteristic features of the American way of life. The whole world is now familiar not only with Coca-Cola, McDonald's fast food, chewing gum, baseball caps, jeans and trainers (and buys them in vast quantities) but with the *mores* of the American people: the ways in which they greet one another (for instance, with 'high-fives'), eat, register their emotions and use the language. Indeed, language is the best barometer of cultural influence. The economic and political ascendancy first of Britain and its empire and then of its former colony, the United States, have made English an international language – that common tongue among people of diverse speech known as a *lingua franca*.

It is perhaps no accident that this expression is Italian, since Italian is the direct descendant of what, thanks to the Roman Empire, was an earlier *lingua franca* of the western world: Latin. But the global status that English has now acquired means that its native speakers, the British, Americans, Australians and so on, no longer 'own' it: that just as in the ancient world there were doubtless Britons, Spaniards and Greeks who were more fluent in Latin than many Romans were, it is now true that there are many Germans, Russians and Japanese with a better command of English than some British or Americans or Australians – a sobering discovery I have made as a teacher. English is ubiquitous: in Thailand or the Ukraine or Rwanda, people wear English slogans on their T-shirts (originally an American garment), of whose meaning they may even be ignorant. In this instance, they use the language less as a means of communication than as a cultural badge.

There is nothing inevitable or permanent about the status of English, nor does it derive from some inherent strength or beauty that other languages lack. The roots of its dominance are merely economic and political. Just as English replaced Latin (and in some circles French) as the *lingua franca*, there is every possibility that within the next century or so, it will itself be replaced by Chinese. One could therefore argue that if the present cultural hegemony were not American, it would belong to some other nation. But is American culture really so pervasive as to be virtually irresistible? And if so, is this aesthetically or morally objectionable? We will consider these questions first in terms of the creative institutions, the 'culture producers', and their political contexts; then of the consumers or audiences; and finally of the products and artefacts.

Perhaps the most convincing instance of American cultural imperialism is its cinema industry – metonymically known to the world by the Los Angeles suburb at its heart: Hollywood. From the 1920s, it became the first cultural industry whose products dominated the international markets (Hesmondhalgh 2002: 187–8), and more recently, it has been joined by television and music production. Television illustrates why this dominion can be so hard for other nations to resist: it can cost the BBC 13 times as much to produce an hour of drama as to import it from the United States (Abercrombie 1996: 101). This is because American television can comfortably recoup its production costs from its huge domestic audience, leaving anything it earns from abroad as pure profit. It can therefore afford to export cheaply (Bignell 2004: 71). Yet despite all this, many scholars now regard cultural imperialism as a somewhat simplistic thesis, feeling that it makes more sense merely to talk about 'globalisation'. Why?

We could regard some media organisations like MTV or CNN as 'imperialist' in the sense that they are based in the United States and broadcast their products to numerous other nations. But not all such organisations are based in the United States. BBC World is similarly imperialist, and the United States is among the countries it broadcasts and exports to. Moreover many other American organisations are becoming internationalised by acquiring additional bases, and investing, in one or more other countries. But again, not all of these are American *in origin*. On the face of it, nothing is more American than the New York-based News Corporation, owned by Rupert Murdoch, a citizen of the United States, and operator of its fourth national TV broadcaster, the Fox Network. But Murdoch and his organisation began in Australia, where they retain substantial media interests. They then expanded to the United Kingdom and Europe and acquired, among other things, the *Sun* and *Times* newspapers and Sky TV. And later they gained control of the Asian satellite broadcaster, Star TV, and of a Hollywood film studio, a television network and other media organisations in the United States. News Corporation has headquarters in Sydney, New York and Los Angeles (Turow 1999: 387), but it was only with its entry into the States that Murdoch was obliged, and readily agreed, to take American citizenship. Other outsiders with substantial film and music interests in the United States are Seagram (Canada), Bertelsmann (Germany) and the Japanese companies Sony and Matsushita.

By moving capital around the world and collaborating with indigenous firms who can circumvent the barriers that individual states raise against outsiders, these 'multinationals' would seem to be able to operate almost as a law unto themselves. But not all scholars accept that they are beyond state control or, indeed, that globalisation is as extensive as is commonly supposed. Colin Sparks (2004: 144) points out that satellite broadcasts can be forced out of certain countries if their governments dislike them, instancing China's refusal to receive Star TV until it agreed to drop the BBC's news service. Content can also be controlled by pay-per-view and subscription systems, and its provision along national lines is convenient to governments, broadcasters and rights holders alike. All in all, the evidence suggests that there is now greater state intervention in the media than hitherto, and that it has proved to be more effective (Sparks 2004: 145, 147). But sometimes the social impact of a new media technology is enough to negate outside influences without the need for state intervention. In the post-war United Kingdom, the growing popularity of television (operated solely by the BBC) caused a huge decline in a cinema industry that was dominated by Hollywood. It could therefore be seen as a reaffirmation, albeit temporary, of British culture against American influence.

Yet while governments are by no means powerless to control individual broadcasters and the material they show, the sheer volume of global traffic – not only in programmes and artefacts but cultural ideas and idioms – seems all but irresistible. Though British television was not screening Hollywood movies during the 1940s and early 1950s, and people in their thousands were deserting the cinema that Hollywood dominated, the BBC's home-grown content on both television and radio – romantic drama, soap opera, quick-fire comedy and above all, popular music – was imbued with American influences. Even within the Soviet Empire at the height of its power between the end of the war and the 1980s, there was a widespread knowledge of, and craving for, American clothes and music. But while these are early instances of straightforward cultural imperialism – of the pervasiveness of American influence – globalisation theorists argue that what is now happening is rather more complicated.

First, there is the simple fact that the different origins and multinational bases of cultural producers like Sony and News Corporation allow the influences to be two-way: America may be influenced as well as influencing. Second, the increasing prosperity of a number of countries and the growing sophistication of their media organisations enable them to circulate programmes and products within their own geolinguistic regions (Hesmondhalgh 2002: 179–80). One such region comprises the Anglophone countries of the United States, Canada, the United Kingdom, Ireland, Australia and New Zealand. Another is Spain and its former empire, notably Hispanic Latin America, together with the huge Spanish speaking population of the United States. A third is Portugal, Brazil and the former Portuguese colonies of Africa and Asia. Other discernible regions include southeast Asia, parts of the former Soviet Empire, the Islamic Middle East, and the Indian subcontinent along with its expatriate communities in the United Kingdom and elsewhere. Some countries manage to create cultural artefacts that are able to transcend their geo-linguistic regions and achieve a wider popularity. The United States is a notable example, and even the United Kingdom is a net exporter of television programmes and products (Abercrombie 1996: 98). Mexico and Brazil have also succeeded with a kind of Latin American soap opera called a *telenovela*, which has been enjoyed in countries as far afield as Russia. However, the frequency with which scholars cite the *telenovela* (for instance, Allen 2004; Bignell 2004; Hesmondhalgh 2002) suggests that, for other than the Anglophone exporters, such success is rare.

The globalisation theorists also point out that these various cultural influences 'bleed into' one another, especially as many consumers have multicultural allegiances. A Mexican living in the United States, for instance, may well have both Hispanic and Anglophone interests. The overall effect is of a kind of global, cosmopolitan culture, for which language is again a useful barometer. The growing economic and cultural significance of the Far East is apparent in words like 'sushi', 'karate' and 'tsunami', the popularity of African-originated music in words like 'jazz' and 'reggae', the enthusiasm for Latin American dance in 'tango' and 'salsa'. All this testifies to the existence of a phenomenon that is not American pure and simple. An optimistic view is that it is colourfully eclectic and miscellaneous, a negative view that it tends to grey uniformity. But one arguably beneficial effect is that in showing viewers in the poorer countries the comfortable lifestyles and abundant consumer goods of the richer ones, it raises material expectations everywhere (Bignell 2004: 71–2).

Nevertheless, the cultural imperialism thesis is not wholly discredited, for while all this can be conceded – while it may be true that many countries have contributed to a global culture, that many cultural producers are not American, and that some of them even own large portions of the American media – the cultural currency in which most prefer to trade is, indeed, American. Even though Sony owns Columbia Pictures and MGM, the films it makes in Hollywood are still 'American', and its records division pumps out what is essentially American music. When outsiders come to America, then, they 'go native', and the evidence suggests that in recent years the dominance of American culture has actually increased. In cinema, for instance, the United States exports far more than it imports. In 1999, and despite the growth of indigenous film industries in Europe, Latin America and

Asia, its movies took 41 per cent of the global market, while foreign films captured less than 3 per cent of its own (Hesmondhalgh 2002: 192). This is not so much the multiple flows and mutual influences of globalisation as plain one-way traffic.

We must now consider the attitudes and roles of the consumers in all this. Again, the evidence is somewhat equivocal. It has been observed that in the majority of countries the most popular programmes are nearly all home produced, even if some are based on American or international formats. Moreover the major media players in Europe are European rather than American (Berlusconi, Bertelsmann and, historically at least, Murdoch), and most television in Europe is nationally rather than transnationally produced and viewed (McQuail 2000: 234–5). In the many countries that import content from America, there are also indications that the viewers absorb it not passively and uncritically but variously, often in resistant or oppositional ways (O'Sullivan *et al* 1994: 294–5; Bignell 2004: 68). Finally, the American transnational broadcasters, CNN and MTV, have had to acknowledge that the world is not a uniform place by adapting their content to meet local tastes and requirements (McQuail 2000: 235). Even so, CNN, the first of the global news providers, has captured only a tiny audience in the United Kingdom – too tiny to warrant a separate mention in the weekly and monthly viewing summaries published by the Broadcasters' Audience Research Board. On the other hand, there are certain American-based broadcasters, such as News Corporation, who have not sought to transmit content to other countries that is materially different from that which the countries would have provided for themselves. Star TV has renounced cultural imperialism to the extent that it has placated the Chinese by dropping BBC World, and offers a programming diet that might have been originated by an Asian-owned service (Hesmondhalgh 2002: 187).

As an example of 'counter-cultural' flow, the United Kingdom exports a considerable number of television programmes to the United States, especially historical dramas and whimsical detective series like *Inspector Morse* (ITV, 1987–2000). The latter posit a quaint, half-deserted and sun-drenched England that seems to exist only in the minds of Americans. But because there is often a need for cultural modification, the formats and concepts it exports are every bit as valuable as actual programmes. Across the Atlantic, *Steptoe and Son* became *Sanford and Son*, *Till Death Us Do Part* (BBC 1, 1966–75) became *All in the Family*, and *Absolutely Fabulous* became *High Society* (O'Regan 2000: 314). More recently, the sitcom *The Office* has been rewritten and re-cast for American consumption. A current success story is the independent production company Endemol UK, which has exported formats for several reality and lifestyle shows to the United States, as well as to many other countries. Yet an intriguing twist to this tale is that Endemol is wholly owned by Spanish telecoms giant, Telefonica, the largest provider of telecom and Internet services to the Hispanic and Portuguese language worlds.

However, when it has been acknowledged that much programming in different parts of the world is still home produced, that audiences do not absorb American culture uncritically, that American broadcasters (and those of other nations) are obliged to adapt their exports to local tastes, that they may even 'go native' rather than taking their culture with them, and that America imports as well as exports programmes, it remains an undeniable fact that the products of the United States are, whether modified or not, universally popular. There is a debate to be had about whether this popularity is a recognition of their intrinsic merit or merely of the economic and political supremacy of the nation that creates them. But if this is 'cultural imperialism', it is at least preferable to the political kind in that those who are subjugated are subjugated willingly (Casey *et al* 2002: 10; Hesmondhalgh 2002: 176). Unless they were able to tap into universal feelings and experiences that transcend local cultural differences, it is difficult to see how so many of these products could be as popular as they are (O'Sullivan *et al* 1994: 294–5).

We need to conclude our discussion of globalisation and cultural influence by taking a closer look at the products and artefacts themselves. These may be transmitted across national borders, for example by satellite, or be exported as programmes – a process which as we have seen confers economic benefits on both exporters and importers – or assume the form of programme concepts or formats. They can also develop as co-productions, especially between countries that share a common language like Britain and the United States or Portugal and Brazil. Since American cinema films, above all others, are not only exhibited in picture-houses overseas but sold to overseas television institutions for local broadcast, they testify to the continuing and overwhelming dominance of Hollywood. But many other countries have important cinema industries, notably India, which is relatively resistant to movies from the United States (Hesmondhalgh 2002: 189–90). In terms of content that television has created for itself, we noted that *telenovelas* are successfully exported by Brazil and Mexico, though they represent only a small proportion of the programmes that those countries create (Hesmondhalgh 2002: 183). No country however can match the scale on which the United States exports television series and programme formats.

Its music enjoys a similar dominance. While much is created in the States, it is true that many important centres of production exist elsewhere in the world. But even when British bands and artists conquer the States, an occasional phenomenon that began with the Beatles and Rolling Stones in the 1960s, the *idiom* of the music remains unmistakably American. In other words, they succeed only by playing the Americans at their own game: for a while, the latter may be matched or beaten, but they do not have a different game imposed on them.

Nevertheless, music gives us a particular insight into the complexity of cultural identities and influences (Hesmondhalgh 2002: 193–4). The cultural imperialism thesis seems to assume that the local and national cultures that are swamped by American exports are themselves 'pure' and indigenous, but this is seldom if ever true. For instance, before they were subjected to bombardment from the north of the continent, the cultures of Central and South America were themselves 'imperial' – hugely mutated by the influence of Spain and Portugal, whose empires had swamped the older civilisations of the Mayas, Incas, Caribs and other peoples. And of course the culture of North America is not thoroughbred, either – anything but. Hence the cultural imperialism thesis is at once true and false: true in the sense that the culture of the United States has achieved global pre-eminence; false, or at least misleading, in the sense that this culture is no purer or more indigenous than any other, probably rather less so. The varieties of (essentially North American) pop and rock music that have conquered the world have some of their roots in 'country and western', which is ultimately of Irish-Scottish origin, and many more in jazz and blues, which are themselves the product of the black African diaspora. It is an extraordinary fact that out of the suffering of people who were uprooted from their homelands, sold into slavery and transported thousands of miles to another continent has come the most popular music of the twentieth century. Who can regret the existence of something that has given pleasure to so many? Yet who can approve of the misery that brought it into being?

Similarly, although the technology of the Hollywood movies has transformed drama and narrative almost beyond recognition, their origins are still traceable to the traditional theatre and to popular fiction, art forms that were every bit as European (and Russian) as American. Not only do many ostensibly diverse and unrelated cultures and art forms seem to tap into universal human values and tastes, but the culture of each country resembles a palimpsest – a document whose earlier contents have been partly erased by the superimposition of more recent material. One could almost regard cultures in general as a kind of macrocosm of the human condition. The individual who remains isolated sooner or later becomes extinct: the individual who unites with another in some sense perpetuates herself. Likewise, a culture (in itself a hybrid) is likely to survive over the longer term only by combining with another or others, sacrificing its own distinctiveness to the new distinctiveness of the combination. It is in this context that questions of globalisation and cultural imperialism should perhaps be considered.

Television, theatricality and public life

If privacy depends upon an expectation of invisibility, the expectation of *visibility* is what defines a public space.
(Jonathan Franzen, *How to be Alone*)

All the world's a stage,
And all the men and women merely players.
(William Shakespeare, *As You Like It*)

Television has gained increasing access to many areas of public life – politics, the law, religion, business, education – and I have argued in this book that its overwhelmingly visual nature has led to a widespread assumption that appearance and reality have a considerable degree of congruence, that the latter is explicable largely in terms of the former. This assumption is not new. We have always been obliged to make judgements, albeit provisional ones, on the basis of appearances. If we interview two applicants for a job, and the first is clean and smartly dressed while the second looks shabby and slovenly, we make the initial judgement that the former is more motivated and suitable, even though subsequent discoveries may cause us to reconsider. When we are likely to encounter others whom we do not know – that is, when we enter the public sphere – we are aware that we will be judged on our appearance, and we therefore create for ourselves a public persona. We adopt a certain demeanour that embraces both dress and behaviour.

However, I would suggest that since the rise of television, the assumption that reality can be judged by appearances has become – certainly within the medium and perhaps outside it – less provisional, more dogmatic. There are a number of reasons for this, some *technological,* to do with the inherent nature of television, and some *organisational*, to do with the competitive way in which it must present its material. Against a fixed background of often familiar household objects, its sharply framed and moving images acquire a peculiar vividness and authenticity and are liable to prevail over any qualifications that are contained in the words that accompany them – a phenomenon we observed in Chapters 5 and 6. Not surprisingly, then, 'contemporary culture has become overwhelmingly a representation through spectacle . . . so that the image has become the paradigmatic means of conceptualisation' (Chaney 1993: 33). To get the audience to question the value or veracity of television's images, programme makers would have to make a sustained demand on its attention: but in a medium whose content is constantly evaporating and which offers a vast choice of channels, that is not something they are willing to do. It is easier for everyone to assume that appearances are a reliable guide to the truth.

Television has created a further problem however. In pre-televisual times a person could be judged on her appearance only by those who were within physical sight of her. At any one time, they would be relatively few – hundreds, at most several thousand – and even fewer would be able to get close enough to observe her in detail. In the political sphere, 'leaders were invisible to most of the people over whom they ruled, and they could restrict the activity of managing their self-presentation to the relatively closed circles of the assembly or the court' (Thompson 1995: 119–20). Now, political and other public figures are under close, and often continual, scrutiny by millions of people. Television has restored the old face-to-face sense of the importance of visibility, making grooming, dress and mannerisms significant factors once more: for public figures, successful self-presentation is not an option but an imperative (Thompson 1995: 136–7; Wernick 1991: 138; Seaton 1998: 3). Moreover, it extends to the institutions they represent or are thought to embody, and to assist both, a whole industry of public relations companies, spin doctors and image and branding consultants has grown up. Though it dates from the early twentieth century, there is no doubt that television has provided the soil in which it has flourished.

The industry's attempts to transform politics first became evident at the end of the 1970s, a time when television was about to change from a closely regulated duopoly into a multi-channelled medium. Saatchi and Saatchi's publicity campaign for the Conservatives during the general election of 1978–9 is thought to have been highly influential, and the Labour Party's similar campaign in 1987 concentrated on television and virtually ignored the press (Negrine 1994: 168). By the 1990s it was being lamented that 'form is more significant than policy content and the essence of political communication has been trivialised and corrupted' (Williams 1998: 254).

One technique of the publicity managers is to encourage television to focus on artificially created events like 'photo opportunities' and politicians' walkabouts that often have no intrinsic news value at all. The advantage to television is that they provide something more visible than issues to point its cameras at, and the advantage to the politicians is that it shows them as friendly, approachable people (Negrine 1994: 166–7). During the 2005 election campaign, the Tory leader Michael Howard sought to present himself in a more humane light by bringing his extended family to the podium at a party conference. This was one of a series of attempts he made to reverse the damage done to him by fellow Tory MP Ann Widdecombe, who some years before had memorably suggested that there was 'something of the night' about him.

The aim of such figures, then, is to create an artifice for a public which consists mostly of television viewers and inclines to the belief that appearance corresponds to reality. But matters are not quite so straightforward. As we have seen, *all* public behaviour is characterised by a degree of artifice that is both desirable and unavoidable. When I emerge from my house washed and dressed, I am in some sense less authentic than my naked and dirtier self – and all those whom I meet are profoundly grateful for the fact. The question of where the irreducibly true and 'real' self lies is one for the philosophers, since the boundaries between authenticity and reality on the one hand and artifice and fiction on the other are by no means clear. But the fact that we are conscious of a degree of self-serving artifice in the behaviour of politicians and other public figures is reflected in our refusal to regard any of the public relations professions as synonymous with that of journalism, which we expect to be objective and disinterested. Yet our attitudes are to some extent equivocal. Just as few of us are ready to admit that we are influenced by advertising even though its success is measurably huge, so the continued existence of spin doctors, publicists and image consultants is testimony to their effectiveness.

It remains true, then, that with or without assistance, public figures in the age of television must strive to appear in the most favourable light. Theirs is an attempt to create 'theatre' in the minimal, prudent sense of seeming clean, smart and benign. But we noted earlier that people not only *believe* what they see; they *enjoy* the activity of seeing: they have scopophilic tendencies that can be satisfied as simply as by sitting on a bench and watching the world go by. Television clearly caters for this enjoyment, and in the early days of technical limitations and channel scarcity did so in relatively 'unspectacular' ways. The BBC, for instance, included within its schedules a number of interludes that consisted of nothing more than images of waves breaking on a shore or a potter's hands at work on a wheel, and many of its programmes showed only 'talking heads' or still photographs.

Not only, however, do people enjoy looking: some people, at least, enjoy being looked at. The counterpart of scopophilia is an exhibitionism of one kind or another. In its strict, pathological sense, exhibitionism is not so much the creation of an artifice as the revelation of what is normally private and hidden – behaviour that television was loath to exploit until forced to do so by the pressure of multi-channel competition. As we noted in Chapters 6 and 7, television has, on a mainly documentary pretext, shown people giving birth, fighting, grieving, having sex and dying. The elements of this behaviour that are voluntary may well be exaggerated for the benefit of the cameras, but its main impulse is reductive rather than enhancive, not so much to create a facade as draw attention to what is behind it.

Television is also interested in a more normal kind of exhibitionism however, one that is on a continuum with the attempt we mentioned earlier to create 'theatre' merely in the sense of decorous self-presentation. This consists of providing *more* of an artifice, of the individual putting on an act which, while a recognisable extension of her character, is not her natural or everyday demeanour. It is theatrical in the same way that stand-up comedy is theatrical, even though the stand-up comedian does not 'inhabit' another character to the extent that, say, Helen Mirren becomes Detective Chief Inspector Jane Tennison. Such performative behaviour was not, of course, brought into being by television, nor does it have to be primarily visual. It may, and often does, express itself verbally – in witty, colourful or persuasive speech. From time immemorial, it has been adopted by those who seek to communicate what their audiences are likely to find tedious or difficult. Over and above mere advocacy, barristers have striven to amuse juries; beyond mere instruction, teachers have sought to divert pupils; in addition to mere officiation, priests have tried to entertain congregations. But the visual adjuncts of posture, gesture and facial expression, clues which among other things tell us how the speech is to be interpreted, are usually crucial. And whereas in non-televisual circumstances this performative behaviour was – and is – merely optional, on multi-channel television it has become more of an imperative, even in serious or educative programming, and likelier to incorporate a stronger visual dimension. Under pressure to maintain audience share, the TV networks must provide content which is, above all, interesting to look at, and they are therefore disposed to give freer rein to exhibitionism than they once were.

The problem is that whereas jurors or pupils or worshippers have had to make the effort to leave their homes for a serious and specific purpose during which 'being entertained' might occur as a kind of unexpected bonus, most people do not have to leave their homes to watch television, and, irrespective of its intentions, switch it on with no other purpose than to be entertained. Yet it is also the medium by which politicians must solicit their support. Although viewers are not a captive audience and have an option to change channels, there is a limit to the performative behaviour that televised politicians can adopt which is consistent with the dignity of public affairs. Their delivery of carefully prepared aphorisms, which are known as 'sound bites' and often as glib as they are memorable, and histrionic moments from their public speeches, are almost at the limits of what modern television is willing to show of them. Hence, aware that the medium must provide spectacle, something interesting to *see* as well as listen to, opposition politicians during election campaigns might attack the government's record on health care not merely with rhetoric but by producing before the cameras an infirm and distressed old lady who has been waiting six months for a hip replacement.

Politicians are not the only ones who understand that in order to gain the attention of television, one must provide a spectacle. While watching a televised cricket match, the viewer can be disconcerted to notice within the crowd a row of spectators dressed up as Father Christmases or red indians. By injecting everyday life with an amusing element of the surreal, they illustrate the extent to which, thanks largely to television, theatricality has informed the public sphere. One could almost say that by prompting people to behave in theatrical ways, television has had the effect of turning reality itself into an artefact or fiction.

There are some in public life who are only too aware that television will not publicise issues that are devoid of visual interest, and who therefore seek to blur the distinction between the playful and entertaining on the one hand and the serious and informative on the other. Among them are the members of the pressure group Fathers 4 Justice, which is campaigning to improve the paternal rights of divorced and separated men in the United Kingdom. While thriving on media coverage of any kind, the group would probably not have devised some of its activities in an age that lacked television. Dressed as the comic superhero Batman, one of its members gained access to Buckingham Palace, climbed to a ledge on one of the upper floors, and declined to come down before he had attracted full media attention. Several others breached security in the House of Commons and threw condoms filled with purple flour at the prime minister and his colleagues. What they no doubt hoped the public would conclude was that if they were prepared to go to such lengths to publicise their case, they must indeed be seriously disadvantaged: such courage and effrontery could only suggest that they had a real grievance. The whole aim of pressure groups is 'to offer a strong emotive and moralistic appeal which can be presented as a simple conflict of good versus evil' (Negrine 1994: 139–40). On the other hand, what Fathers 4 Justice brought off were nothing other than *stunts* – entertaining spectacles that pricked the pomposity of certain national institutions: royalty, parliament, the police. Hence their aim was to win public support by being at once amusingly flippant and deadly serious.

As we might expect, the facts about paternal access are rather more complex and finely balanced than such activities would imply. In some cases, fathers are indeed denied contact with their children by mothers who refuse to obey court orders. But in many others, fathers provide inadequate maintenance for their children and seldom if ever avail themselves of the access that is granted. What Fathers 4 Justice provides is not a properly argued case: it is a mere spectacle that is offered, and perhaps taken, as proof that a case exists. And it has been contrived because we live in 'a culture in which public discourse increasingly takes the form of entertainment. Our politics, religion, news, athletics, education and commerce have been transformed into congenial adjuncts of show business, largely without protest and even much popular notice' (Postman 1986: 3–4). The stunts had sufficient impact for the government to promise to consider changes in the law of paternal access. There was, of course, serious debate on the matter, mainly in the press and radio, but the great majority of the public get their information primarily if not exclusively from television news – and it is to majorities that governments owe their power. If the government was not primarily swayed by the televised pictures of Batman on a ledge and exploding condoms in the Commons, it is pertinent to ask why such changes had not been considered before.

To sum up, then. Because sight is our primary sense, we tend to believe what we see: yet because we believe what we see, we prompt people to present themselves in a way that is not a wholly accurate reflection of the truth. Thanks to television, this problem has become somewhat magnified: because our access to public conduct and public institutions is more visual than in the old days of press and radio coverage, these things have in some sense become more theatrical – more guardedly self-conscious. The primary mode of communication remains, of course, verbal. But television's words are limited in number and largely incapable of qualifying the meanings suggested by the images they accompany. However, it is not simply that we *believe* what we see: we *enjoy* the act of looking. Hence people in the public sphere have an incentive to behave even more theatrically, to 'put on a show' that so entertains us that we accept the validity of their cause even though it is not logically made out and is, indeed, sidelined by the spectacle itself.

It should be stressed that these problems are of variable seriousness: television is sometimes capable of treating serious issues without recourse to amusingly distracting pictures, and it may also be true that many viewers can enjoy the antics of Fathers 4 Justice without ever being impressed by the merits of their case. But the aim of this chapter has been to remind us that television has its limitations: because it gets closer than the older mass media to the visual and temporal aspects of reality, we should not assume that it is necessarily more 'truthful' than they are.

Conclusion

The basic question this book set out to answer has proved unexpectedly difficult: What is television? In reviewing our findings, we will first focus on the medium itself and its messages – matters which we considered in the introduction and in the chapters on genres (Part II). It seems logical to begin with these since in being technologically determined they are the least variable, but we will also need to set them within the contexts of production and reception. Adopting the suggestion of Dahlgren (1995: 25), we have therefore treated television as a sort of prism consisting of a medium that contains audio-visual texts, an industry or set of institutions more or less regulated by government, and a socio-cultural experience.

Yet even defining the medium has proved far from straightforward. As its name suggests, vision provides its primary appeal: but that is equally true of cinema and video, and since sight is our main cognitive faculty – the one we attach most credence to and which we often gain pleasure from exercising – it is hard to identify the distinctiveness of television in the way that, for instance, we can identify that of the 'blind' medium of radio. A historical perspective is helpful. Where previously content was textual (newspapers and books), or consisted of fixed images (photographs) or only of sounds (radio), television provides both moving images and sounds. Later moving images and sounds were pre-recorded and received in a public space (cinema), but television provides live images and sounds in the audience's own homes. We have therefore defined television as a medium for the instantaneous ('live') transmission of messages which consist of sounds and moving images to a large, remote, dispersed and mostly domesticated audience. Since radio, newspapers and books are also domestic media – if not always in fact then certainly in potential – we can regard the *liveness* of television's images and sounds as being at the core of our definition. Yet television is best seen as the composite of *all* its characteristics, since different ones assume priority in different circumstances: in other words, the liveness that is its unique advantage may sometimes yield precedence to the needs of its other characteristics. It seems helpful to discuss television in terms of a series of dichotomies.

Liveness–recordedness

I have just suggested that the primary appeal of television lies, like that of cinema, in its images, but that its unique appeal is that the images (and sounds) are always and ineluctably *live*. The value of its liveness is declared by the fact that other media covet it, notably writing and print. In the course of this book, I have used phrases like 'We said earlier that . . .' and 'Let us consider for a few moments . . .' rather than 'On a previous page I wrote that . . .' and 'I need to consider for a few paragraphs . . .'. Why? By suggesting that I am talking to you during a period of time rather than writing to you across an expanse of space, I am trying to simulate the conditions of co-presence – that is, liveness – with you, the reader: I prefer to think of you as my listener and collaborator. This desire among writers is so instinctive, so ineradicable, that even in our era of newspapers, magazines, books and universal literacy, writing and print are still pervaded by a sense of orality and liveness (Ong 1982: 40–1, 115, 149). Why, then, should television compromise the advantage it enjoys over the other visual media by making use of pre-recordings – and sometimes, as we noted in Chapter 5, with such a bad conscience that it disguises the fact?

The answer, as we saw in Chapter 9, is that in certain circumstances another aspect of the medium – its domesticity – assumes an even greater importance than its liveness, and we might also note at this point how our attempt to create an essentialist definition of television slides unavoidably into a consideration of television as a socio-cultural experience. Because it is an easily accessible feature of the household, there is an incessant demand for its content, and the only economical means of supply is by pre-recording much of it. The domesticity of television is, then, almost as singular and important a characteristic as its liveness: to enjoy movies, and even the DVDs to which they transfer, viewers must leave their homes for the cinema and the rental shop (although this may not apply to all DVDs in the future).

Factuality–fictionality

Though unavoidably crude, some generalisations may be helpful here. Liveness tends to be most valued in factual programmes and pre-recordedness most acceptable in fictional programmes. Within this, a further and less sweeping generalisation is possible: because television's primary appeal is visual, pre-recordings are acceptable within factual programmes if the alternative would be uninteresting pictures. In other words, just as in certain circumstances the liveness of television will yield to the needs created by its domesticity, so in other circumstances it will yield to visuality – to the medium's need for interesting pictures. But factual pre-recordings are used, as far as possible, to support the *semblance* of liveness, whereas in fictional content, pre-recording is openly acknowledged and, indeed, may confirm its claim to be 'art'. We might say that those images in news and sports programmes that are not actually live are likely to be recent – at least broadly contemporaneous: they provide a quasi-liveness. Again, the celebrity chat shows that are pre-recorded (many are live) will offer a pretence of liveness, since historical factors are often relevant. But at the other extreme, it would be not merely absurd but self-defeating for television to pretend that the classic cinema movie it is showing is live. Recording underwrites its claim to artistic status, since most works of art are 'timeless'. We might therefore venture to suggest that television can use recording technology to subserve liveness and ephemerality on the one hand and express permanence and continuity on the other.

Nevertheless we have seen that the distinction between fact and fiction is in some respects porous and elusive. This is fundamentally a philosophical matter but is also complicated by the social effects of television itself. We could say that fictional programmes are those which the medium creates, or acquires from the cinema, and factual programmes are those through which it reflects the outside world. One problem, however, is that the outside world is itself permeated with fictions of various kinds. We noted that those who will be seen in public are obliged in their dress and conduct to construct what are more or less 'fictional' versions of themselves. Indeed, by extending and intensifying public observation, television not only reminds us of the degree of artifice that exists in everyday life but encourages it. To command the medium's attention, people feel they must behave in theatrical ways, whether they are electioneering politicians, fathers separated from their children or mourners of a dead pope or princess. Through various forms of 'reality TV', television explores the connections between authenticity and artifice. We also observed that at a more organised, institutional level, sporting fixtures and theatrical entertainments are both actual events and artefacts that are in some sense distinct from everyday reality.

If, for simplicity's sake, we regard all those events that originate in 'the outside world' as straightforward matters of fact, we might be tempted to conclude that the only real programmes on television are those that it generates from fictional materials: in all other respects it is merely a passive 'window on the world'. During outside broadcasts, there are certainly times – perhaps in the middle of a religious service or a languid spell in a cricket match – when the medium can seem so transparent, so self-effacing, that we are barely conscious of it. Nevertheless we know that its actual or potential presence can have a considerable impact on the outside world – for instance, on the conduct of parliamentary debates and on the presentation and organisation of many sports. Penalty shoot-outs in soccer and limited-over games in cricket are just two of the palpable consequences of television. Moreover, we know that in its own coverage of the outside world television is never really self-effacing – that in one way or another it always transforms what it shows into something vastly different from unmediated perception. In its most discreet coverage of a Remembrance Day service, with all the ceremony and silences that are involved, television still proclaims itself in the range and selection of camera shots and the sporadic, murmured commentary. We also saw how the factual content of its news, current affairs, documentary and features programmes is editorially mediated – shaped by elements of production, narration and presentation. In its coverage of sport, the actual events are not only punctuated by video reprises but part of a package of studio discussion and analysis. In the Introduction we described all these mediating elements as 'fictive', a word that usefully implies an element of creativity and rearrangement but not necessarily one amounting to fiction, untruth or make-believe.

Whether its programmes deal in fact or fiction, it is hard to decide how far television has created genuinely new art forms. Much depends on how we define the term. 'New forms of cultural expression' perhaps does fuller justice to the breadth of television's content. What we regard as characteristic forms of TV, such as the documentary, the soap opera and the 'reality' show, existed – or have clear antecedents – in older media. We saw in Chapter 6 that documentary was originally a cinematic form, and in Chapter 9 that soaps flourished on the radio for many years before television adopted them. The reality show, which explores the fusion of normal and theatrical behaviour that television has itself stimulated, has perhaps the best claim to be regarded as a new form of cultural expression, but despite critical as well as popular interest, there are signs that it may not endure. Many of the series, even *Celebrity Love Island* (ITV 1, 2005), have proved more banal than titillating, and the genre may be sustainable only if it merges itself into the conventional competition show.

In Chapter 9, I suggested that television's main cultural innovation has been *seriality*, especially in respect of drama. Radio's seriality preceded it but was, of course, non-visual, while seriality in the cinema has existed on nothing like the same scale. Curiously enough, with sequences like *Star Wars*, *Lord of the Rings* and the *Harry Potter* films, cinematic series have become more common in recent years: yet the explanation for this is at least partly televisual. Since the end of the 1990s, film distributors have derived more revenue from the sale and rental of video cassettes and DVDs than from cinema screenings (Turow 1999: 262). Because films, like TV programmes, are now as often as not viewed on television screens, domestically and over short sequences of time, it is logical that they, too, might be serial in character.

Mainly as sitcom, seriality has also brought innovation to comedy. But comedy is not an analogous category to drama since it is a matter of content, not form, and adopts many other guises, including those of the programme categories it seeks to parody: recently, the pseudo-documentary has been fashionable. Indeed, in Chapter 10, I ventured to suggest that despite its huge popularity, comedy has not been transformed by television to the extent that sport has. My argument was that much, though by no means all, humour is at bottom verbal, and therefore that television's contribution has been merely to magnify those ancillary visual elements that were already apparent in stage and cinematic comedy. In sport, on the other hand, spectacle is everything, and with its multiple viewpoints, graphics and playback facilities, television could offer not only new pictures but new insights into technique and tactics.

It is hardly surprising that seriality should stand out as television's main innovation, since the medium's defining element is – like that of music and the theatre arts – *time*, whereas the defining element of literature and the graphic arts is *space*. It seems fair to say that those things that exist in time pose a bigger challenge to our analytical and critical skills than those that exist in the more stable element of space. But television is even more in thrall to time than are music and theatre, and we must now consider some of the artistic and critical issues that this raises.

Extended programming: self-contained programmes

Television's output is continuous. Many channels transmit round the clock, conveying a sense of the medium as a domestic utility: like the electricity or water supply, it can be turned on at any time. Some forms of programming acknowledge that continuity by lasting for many hours. They may include live coverage of a major event, such as a coronation, fund-raising marathon or cricket test match, but in a formatted network like MTV or a home-shopping channel they may be coextensive with the totality of its output. They are likely to be segmented in the way that much television content is (Ellis 1982: 122), but the segments will not amount to, or generally correspond with, programme boundaries: such programming is often, quite literally, endless. Other forms – 'programmes' rather than 'programming' – cut slices out of television's continuity: they are more clearly artefactual and demarcated. And somewhere between the two lies television's main cultural innovation: serial and series programming.

These different forms of output are in essence television's attempt to make sense of the unprecedented domesticity of its viewers. It is true that for much of the time TV is used as casually and intermittently as the water supply, turned on and off – or, if always on, viewed – at times that do not match the beginnings and endings of the programmes. But sometimes it is also used to mark the sense of occasion that surrounds a trip to the theatre or cinema: people will make time to sit down and do nothing but watch the television. Extended programming and self-contained programmes thus serve paradoxical purposes. Extended programming caters for distracted viewing, for those who are watching television in the course of doing several other things and who, when they return to it, wish to feel that they have missed nothing crucial. Self-contained programmes cater for continuous and attentive viewing from their beginnings to their ends: they are 'occasional' both in the sense of aiming at those who view sporadically and selectively rather than indiscriminately, and in the older sense of seeking to mark an occasion, a special event.

Seriality is an attempt to face both ways. By, so to speak, turning extended programming on its side and dividing it into separate episodes spread over days, weeks or months, it seeks to persuade the casual and distracted viewers to adopt more regular and attentive habits and the already attentive viewers to stretch their sense of occasion over a number of programmes that are sequentially or thematically linked.

Yet whatever forms television's output may take, the fact of its continuousness remains. The medium exists in an eternal, overweening present that dismisses the past and ignores the future. Nowness is all. Even separate, well-crafted programmes are instantly superseded by other material. Consequently, as the scholar Stephen Heath remarks, 'television produces forgetfulness, not memory, flow, not history' (quoted in Kavka and West 2004: 137). Its artefacts are not 'framed': they are surrounded by neither space nor silence, and this has had a curious cultural consequence. Despite its promise of audiences who can be reached in the most intimate circumstances and often in their millions, there are relatively few artists, sculptors, choreographers, composers or dramatists who have fallen under the spell of television or adapted their work for it. We have instanced a number of distinguished playwrights who have written for the medium, but, for most, the primary yardstick of their success seems to be the stage. Likewise, many actors in search of critical recognition look to the theatre or cinema, rather than the small screen. Even journalists who work in television show a similar wariness about the medium, believing they acquire respectability only when they write newspaper and magazine articles or books.

Several reasons could be advanced for this. One is that the very size of television's audiences prompts an intellectual snobbery among those with serious cultural ambitions. But perhaps the more compelling reasons relate to the temporality of television – to what we have perceived as its imprisonment in the present. We have seen that in order to keep the medium fed, much programme production has to be collaborative, even industrial: hence the dedicated writer always runs the risk that her individual contribution will be submerged or compromised. But for creative people of all kinds, what is more significant is the fact that the individual programme is not clearly isolated from all television's other content: it is rapidly succeeded and often soon forgotten. Stage plays and cinema films also exist in time rather than space, but at least each does so in isolation from other such artefacts and requires its audience to step out of their normal existence in order to watch it. Thus it would appear that most creative people would prefer to make a lasting impact on a relatively small audience than a momentary impact on a large one. The old notion persists that artefacts should be in some sense detachable from the temporal flow that also happens to be television's element. If this makes television a relatively difficult and unattractive medium for creative people, we will hardly be surprised when some take the view that it has been responsible for few, if any, new forms of cultural expression (Williams 2004: 230).

The television medium: strengths and limitations

In this respect, the problem raised by television is not only one of temporality – how, for instance, can a sculpture maintain a continuous presence in an evanescent medium? – but of what is, in a sense, its transparency and insubstantiality: how would a dance that has been commissioned for television differ in essence from conventional theatrical dance? Yet this is also to overlook the obvious fact that television is, *in itself*, a new form of cultural expression. In terms of the numbers it reaches, the circumstances in which they can access it, and the quality and cost of what they watch, it has transformed the common awareness of the factual and fictional worlds – of news, sport, the arts and light entertainment. It is able to extend our experience in valuable ways, to enlarge rapidly, often instantaneously, our understanding of nature and society. It alerts us to certain key issues, albeit in often simple and rudimentary ways. Using hidden cameras, journalistic investigations bring facts and scandals to light, forcing politicians to address problems of human trafficking or school meals or the arms trade. Television's more overt, routine surveillance promotes the rapid relief of natural disasters such as famines, floods and earthquakes and inhibits the belligerency of governments and paramilitary groups – or at any rate, prompts other parties to try to contain it. In cultural terms, television has immeasurably increased public access to the natural world, to the visual arts, history, drama (and through drama, literature), music and sport. It has expanded our knowledge of cuisine, gardening, fashion and décor and perhaps cultivated our sense of taste in these things. And in almost every instance, it has not only increased access to the things it shows but shown them in ways that transcend first-hand observation. We noted in respect of sport and drama that the mediated absence from an event that constitutes the viewing experience is usually far better than an unmediated presence at it: the viewer half a world away sees better than the spectator in the stadium.

We must, however, balance these huge and palpable achievements with a reminder of television's limitations as an informative and intellectual medium. Images are its lifeblood, and we tend to believe what we see. Sight, after all, is our primary cognitive faculty: up to a point, to look is to learn. But images are only part of the matter: they need the accompaniment of words to explain, qualify, sometimes even contradict them. Television's are moving images, and images can only move through time. Consequently it contains a much lower ratio of words to images than is possible in the print media. I have argued that the information we derive from television is therefore likely to be rudimentary. There is little time for backgrounding or contextualisation, and the words that diverge from the images they accompany are likely to be ignored or disbelieved. This has prompted the complaint that television news offers 'sequences of events that, having appeared with no explanation, will disappear with no solution' (Bourdieu 1998: 7). Moreover the dominance of images has led to a widespread assumption that seeing is a reliable guide to knowing, that there is a harmony, a straightforward correspondence, between appearance and reality. By concentrating on what is visible and ignoring or relegating what is invisible, television can distort: it can exaggerate even while telling the literal truth, and so lead to stereotyping and moral panics. Moreover because what is seen on television is generally believed, we have argued that the medium encourages people to behave in theatrical and inauthentic ways.

All of this suggests that there is an incipient conflict, as well as a correspondence, between knowing, whose main currency is words, and seeing. In Chapter 6, we noted that the main impulse of instruction is abstract. It is not preoccupied with the visible world *per se* but seeks to elicit from it a body of principles that will help us to make sense of it. Television, on the other hand, is attracted to the visible world for its own sake: seeing is indeed our primary – albeit limited – means of finding out about things, but with all the plenitude it affords, it can also be overwhelming and confusing.

Yet the conflict between seeing and knowing is only incipient and one which, in theory at least, television could easily resolve. It is, after all, nothing more than a technology for sending images and sounds over distances, and there need be no restraint on the duration of its transmissions. It could, for instance, offset the quantitative limitations from which it suffers in comparison with print by broadcasting news bulletins that last for long periods of time. (This is no doubt the laudable idea behind *Channel 4 News*, which runs for no less than 55 minutes.) Such bulletins would afford the opportunity to provide extensive backgrounding and discussion and qualify the impact of the images. Television could, in other words, increase the ratio of words to pictures, which is exactly what it aims to do in its more responsible documentary programmes.

Moreover, while television must always show something, it is not even obliged to show its subject matter: a news bulletin might contain a report of a landslide but it does not have to show pictures of the landslide, and indeed the subject matter of some news items is literally invisible. What it can show instead is a person or persons talking *about* that subject. Such 'talking heads' are shown not because there is anything special or striking about their appearances, but merely as the adjunct of their remarks. The primary point of interest lies in what they are saying and our purpose in watching them is merely to gain a fuller understanding of it. As we noticed with our smartly presented weather forecaster in Chapter 11, there will be an element of redundancy and distraction even here, but it will be tolerably minimal. This is, in effect, television as 'radio with added pictures'. Indeed, it seems to be the most effective way in which ideas can be conveyed on television, and the medium continues to use numerous talking heads – in news bulletins and on breakfast and chat shows, studio debates and discussions. Yet it makes much less use of them than it used to. Why?

Sight, to repeat, is our primary faculty – usually the initial means by which we know about things – and we tend to believe what we see. But we noted earlier that we also *enjoy* the act of looking, an experience we termed 'scopophilia'. However, we cannot regard television as nothing more than a technology that allows us to look at things over distances: it is also an organised activity, an institution that has to operate in a context of political, economic and cultural pressures and, above all, competitively. Under competition, the dominant source of its appeal is what it must exploit, and the channel that provides the most enjoyable or interesting things *to look at* is the one that will do best, while the ancillary, essentially verbal, possibilities of the medium can be ceded to its blind rivals: radio and print. Even when competition was restricted to just three channels, it was observed that 'Television does not simply need pictures. It needs interesting pictures. But people are not disposed to be interested by what they see every day. So there is a premium on the unusual, the abnormal' (Whale 1969: 25).

In a perceptive newspaper article, David Herman has shown how the 'ideas' programme on television declined as the number of channels increased. It developed during the 1960s and 1970s with *Civilisation* (1969), *Ways of Seeing* (1972), *The Ascent of Man* (1973) and *The Body in Question* (1978), all broadcast on BBC 2.

There are a number of things that are striking about these series now. First, how little gimmickry there is: almost laughably primitive graphics, no dramatisation, no computer-generated imagery.

> The programmes relied on the intelligence of three people: the presenter, the producer and the viewer.
>
> (Herman 2003: 18)

When Channel 4 was launched in 1982, it was not obliged to sell its own advertising, which meant that it could sometimes serve unprofitable minorities and push against the boundaries of the medium. Its arrival therefore gave an impetus to the ideas programme. In *Opinions* (Channel 4, 1982–94), individuals like the novelist Salman Rushdie and the historian E.P. Thompson each spoke to the camera for half an hour on a subject that interested them, and over six series *Voices* (Channel 4, 1982–7) focused on some leading intellectual and cultural figures of the late twentieth century – among them, Umberto Eco, Edward Said and Bruno Bettelheim. This was also the focus of *After Dark* (Channel 4, 1987–91) and BBC 2's *The Late Show*, which was launched in 1989 and adopted a variable format of lectures, interviews, documentaries and studio discussions. But thanks to the proliferation of satellite and cable channels and, from 1993, the requirement on Channel 4 to sell its own advertising, interchannel competition intensified, and BBC 2 dropped *The Late Show* in 1995. Increasingly, television had to fall back on its core strength: the provision of spectacle – interesting pictures.

Today, every terrestrial channel will insist that it has retained its quota of documentary and ideas programmes: the BBC, for instance, boasts of its *Great Britons* series (BBC 2, 2002). But such programmes are not what they were:

> Last year, the BBC repeated the episode on Newton from *The Ascent of Man*. The contrast with the *Great Britons* programme on Newton was telling. The earlier programme's presenter, Jacob Bronowski, was a polymath, at home discussing the humanities and the sciences, with a Cambridge PhD in maths and the author of a book on Blake. . . . By contrast, *Great Britons'* use of a video sequence of gay clubs in Soho to explain Newton's sexuality was a world away, and spoke of the anxiety of executives at losing an audience unless it is constantly titillated.
>
> (Herman 2003: 18)

While planning a modern series about philosophy, producer Stuart Jeffries neatly summed up the way in which the ethos of television has changed:

> Time was when people who made television programmes about philosophy didn't worry about . . . visual matters. Rather, TV philosophy was about two men sitting in a studio, swivelling their

chairs while their trouser legs rode up exposing unalluring inches of calf . . . . Television is different now, and editors wouldn't dare commission [such] series . . . although perhaps to do so in our image-insatiable TV age might be a good thing . . .

(Jeffries 2003: 17)

But then Jeffries rather risibly declines to take his own point:

That said, the history of modern philosophy is a visually untapped mine of great stories. Hegel put the finishing touches to the Phenomenology of the Spirit as the Battle of Jena raged outside the city walls. Wittgenstein wrote the Tractatus Logico-Philosophicus while serving in the Austrian army in the first world war.

(Jeffries 2003: 17)

His position therefore seems to be that television programmes about philosophy should not be about philosophy at all, but merely focus on the televisable contexts in which it is written.

What we have been suggesting, then, is that television suffers from a number of limitations, especially in its informative and intellectual functions. Because it is a time-based medium, the amount of information it can convey is minimal and dominated by its images – a phenomenon which encourages the belief that seeing is an adequate guide to knowing and which heightens the risk of stereotyping and moral panics. Its unease with ideas and abstractions could be alleviated in an ideal world, but not in the competitive one in which it is obliged to operate. Many years ago it was observed that:

Television's special strengths are matched by special weaknesses. Born late into the same world as newspapers and the radio, television is heir to different but equally numerous ills; and the viewer, no less than the reader or the listener, is right to treat the evidence of his senses with a due scepticism.

(Whale 1969: 204)

Having considered the character, strengths and limitations of the medium, we must now turn to the behaviour of its audiences and the discernible influences it has on them.

Television as a socio-cultural experience

Thanks to the relative cheapness of its receivers, television's audiences, like those for radio, are becoming increasingly individualised as well as domesticated. But wherever the individual viewer might be – communal sitting room, bedroom, study or picnic table – the distractions of her personal space persist, and it is therefore hard to say exactly what 'a viewer' is. There are degrees of distraction and no obvious correlation between the viewer's attentiveness and the effects that the medium has on her. Moreover, when studying the audience we can perceive yet another dichotomy in the medium: between 'public' and 'private'. Television brings public events into the private sphere. Yet also, in such genres as reality TV and documentary, it often takes aspects of private life and transforms them into a public spectacle. In addition, and particularly when watching big 'media events', the individual viewer has a vivid sense of being positioned within the public sphere, as part of a mass audience.

What influence the various forms of content have on the audience is, as we have seen, impossible to gauge. Television has surely increased global cultural traffic at popular levels. It adopts, adapts and permutates genres, and if its influences seem to be rather more one-way than mutual – the phenomenon of 'cultural imperialism' – we should remember that the conquest is consensual and that both conquered and conquering cultures are likely to be hybrid and depend on further hybridisation for their survival. We may feel that most of the influences are 'popular', superficial and unimportant – ephemeral matters of food, drink, fashion products and music. But because deeper influences are harder to detect, we should not assume that they do not exist.

We have suggested that, over time, shifts in basic values have occurred, in attitudes to race, the environment, women, sexuality and economic inequalities, and that in our hyper-visual world, the daily social rituals and conventional human expressions of feeling may have become rather more demonstrative than they once were. Though impossible to prove, it is reasonable to assume that television has had a big hand in all of this. And so we come finally to institutional and even philosophical issues: in the light of the social and cultural significance we attach to television, how do we wish it to be funded and organised now, and in the future?

Institutional and philosophical issues

We have seen that television has been shaped by two main broadcasting philosophies. First, there is the old 'public service' view that it is a common cultural resource rather like schools, libraries, museums and art galleries and spiritually analogous to universal health-care. It should therefore be funded by all viewers to ensure comprehensive provision, even for certain minority tastes. The second view is that television is predominantly a medium of entertainment and abbreviated news, whose products exist in a market where, in accordance with the demand for them, they are bought by viewers and/or paid for by advertisers.

Historically, the public service case was predicated on the *scarcity* of broadcasting: if relatively little of it existed, it should serve as wide a range of people as possible. The case has been weakened by the growing abundance of channels, since these have provided the mechanisms of competition, diversity and choice that are more efficient and equitable than a levy on all viewers. But though weakened, the case has not been destroyed, for it is clear that the market cannot cater as adequately for the range of tastes as public service broadcasting can. Some programming is simply too costly to provide for the size of audience it would attract, so for some viewers the market system would cater insufficiently, and for others not at all. The largest minority to suffer would be the devotees of 'serious' content: extended news, intellectual discussions, documentaries, highbrow art forms like opera, ballet, traditional theatrical drama and classical music.

This minority is for the most part affluent – not perhaps affluent enough to pay for televisual forms of this content to an acceptable standard and quantity, but able to acquire it through other and comparable media: newspapers, magazines, books, live theatre, concert halls, radio. Moreover, it is arguable that some of these media, being spatial rather than temporal, may be a more efficient means of providing it, and even VCRs and DVDs are more 'stable' media than live television. If so, the case for public service would appear to dissolve, and in those countries without a public service tradition it seems to be true that serious people do not take television seriously. They use it, and appreciate it, for light entertainment and for summary news and information, but for their weightier intellectual and cultural needs they turn to other media. Does this matter? Everything depends on our estimate of television's strengths and limitations and the purposes we wish it to serve.

Bibliography

Abercrombie, N. (1996) *Television and Society*, Cambridge: Polity.

Adams, J. (1993) 'Social reality and comic realism in popular television drama' in Brandt, G. (ed.) *British Television Drama in the 1980s*, Cambridge: Cambridge University Press.

Allen, R. (2004) 'Making sense of soaps' in Allen, R. and Hill, A. (eds) *The Television Studies Reader*, London and New York: Routledge.

Bakewell, J. and Garnham, N. (1970) *The New Priesthood: British Television Today*, Harmondsworth: Allen Lane/Penguin.

Barr, C. (1996) 'They think it's all over: the dramatic legacy of live television' in Hill, J. and McLoone, M. (eds) *Big Picture, Small Screen: The Relations between Film and Television*, Luton: John Libbey Media/University of Luton Press.

Barwise, P. and Gordon, D. (2002) 'The economics of the media' in Briggs, A. and Cobley, P. (eds) *The Media: An Introduction*, Harlow: Longman, second edn.

Bignell, J. (2004) *An Introduction to Television Studies*, London and New York: Routledge.

Blain, N. and Boyle, R. (2002) 'Sport as real life: media sport and culture' in Briggs, A. and Cobley, P. (eds) *The Media: An Introduction*, Harlow: Longman, second edn.

Boddy, W. (2001) 'The quiz show' in Creeber, G. (ed.) *The Television Genre Book*, London: BFI.

Bonner, P. with Aston, L. (1998) *Independent Television in Britain: Volume V – ITV and the IBA, 1981–1992*, London: Macmillan.

Bourdieu, P. (1998) *On Television and Journalism*, trans. Priscilla Parkhurst Ferguson, London: Pluto Press.

Bowes, M. (1990) 'Only when I laugh' in Goodwin, A. and Whannel, G. (eds) *Understanding Television*, London and New York: Routledge.

Brandt, G. (ed.) (1993) *British Television Drama in the 1980s*, Cambridge: Cambridge University Press.

Branigan, T. (2004) 'Jungle celebs . . . we can't get enough of them', *The Guardian*, 31 January.

Briggs, A. (1961) *The History of Broadcasting in the United Kingdom: Volume I – The Birth of Broadcasting*, London: Oxford University Press.

—— (1979) *The History of Broadcasting in the United Kingdom: Volume IV – Sound and Vision*, Oxford: Oxford University Press.

—— (1995) *The History of Broadcasting in the United Kingdom: Volume V – Competition*, Oxford: Oxford University Press.

Brooker, W. (2004) 'Living on *Dawson's Creek*: teen viewers, cultural convergence, and television overflow' in Allen, R. and Hill, A. (eds) *The Television Studies Reader*, London and New York: Routledge.

Burns, T. (1977) *The BBC: Public Institution and Private World*, London: Macmillan.

Casey, B., Casey, N., Calvert, B., French, L. and Lewis, J. (2002) *Television Studies: The Key Concepts*, London: Routledge.

Caughie, J. (2000) *Television Drama: Realism, Modernism and British Culture*, Oxford: Oxford University Press.

Chaney, D. (1993) *Fictions of Collective Life: Public Drama in Late Modern Culture*, London and New York: Routledge.

Clissold, B. (2004) '*Candid Camera* and the origins of reality TV: contextualising a historical precedent' in Holmes, S. and Jermyn, D. (eds) *Understanding Reality Television*, London and New York: Routledge.

Cooke, L. (2003) *British Television Drama: A History*, London: BFI.

Corner, J. (1996) *The Art of Record: A Critical Introduction to Documentary*, Manchester: Manchester University Press.

—— (1999) *Critical Ideas in Television Studies*, Oxford: Oxford University Press.

—— (2001) 'Documentary fakes' in Creeber, G. (ed.) *The Television Genre Book*, London: BFI.

—— (2004) 'Afterword: framing the new' in Holmes, S. and Jermyn, D. (eds) *Understanding Reality Television*, London and New York: Routledge.

Crisell, A. (1994) *Understanding Radio*, London and New York: Routledge, second edn.

—— (2002) *An Introductory History of British Broadcasting*, London and New York: Routledge, second edn.

—— (2004) 'Look with thine ears: BBC Radio 4 and its significance in a multi media age' in Crisell, A. (ed.) *More than a Music Box: Radio Cultures and Communities in a Multi Media World*, New York and Oxford: Berghahn Press.

Cumberbatch, G. (1998) 'Media effects: the continuing controversy' in Briggs, A. and Cobley, P. (eds) *The Media: An Introduction*, Harlow: Addison Wesley Longman.

—— (2002) '"Effects": media effects – continuing controversies' in Briggs, A. and Cobley, P. (eds) *The Media: An Introduction*, Harlow: Longman, second edn.

Cumberbatch, G. and Howitt, D. (1989) *A Measure of Uncertainty: The Effects of the Mass Media*, London: John Libbey.

Curran, J. and Seaton, J. (1997) *Power without Responsibility*, London: Routledge, fifth edn.

Dahlgren, P. (1995) *Television and the Public Sphere*, London: Sage.

Davies, N. (1999) *The Isles: A History*, London: Macmillan.

Davis, A. (1976) *Television: Here is the News*, London: Independent Television Books.

Day-Lewis, S. (1992) *TV Heaven*, London: Channel 4 Television.

Dovey, J. (2001) 'Big Brother' in Creeber, G. (ed.) *The Television Genre Book*, London: BFI.

Dyer, R. (1973) *Light Entertainment*, London: BFI Television Monograph, no. 2.

Ellis, J. (1982) *Visible Fictions*, London: Routledge and Kegan Paul.

—— (2002) *Seeing Things: Television in the Age of Uncertainty*, London: I. B. Tauris.

Fanthome, C. (2004) 'The contribution of reality TV in the critique and creation of lifestyle choices' in Kennedy, E. and Thornton, A. (eds) *Leisure, Media and Visual Culture: Representations and Contestations*, LSA Publication No. 83, Eastbourne: Leisure Studies Association.

Fiske, J. (1987) *Television Culture*, London: Methuen.

Foster, A. and Furst, S. (1996) *Radio Comedy 1938–1968: A Guide to 30 Years of Wonderful Wireless*, London: Virgin Books.

Franklin, B. (1997) *Newszak and News Media*, London: Edward Arnold.

—— (ed.) (2001) *British Television Policy: A Reader*, London and New York: Routledge.

Freud, S. (1976) *Jokes and their Relation to the Unconscious*, trans. and ed. James Strachey, revised Angela Richards, Harmondsworth: Penguin.

Geraghty, C. (1996) 'The continuous serial: a definition' in Marris, P. and Thornham, S. (eds) *Media Studies: A Reader*, Edinburgh: Edinburgh University Press.

Gillan, J. (2004) 'From Ozzie Nelson to Ozzy Osbourne: the genesis and development of the reality (star) sitcom' in Holmes, S. and Jermyn, D. (eds) *Understanding Reality Television*, London and New York: Routledge.

Goddard, P. (1991) '*Hancock's Half Hour*: a watershed in British television comedy' in Corner, J. (ed.) *Popular Television in Britain*, London: BFI.

Goodwin, P. (1998) *Television under the Tories: Broadcasting Policy 1979–1997*, London: BFI.

Grierson, J. (1979) *On Documentary*, ed. Forsyth Hardy, London: Faber and Faber, abridged edn.

Gripsrud, J. (1998) 'Television, broadcasting, flow: key metaphors in TV theory' in Geraghty, C. and Lusted, D. (eds) *The Television Studies Book*, London: Edward Arnold.

Hadfield, D. (1995) 'Television threatens tyranny: game falling into the hands of the lawyers', *The Independent*, 20 December.

Hartley, J. (1999) *Uses of Television*, London and New York: Routledge.

—— (2001) 'Situation comedy, Part 1' in Creeber, G. (ed.) *The Television Genre Book*, London: BFI.

Harvey, S. (2002) 'Making media policy' in Briggs, A. and Cobley, P. (eds) *The Media: An Introduction*, Harlow: Longman, second edn.

Hendy, D. (2000) *Radio in the Global Age*, Cambridge: Polity.

Herman, D. (2003) 'Thought crime', *The Guardian Review*, 1 November.

Hesmondhalgh, D. (2002) *The Cultural Industries*, London: Sage.

Hill, J. (1996) 'British television and film: the making of a relationship' in Hill, J. and McLoone, M. (eds) *Big Picture, Small Screen: The Relations between Film and Television*, Luton: John Libbey Media/University of Luton Press.

Hodgson, G. (1995) 'TV's power behind the screens: snooker', *The Independent*, 21 December.

Holmes, S. (2004) '"All you've got to worry about is the task, having a cup of tea and doing a bit of sunbathing": approaching celebrity in *Big Brother*' in

Holmes, S. and Jermyn, D. (eds) *Understanding Reality Television*, London and New York: Routledge.

Holmes, S. and Jermyn, D. (2004) 'Introduction: understanding reality TV' in Holmes, S. and Jermyn, D. (eds) *Understanding Reality Television*, London and New York: Routledge.

Horsman, M. (1997) *Sky High: The Inside Story of BSkyB*, London: Orion Business Books.

Jacobs, J. (2000) *The Intimate Screen: Early British Television Drama*, Oxford: Oxford University Press.

Jeffries, S. (2003) 'Beautiful minds', *The Guardian G2*, 3 November.

Jermyn, D. (2004) 'This IS about real people! video technologies, actuality and affect in the television crime appeal' in Holmes, S. and Jermyn, D. (eds) *Understanding Reality Television*, London and New York: Routledge.

Kaplan, E. (1987) *Rocking Around the Clock: Music Television, Postmodernism and Consumer Culture*, New York and London: Routledge.

Kavka, M. and West, A. (2004) 'Temporalities of the real: conceptualising time in reality TV' in Holmes, S. and Jermyn, D. (eds) *Understanding Reality Television*, London and New York: Routledge.

Kerr, P. (1990) 'F for fake? Friction over faction' in Goodwin, A. and Whannel, G. (eds) *Understanding Television*, London and New York: Routledge.

Kilborn, R. and Izod, J. (1997) *An Introduction to Television Documentary: Confronting Reality*, Manchester: Manchester University Press.

Lewis, J. (1990) 'Are you receiving me?' in Goodwin, A. and Whannel, G. (eds) *Understanding Television*, London and New York: Routledge.

Liddiment, D. (2003) 'Reality TV's ultimate trick', *Media Guardian*, 28 April.

Livingstone, S. (1990) *Making Sense of Television: The Psychology of Audience Interpretation*, Oxford: Pergamon.

McNair, B. (1998) *The Sociology of Journalism*, London: Edward Arnold.

McQuail, D. (2000) *McQuail's Mass Communication Theory*, London: Sage, fourth edn.

McQueen, D. (1998) *Television: A Media Student's Guide*, London: Edward Arnold.

Mills, B. (2001) 'Studying comedy' in Creeber, G. (ed.) *The Television Genre Book*, London: BFI.

Moores, S. (1993) *Interpreting Audiences: The Ethnography of Media Consumption*, London: Sage.

Morley, D. (1992) *Television, Audiences and Cultural Studies*, London and New York: Routledge.

Morse, M. (2004) 'News as performance: the image as event' in Allen, R. and Hill, A. (eds) *The Television Studies Reader*, London and New York: Routledge.

Mumford, L. (1998) 'Feminist theory and television studies' in Geraghty, C. and Lusted, D. (eds) *The Television Studies Book*, London: Edward Arnold.

Nathan, D. (1971) *The Laughtermakers: A Quest for Comedy*, London: Peter Owen.

Negrine, R. (1994) *Politics and the Mass Media in Britain*, London and New York: Routledge, second edn.

—— (2002) 'Media institutions in Europe' in Briggs, A. and Cobley, P. (eds) *The Media: An Introduction*, Harlow: Longman, second edn.

Neale, S. and Krutnik, F. (1990) *Popular Film and Television Comedy*, London and New York: Routledge.

Nelson, R. (1997) *TV Drama in Transition: Forms, Values and Cultural Change*, Basingstoke: Macmillan.

—— (2001) 'Studying television drama' in Creeber, G. (ed.) *The Television Genre Book*, London: BFI.

O'Hagan, S. (1995) 'Murdoch demands veto rights on player transfers', *The Independent*, 20 December.

Ong, W. (1982) *Orality and Literacy*, London and New York: Methuen.

O'Regan, T. (2000) 'The international circulation of British television' in Buscombe, E. (ed.) *British Television: A Reader*, Oxford: Oxford University Press.

O'Sullivan, T., Dutton, B. and Rayner, P. (1994) *Studying the Media: An Introduction*, London: Edward Arnold.

Paget, D. (1998) *No Other Way to Tell It: Dramadoc/Docudrama on Television*, Manchester: Manchester University Press.

Paulu, B. (1961) *British Broadcasting in Transition*, Minneapolis: University of Minnesota Press.

—— (1981) *Television and Radio in the United Kingdom*, London: Macmillan.

Persaud, R. (2000) 'Car-crash television', *Media Guardian*, 17 July.

Postman, N. (1986) *Amusing Ourselves to Death: Public Discourse in the Age of Show Business*, London: Heinemann.

Scannell, P. (1986) '"The stuff of radio": developments in radio features and documentaries before the war' in Corner, J. (ed.) *Documentary and the Mass Media*, London: Edward Arnold.

—— (1990) 'Public service broadcasting: the history of a concept' in Goodwin, A. and Whannel, G. (eds) *Understanding Television*, London and New York: Routledge.

—— (1996) *Radio, Television and Modern Life*, Oxford: Basil Blackwell.

Seaton, J. (ed.) (1998) *Politics and the Media: Harlots and Prerogatives at the Turn of the Millennium*, Oxford: Basil Blackwell.

Selby, K. and Cowdery, R. (1995) *How to Study Television*, London: Macmillan.

Sendall, B. (1982) *Independent Television in Britain: Volume I – Origin and Foundation, 1946–1962*, London: Macmillan.

Seymour-Ure, C. (1996) *The British Press and Broadcasting since 1945*, Oxford: Basil Blackwell, second edn.

Shattuc, J. (2001) 'The confessional talk show' in Creeber, G. (ed.) *The Television Genre Book*, London: BFI.

Sparks, C. (2004) 'The global, the local and the public sphere' in Allen, R. and Hill, A. (eds) *The Television Studies Reader*, London and New York: Routledge.

Thompson, J. (1995) *The Media and Modernity: A Social Theory of the Media*, Cambridge: Polity.

Thorne, T. (1991) *Dictionary of Contemporary Slang*, London: Bloomsbury, paperback edn.

Tincknell, E. and Raghuram, P. (2004) 'Big Brother: reconfiguring the "active" audience of cultural studies?' in Holmes, S. and Jermyn, D. (eds) *Understanding Reality Television*, London and New York: Routledge.

Tolson, A. (1996) 'Televised chat and the synthetic personality' in Marris, P. and Thornham, S. (eds) *Media Studies: A Reader*, Edinburgh: Edinburgh University Press.

Took, B. (1976) *Laughter in the Air*, London: Robson Books/BBC.

Tulloch, J. (1990) *Television: Agency, Audience and Myth*, London and New York: Routledge.

Tunstall, J. (1996) 'Producers in British television' in Marris, P. and Thornham, S. (eds) *Media Studies: A Reader*, Edinburgh: Edinburgh University Press.

Turow, J. (1999) *Media Today: An Introduction to Mass Communication*, Boston and New York: Houghton Mifflin.

Wernick, A. (1991) *Promotional Culture: Advertising, Ideology and Symbolic Expression*, London: Sage.

Whale, J. (1969) *The Half-Shut Eye*, London: Macmillan/St Martin's.

Whannel, G. (1992) *Fields in Vision: Television Sport and Cultural Transformation*, London and New York: Routledge.

Williams, J. (2004) *Entertaining the Nation: A Social History of British Television*, Stroud: Sutton.

Williams, K. (1998) *Get Me a Murder a Day! A History of Mass Communication in Britain*, London: Edward Arnold.

Williams, R. (1974) *Television: Technology and Cultural Form*, Glasgow: Fontana.

Winston, B. (1998) *Media Technology and Society*, London and New York: Routledge.

Woollacott, J. (1996) 'Fictions and ideologies: the case of situation comedy' in Marris, P. and Thornham, S. (eds) *Media Studies: A Reader*, Edinburgh: Edinburgh University Press.

Index

625 lines/UHF, 26, 27, 54–5

A
ABC (American Broadcasting
  Company), 115
Abercrombie, N., 1, 60, 116, 131,
  139, 147, 149
Absolute Power, 121
Absolutely Fabulous, 121, 150
Adam Smith Institute, 43, 136
Adams, J., 122, 123, 126
After Dark, 168
Airport, 89
All in the Family, 150
Allen, Gracie, 97
Allen, R., 116, 149
American football, 105
Anatomists, The, 77
Annan Committee, 28
AOL/Time-Warner, 38
Are You Being Served?, 121
'Armchair Theatre', 113
Arnaz, Desi, 97
Ascent of Man, The, 167
Aston, L., 55
athletics, 106
Attenborough, David, 71–2, 73, 76
Avengers, The, 111
Ayckbourn, Alan, 6, 7

B
Baird, John Logie, 17–18, 20
Bakewell, J., 95
Ball, Lucille, 97
Barr, C., 110, 112
Barwise, P., 41, 44–5, 45, 137
baseball, 105
basketball, 105
BBC, 10, 18–23, 24–9, 31–3, 34–5,
  36–9, 42–3, 43–5, 52–3, 57, 67,
  86, 87, 108, 111, 115, 121, 125,
  127, 147, 148, 155
BBC 1, 35, 55, 77, 79, 83, 87, 89,
  113, 121, 122, 123, 125, 128,
  138, 150
BBC 2, 26–7, 35, 55, 70, 73, 83,
  113, 121, 122, 123, 125, 128,
  138, 167–8
BBC News 24, 37, 56
BBC World, 147, 150
BBC Worldwide, 43
Bennett, Alan, 7
Berlusconi, Silvio, 150
Bertelsmann, 38, 147, 150
Big Brother, 79, 89, 90, 92, 94
Bignell, J., 123, 135, 137, 145, 147,
  149, 150
Blain, N., 108–9
Bleasdale, Alan, 7
Boddy, W., 128
Body in Question, The, 167
BodySnatchers, 77
Bonner, P., 55
books, 1, 9, 12, 21, 38, 116, 140,
  142, 152, 159, 160, 164, 171
Bourdieu, P., 62, 166
Bowes, M., 121, 122, 123
boxing, 105, 106
Boyle, R., 108–9
Brandt, G., 9
Branigan, T., 92
Braun, Karl, 17
Bridson, D. G., 66
Briggs, A., 19, 22, 55
Broadcasting Act 1990, 32, 34, 44
Broadcasting Act 1996, 36
Brooker, W., 137
Brunsdon, C., 117
BSB, 33, 36
BSkyB (formerly Sky TV), 33–4,

36–8, 42, 56, 98, 103, 106, 108, 118, 137, 145, 147
Burns, George, 97
Burns, T., 44

C
cable television, 31–2, 33, 34, 35, 36, 42, 55, 56, 144, 168
Campaign for Press and Broadcasting Freedom, 136–7
Campbell-Swinton, A. A., 17
Candid Camera, 94
Carlton Television, 35, 36
Casey, B., 1, 3, 49, 80, 105, 115, 121, 129, 130, 145, 151
Cathy Come Home, 86, 87
Caughie, J., 110
Cawston, Richard, 67
Celebrity Big Brother, 79
Celebrity Love Island, 162
Chaney, D., 154
Changing Rooms, 83
Channel 4, 27–9, 32, 37, 42, 44, 70, 77, 79, 80, 87, 89, 95, 107, 113, 118, 126, 128, 168
Channel 4 News, 166
Channel 5, 32, 35, 37, 38, 42, 76
Channel 9 TV, 106
Cheyenne, 115
cinema, 1, 1–3, 4–6, 7, 8, 12, 21, 25, 27, 31, 38, 51–3, 54, 66–7, 68, 91, 110–13, 114–16, 117–18, 121, 123–4, 126, 127–8, 141, 142, 146, 147, 148, 149–50, 151, 152, 159, 160, 161, 163–5
Cinema Exhibitors' Association, 112
Civilisation, 167
Cleese, John, 124–5
Clissold, B., 93, 94
CNN, 56, 147, 150
colour television, 26, 27, 104, 111
Columbia Pictures, 149
Communications Act 2003, 37
Consumers' Association, 43
Cooke, L., 9, 111, 112, 113, 115, 116, 118
Corner, J., 58, 71, 79, 87, 89, 135

coronation of Elizabeth II, 22
Coronation Street, 87
Countdown, 128
Cowdery, R., 121, 123
cricket, 4, 104, 105, 106, 107, 161
Crimewatch UK, 87, 94
Crisell, A., 60, 63, 79, 140
cross-country running, 103
cultural imperialism, 145–7, 148, 149–50, 151–2, 170
Cumberbatch, G., 139, 141, 142
Curran, J., 19, 22

D
Dad's Army, 121
Dahlgren, P., 1, 79, 135, 159
darts, 103, 104
Davies, N., 88
Davis, A., 54, 61
Day-Lewis, C., 87
Deal, The, 87–8
Death of a Princess, 86, 87
digital television, 35–9, 137, 144
Dovey, J., 91, 93
Drop the Dead Donkey, 126
Dwarves in Showbiz, 76–7
Dyer, R., 124

E
Early Doors, 121
Edison, Thomas, 17
electronic newsgathering, 55
Ellis, J., 1, 45, 46, 53, 57–8, 84, 86, 96, 110–11, 113, 122, 126, 163
Elster, Julius, 17
Emergency – Ward 10, 87
Endemol UK, 150–1
Extras, 121
Eyre, Richard, 40, 113

F
Fanthome, C., 89, 94
Farnsworth, Philo, 18
Fathers 4 Justice, 157–8
Fawlty Towers, 123
Federal Radio Commission, 18
figure skating, 107

'Film on Four', 113, 118
Fiske, J., 117, 139
Flaherty, Robert, 66
Foster, A., 121
Fox Network, 147
Franklin, B., 43, 57
Frears, Stephen, 113
Freeview, 37, 38
Freud, Sigmund, 120
Furst, S., 121

G
Garnham, N., 95
Geitel, Hans, 17
Geraghty, C., 117
Gielgud, Val, 110
Gillan, J., 97
Gladiators, 108
Goddard, P., 123
Gold, Jack, 113
golf, 103
Goodwin, P., 35
Gordon, D., 41, 44–5, 45, 137
Graef, Roger, 67
Granada Television, 35, 36
Great Britons, 168
Grierson, John, 65, 66, 68, 69
Griffiths, Trevor, 112–3
Gripsrud, J., 5, 54
Ground Force, 83, 84

H
Hadfield, D., 106
Haley, Sir William, 21
Hancock, 121, 123
Harding, A. E., 66
Harry Potter, 162
Hartley, J., 122, 143
Harvey, S., 41, 43
Have I Got News for You, 128
Heath, S., 164
Hendy, D., 144
Herman, D., 167–8, 168
Hesmondhalgh, D., 145, 147, 148, 149, 150, 151, 152
High Society, 150
Hill, Benny, 124–5

Hill, J., 118
Hillsborough, 87
Hodgson, G., 104
Hole, Tahu, 52–3, 58, 59
Holmes, S., 88, 89, 92
Hopkins, John, 112
horse-racing, 103
Horsman, M., 98
Hotel, 89
Howitt, D., 142
Hunt Committee, 31

I
IBA, 28, 33, 35
ice hockey, 105
I'm a Celebrity – Get Me Out Of Here!, 89
Inspector Morse, 150
Institute for Public Policy Research, 43, 135
interactivity, 137–8
ITA, 24–5, 28, 33, 34–5
ITC, 34, 35, 36–7
ITN, 53, 54–5
It's a Knockout, 108
ITV (also ITV 1), 11, 24–9, 31–3, 34–5, 37, 41, 42, 43, 44–5, 55, 67, 70, 86, 87, 89, 95, 108, 111, 113, 121, 123, 125, 128, 150, 162
Izod, J., 66, 71

J
Jacobs, J., 20, 111, 112
Jeffries, S., 168–9, 169
Jermyn, D., 88, 89, 94
Jerry Springer Show, The, 95–6
Joffe, Roland, 113

K
Kaplan, E., 130
Kavka, M., 99, 164
Kerr, P., 67, 87
Kilborn, R., 66, 71
Krutnik, F., 119, 120, 121, 126

L
La Plante, Lynda, 7

Late Show, The, 168
Law and Order, 87
Lewis, J., 143
Liddiment, D., 91, 92
Likely Lads, The, 122
Livingstone, S., 139
Loach, Ken, 112
Lord of the Rings, 162

M
Mastermind, 128
Matsushita, 147
Maverick, 115
McNair, B., 51, 56, 59, 61
McQuail, D., 137, 141, 142, 150
McQueen, D., 128, 129
Mediawatch-UK, 43, 136
Mercer, David, 112
MGM, 149
Miller, Jonathan, 95
Mills, B., 119
Minder, 123
Monocled Mutineer, The, 86, 88
Monty Python's Flying Circus, 125, 126–7
Moores, S., 137, 140
moral panics, 62, 141–2, 166, 169
Morley, D., 138
Morse, M., 96
Mr Bean, 128
MTV, 147, 150, 163
Mumford, L., 117

N
Nathan, D., 119, 121, 124, 125
Neale, S., 119, 120, 121, 126
Negrine, R., 45, 64, 154, 155, 157
Nelson, R., 9, 113, 117
Never Mind the Buzzcocks, 128
News Corporation (formerly News International), 33, 147, 148, 150
newspapers, 4, 12, 25, 29, 31, 38, 50–1, 52, 56–7, 60, 61–4, 69, 91, 147, 158, 159, 160, 164, 169, 171
Nineteen Eighty Four, 79, 93, 111
Nipkow, Paul, 17
Norden, Denis, 119

NTL, 36

O
Ofcom, 37
Office, The, 121, 122, 150
O'Hagan, S., 108
ONdigital, 36–7
Ong, W., 160
Only Fools and Horses, 123
Open All Hours, 123
Opinions, 168
Oprah Winfrey Show, The, 95
O'Regan, T., 150
O'Sullivan, T., 150, 151

P
Packer, Kerry, 4, 106, 107
Paget, D. ,87
para-sports, 108–9
parlour games, 4, 12, 25, 128
Paulu, B., 21, 22
Peacock Committee, 32
Persaud, R., 91
Pilkington Committee, 26–7
Plater, Alan, 7, 122
'Play for Today', 113
Pop Idol, 89
Popular Television Association, 23
Porridge, 121
Postman, N., 82, 119, 158
postmodernism, 130–1
Potter, Dennis, 7, 112
Prior, Allan, 112
public service broadcasting, 10–11, 19–20, 21, 25–6, 28, 31, 32, 34, 35, 38–9, 40–44, 67, 68, 80, 111, 136, 170–1

Q
Quatermass Experiment, The 115

R
radio, 4, 7, 20, 21–2, 25, 31, 51–3, 58–9, 63, 66, 77, 91, 115, 121, 123–5, 128, 140, 141, 144–5, 158, 159, 162, 167, 169, 171
Radio Newsreel, 53

Raghuram, P., 90, 94
rally driving, 103
RCA Company, 18
Ready Steady Cook, 83
recorded programming (by broad-
    casters), 27, 53–4, 98–9, 104, 107,
    111–12, 113–14, 115, 117,
    159–61, 162
Reith, John, 19, 21, 23
Rising Damp, 121
Rosenthal, Jack, 112
Rotha, Paul, 66
Royle Family, The, 121, 138
rugby league, 106, 107, 108
rugby union, 103, 106

S
Saatchi and Saatchi, 154
Sanford and Son, 150
satellite television, 29, 32–4, 36–7,
    55–6, 105, 136, 144, 148, 151,
    168
Scannell, P., 32, 66, 79, 135
Schama, Simon, 70, 71, 73
'Screen on One', 113
'Screen Two', 113
'Screenplay', 113
Seagram Company, 147
Seaton, J., 19, 22, 154
Selby, K., 121, 123
Selsdon Committee, 20
Sendall, B., 25, 53
serials, 2, 4, 7, 114–17, 162–4
series, 7, 25, 114–17, 163–4
Seymour-Ure, C., 24, 41, 135
Shapley, Olive, 66
Shattuc, J., 96
showjumping, 104–5
situation comedy ('sitcom'), 2, 25,
    115, 119, 121–6, 138, 142
snooker, 103, 104, 107
soap opera, 2, 4, 7, 9, 25, 80, 87, 89,
    91, 114–17, 138, 148, 162
soccer, 100, 100–1, 105, 105–6, 106,
    107, 108, 124, 161
Sony Corporation, 38, 147, 148, 149
Sparks, C., 145, 148

spin doctors, 154–5
squash, 106, 107–8
Star TV, 147, 148, 150
Star Wars, 162
Starkey, David, 70, 71
Steptoe and Son, 121, 123, 150
stereotyping, 62, 122, 166, 169
Stoppard, Tom, 7
Sugarfoot, 115
sumo wrestling, 104–5
*Sunday Night at the London
    Palladium*, 108
Survivor, 89

T
Telefonica, 151
telenovela, 149, 151
teletext, 30
Television Act 1954, 11, 23
Telewest, 36
Telstar, 27, 55
Temptation Island, 80
tennis, 106
That Was the Week That Was, 53
Thatcher, Margaret, 30, 31, 70–1,
    84, 93–4
theatre, 1, 4, 5–8, 12, 13, 91, 100,
    101–2, 105–6, 109, 110–13,
    114–17, 118, 121, 123, 123–6,
    127–8, 137, 141, 155, 156–8,
    161, 162, 163–5, 166, 171
'Theatre 625', 113
They Think It's All Over, 128
Thompson, J., 141, 145, 154
Thorne, T., 84
Till Death Us Do Part, 150
Tincknell, E., 90, 94
TiVo, 54
Tolson, A., 97
Took, B., 121
Tulloch, J., 9, 113
Tunstall, J., 43, 44
Turow, J., 18, 115, 147, 162

V
video recording (by viewers) 8–9, 29,

30–1, 32, 38, 54, 114, 138, 159, 162, 171
Voice of the Listener and Viewer, 43, 136
Voices, 168

W
War Game, The, 87
Warner Brothers, 115
Watson, Paul, 67
Ways of Seeing, 167
'Wednesday Play, The', 113
Weldon, Fay, 112
Wernick, A., 154
West, A., 99, 164
Westinghouse Company, 18
Whale, J., 167, 169
Whannel, G., 98, 101, 102, 103, 106, 107, 108

What Not to Wear, 83, 85
Whatever Happened to the Likely Lads?, 122
Who Wants to be a Millionaire?, 128
Wife Swap, 80
Williams, J., 103, 121, 123, 136, 165
Williams, K., 66, 118, 154
Williams, R., 4
Winston, B., 19, 112
Woollacott, J., 122
wrestling, 109

Y
Yes, Minister, 123

Z
Zworykin, Vladimir, 18